Getting by in Europe's Urban Labour Markets

IMISCOE (International Migration, Integration and Social Cohesion)

IMISCOE is a Network of Excellence uniting over 500 researchers from various institutes that specialise in migration studies across Europe. Networks of Excellence are cooperative research ventures that were created by the European Commission to help overcome the fragmentation of international studies. They amass a crucial source of knowledge and expertise to help inform European leadership today.

Since its foundation in 2004, IMISCOE has advanced an integrated, multidisciplinary and globally comparative research programme to address the themes specified in its name, short for: International Migration, Integration and Social Cohesion in Europe. IMISCOE members come from all branches of the economic and social sciences, the humanities and law. The Network draws from existing studies and advances innovative lines of inquiry key to European policymaking and governance. Priority is placed on developing a theoretical design to promote new research and offer practical alternatives for sound policy.

The IMISCOE-Amsterdam University Press Series was created to make the Network's findings and results available to researchers, policymakers, the media and the public at large. High-quality manuscripts authored by IMISCOE members and cooperating partners are published in one of four distinct series.
   Research
   Reports
   Dissertations
   Textbooks

The RESEARCH series presents empirical and theoretical scholarship addressing issues of international migration, integration and social cohesion in Europe. Authored by experts in the field, the works provide a rich reference source for researchers and other concerned parties.

The REPORTS series responds to needs for knowledge within IMISCOE's mandated fields of migration research. Compiled by leading specialists, the works disseminate succinct and timely information for European policymakers, practitioners and other stakeholders.

The DISSERTATIONS series showcases select PhD monographs written by IMISCOE doctoral candidates. The works span an array of fields within studies of international migration, integration and social cohesion in Europe.

The TEXTBOOKS series produces manuals, handbooks and other didactic tools developed by specialists in migration studies. The works are used within the IMISCOE training programme and for educational purposes by academic institutes worldwide.

IMISCOE Policy Briefs and more information on the Network can be found at www.imiscoe.org.

Getting by in Europe's Urban Labour Markets

Senegambian Migrants' Strategies for Survival, Documentation and Mobility

Inge Van Nieuwenhuyze

IMISCOE Dissertations

AMSTERDAM UNIVERSITY PRESS

The author gratefully acknowledges the King's College London School of Social Science and Public Policy Research Studentship that funded this project and the three-month doctoral fellowship at the AMIDSt UrbEUROPE Research and Training Network in Amsterdam.

Cover design: Studio Jan de Boer BNO, Amsterdam
Layout: The DocWorkers, Almere

ISBN   978 90 8964 050 5
e-ISBN   978 90 4850 635 4
NUR   741 / 763

© Inge Van Nieuwenhuyze / Amsterdam University Press, Amsterdam 2009

All rights reserved. Without limiting the rights under copyright reserved above, no part of this book may be reproduced, stored in or introduced into a retrieval system, or transmitted, in any form or by any means (electronic, mechanical, photocopying, recording or otherwise) without the written permission of both the copyright owner and the author of the book.

For Modou and Karim

Table of contents

List of tables and figures		9
Abbreviations and terms		10
1	**Understanding labour migration trajectories**	11
	1.1 The research question: Understanding trajectories	13
	1.2 Research design	18
	1.3 Structure of the book	24
2	**Embarking on an explanatory framework**	27
	2.1 What is new about recent labour migration?	28
	2.2 The explanatory structural factors	32
	2.3 The two case studies	38
	2.4 Conclusion: Summarising hypotheses	52
3	**Data collection: Interviews and participant observation in a hidden population**	55
	3.1 A new world opening up	56
	3.2 The interviews	59
	3.3 Conclusion: Limits and advantages of the data	63
4	**How migration from Senegal and the Gambia became an institution**	67
	4.1 Why leave Senegal or the Gambia?	68
	4.2 Making it to Europe	77
	4.3 Senegalese business tradition	83
	4.4 The importance of migration back home	88
	4.5 The sample	92
	4.6 Conclusion: Senegambian migration	94

5	**Survival strategies as an undocumented migrant**	97
	5.1 Work experiences of undocumented migrants	98
	5.2 The functioning of the informal labour market	110
	5.3 Reciprocity strategies	117
	5.4 Conclusion: Better off in Spain	127
6	**Documentation strategies as an undocumented migrant**	131
	6.1 Being able to stay	132
	6.2 Being allowed to stay	142
	6.3 Conclusion: Different ways of 'being undocumented'	155
7	**Mobility strategies as a legal migrant**	159
	7.1 Work experiences for documented migrants	159
	7.2 Some remarks about the formal labour market	175
	7.3 Other mobility strategies	182
	7.4 A better life realised, but...	187
	7.5 Conclusion: Better off in Antwerp	190
8	**Conclusions**	191
	8.1 General research conclusions	192
	8.2 Policy implications	196
Appendix A	**Topic list for questionnaire**	201
Appendix B	**List of key informants**	203
Appendix C	**Letter**	205
Notes		207
References		217
Abstract		233

List of tables and figures

Table 2.1	Key labour market indicators for Belgium and OECD Countries	41
Table 2.2	Key labour market indicators for Spain and OECD Countries	47
Table 2.3	Theoretical elements of comparison	53
Table 4.1	Most recent key data for Senegal and the Gambia, 2004	70
Table 4.2	Overview of respondents by key categories	93
Table 5.1	Overview of jobs in Antwerp and Barcelona for undocumented migrants	111
Table 6.1	Number of years in illegality before being regularised	142
Table 6.2	Successful documentation strategies in Spain and Belgium	144
Figure 1.1	Maps of Belgium and Spain	23
Figure 2.1	Foreign residents in Spain, evolution 1955-2008	49
Figure 4.1	Map of Senegal and the Gambia	69
Figure 4.2	Key migrant routes from Africa to Europe	82
Figure 5.1	Domains of economic help	98

Abbreviations and terms

AU	African Union
GDP	Gross Domestic Product
ILO	International Labour Organisation
IOM	International Organisation for Migration
Modu-modu	Wolof term for 'hawkers'
NGO	Non-governmental organisation
OCMW	Openbare Centra voor Maatschappelijk Werk (Social Welfare Agency)
OECD	Organisation for Economic Cooperation and Development
UN	United Nations
Vlaams Belang	Extreme rightwing political party in Flanders
VDAB	Vlaamse Dienst voor Arbeidsbemiddeling (Flemish Employment Office)

1 Understanding labour migration trajectories

> I tread European ground, my feet sculpted and marked by African earth. One step after another, it's the same movement all humans make, all over the planet. Yet I know my western walk has nothing in common with the one that took me through the alleys, over the beaches, paths and fields of my native land. People walk everywhere, but never towards the same horizon. In Africa, I followed in destiny's wake, between chance and infinite hopefulness. In Europe, I walk down the long tunnel of efficiency that leads to well-defined goals. (Diome 2006: 3)

Labour migration is as old as humanity, an ageless human strategy to improve life. It is a manifestation of imbalances between parts of the world as well as an expression of links between them; major population movements at different episodes have shaped the world as we know it today. Many of the world's estimated 175 million migrants (IOM 2005) are people searching for improved economic opportunities abroad: they travel in search of work, a higher wage, or simply the chance for a better life – and there is no reason to expect this tendency to diminish in the near future. This panorama is one of diversity, complexity and new tendencies of international migration, and therefore impossible to stereotype or interpret simplistically. In the fortunate cases, the migrant belongs to the top layers of the international labour market, moving around between the major global cities, with well-paid employment contracts. However, a large group of migrants do not fit these profiles: they were not invited; their skills are limited or not recognised; they face difficulties finding a job, or have to accept inferior working conditions in order to make a living.

This topic caught my attention when a Senegalese family had tried to involve me in the migration plans for their oldest son, and when I was visiting him later, after he came over as a migrant worker in Europe. He and his friends drew their motivation from the example of 'the lucky ones' who manage to support their family with money from paradise; this conflicted with my knowledge as a sociologist, aware of the difficulties in European labour markets. I was left wondering how they do it: how do they manage to organise a life on unwelcoming territory? My initial interest lay in the labour dimension, but as the research evolved, I realised other areas of life had to be taken into account. Fatou Diome's illustrative novel about a Senegalese migrant woman in France provided me with the quote above, which paraphrases the journey of African migrants in Europe. This curiosity about West African labour migrant trajectories lays at the basis of this study, and forms its main topic.

The arrival of considerable numbers of migrant workers in European societies during the last couple of decades has raised a number of challenges for the individuals involved, as well as for the host societies. Taken together the group of migrants constitutes only 3 per cent of the world population, and those coming to western countries form a minority, but they attract attention that is disproportionate to their numbers. Labour migration has, in the 21st century, moved to the top of the policy agendas of many countries: debates about the 'migration crisis' have affected politics, public opinion, media, academia and society as a whole for the last decade (Schierup 2006). Stalker (2003) explains this by pointing at how labour migration confronts us with fundamental and hard questions about our society: about solidarity in and between countries, about identity and culture, about political status and moral duties (Sayad 1993). The number of conferences, publications and meetings is rife; labour unions, employers' organisations, government officials and journalists launch communications and initiatives; international organisations like the UN, the OECD, the ILO, the EU and the IOM coordinate activities in countries of origin, transit and destination. This reflects the shift in emphasis of the international debate on labour migration from its narrow focus on asylum seekers and refugees to a more broad-based view of linkages among migration, globalisation and development and sharing of benefits by both receiving and sending countries.

As both the receiving societies and the migration flows themselves evolve, it seems clear that the social and economic processes by which immigrants are received and incorporated will change as well. Understanding these processes will be important: the rapid changes have far-reaching implications for how new immigrants can gain a place in the economic and social life of their host countries. They are also significant for certain geographical areas where concentration of immigrants becomes a key factor in social transformation. In what follows, the 'dependent variable' of this study will be outlined: employment patterns and coping strategies of newly arrived migrants in host societies. The research question will be narrowed down and formulated, and some fundamental choices in the research design will be explained.

1.1 The research question: Understanding trajectories

Our knowledge of how recent immigrants manage to organise their lives and find their way in the complex labour markets is rather limited; there is a serious lack of insight in the nature and structure of the complexities of survival strategies and settlement. In this research I want to gain a better understanding of the trajectories of newly arrived low-skilled labour migrants in Europe: how they perceive and maximise their chances and what determines their decisions and strategies. Given that economic immigrants come in search of a better life, and that the context in which they arrive does not automatically provide them with the means to achieve that, how do they develop strategies to realise their goal? What kind of life-course patterns can be identified? How do they change over time?

In terms of trajectories, the only scenario that underlies most current appraisals of migration processes dates back to Piore (1979). He suggests that the transition from temporary migrant to permanent settler consists of several stages: initially, migrants behave like purely economic beings divorced from their social settings. They work for long hours in poor conditions, avoiding leisure and social contacts that may hinder the accumulation of funds and therefore their return aspirations. This initial commitment, however, cannot be sustained for long periods: as the need for companionship and community grows, the migrants work fewer hours, socialise more, send less money home and have to stay longer to reach their economic goals. Gradually, the migrants establish households in receiving places; a resident community grows with new social structures and new generations that may share the aspirations of native residents. According to Piore, those who settle permanently in these enclaves are concerned with upward mobility, job stability and their future in the receiving places.

However, this seems to be a rather individualistic appraisal of the process of settlement. De Lourdes Villar (1990) criticises this overly adaptationist framework in which migrants take advantage of the opportunities and cope with the constraints imposed by life in places of settlement, resulting in necessarily progressive accommodation. She stresses the role of adverse economic factors and new circumstances in pressing migrants to modify traditional behaviours and attitudes, while at the same time curtailing the migrants' potential to accumulate resources. In order to understand the possibilities and constraints they encounter over their trajectory as labour migrant, their micro-level individual decisions should be put in a broader perspective about the functioning of labour markets and states. The structural context will be fundamental to my research project.

Several studies have investigated how recently arrived migrants manage to survive in large cities. The first were published in the US (Briggs 1984; Chavez 1992; Chiswick 1984; Cornelius 1982); later, the topic saw a greater impetus in Europe as well (Engbersen 1995; Leman 1997; Leman et al. 1994; Tarrius 1992). These studies revealed a huge diversity and heterogeneity in groups of undocumented migrants in terms of their origins, the way in which they enter the country, their work and the structure of their family life. In general, the early years were characterised by case studies of particular migrant groups rather than generalisations for abstract theorising. Immigration was studied from an anthropological micro perspective, or as statistics in a macro-economic framework, but little attention was paid to the strategies themselves. Later studies have tried to put migration in its wider perspective, 'from geopolitics to micro politics', as in the study of Knights about Bangladeshi immigrants in Italy (1996). She includes the change of government in Bangladesh, the Italian legislation, the opening of Eastern Europe as a migration route, as well as the mechanisms of immigration, migration sponsorship, connections to Italian political groups and clientelistic relationships within the community. The Dutch in depth field study 'The Unknown City' is also proof of a comprehensive vision (Burgers & Engbersen 1999).

From these studies of migrants' experiences in the labour market and the 'gaps' they leave, the main points of attention for my research project will be discussed below. The trajectories of newly arriving migrants are the central topic, and form the 'dependent' variable. In order to study them, a number of fundamental choices were made from the start. The first is situated at the macro-level where I will look at political and economic opportunity structures and compare them between countries. Second, at the micro-level, is the choice of a model based on individual agency. Last is a focus on mobility in its widest sense, including legal categories, geography, as well as employment.

The macro-context: Labour market and state

The trajectory of an immigrant depends of course on individual characteristics, such as educational background or professional experience, but here I opt for a more structural approach. In her discussion of 200 years of migration in Europe, Sassen argues that international migrations are produced, they are patterned, and they are embedded in specific historical phases; this is why one should look at larger social, economic and political structures (Sassen 1999: 155). The socio-economic position of immigrants and the dynamics in their labour market position, their prospects with respect to their original goal, can only properly be understood by taking into account the socio-economic and politico-institutional environment of the country of settlement.

A first element is economic in nature: when trying to understand the place and position migrants are most likely to occupy in the host countries, an insight into the very dynamics of the labour market in which migrants arrive is crucial. In the post-war guestworker age of migration a specific balance between economic mode of production and migration existed. Drastic changes in the relationship between economic structures and their demographic bases have made the relationship between newly arriving migrant populations and the urban labour markets central to research and policy. Therefore, the realities of a changing post-industrial labour market should be analysed, with special attention to the built-in demand for immigrant labour. However, the migration flows also require responses from the state, stressing a second structural factor. The ways in which political bodies have tried to regulate and influence these market tendencies constitutes another theme, although it is difficult to separate between state and labour market dynamics. The state influences the labour market through regulating the principle cornerstones of entrance, retirement and paid absence; it also sets the conditions for migration, by allowing certain categories to enter the country, by attributing them with certain rights, and by controlling the territory.

These macro-scale structural factors result in a set of opportunities influencing the newly arrived migrants' mobility in the labour market: they offer a set of legitimate and illegitimate opportunities. A framework of 'independent variables' building on the interaction between the state, the labour market and migration will be developed in the next chapter. In order to highlight the importance of the labour market as well as the state, several authors have called for more explicitly comparative research on immigration in different countries and systems, testing explanations comparatively across nations and migratory systems to determine which ones prevail under what circumstances and why (Massey & Taylor 2004; Portes 1997; Reitz 2002).

The micro-level: Agency

Both the methodological individualism of neo-classical approaches and the legal positivism of state actors have ignored the agency of migrants and their families in different fields of reality; another tendency is to victimise migrants, seeing them merely as passive recipients of the macro-influences. Here, they are considered to be partly producers of their own process, with the capacity to mobilise resources, activate options and create or broaden their own spaces of control, be it in an arena that they do not have power over, where choices are limited by a range of factors including migration regimes, social networks and personal characteristics. These factors are not taken into account in a traditional neo-classic approach; the actor perspective used in this book will go beyond that of homo economicus, rationally looking for profit maximisation; those involved in the migration experience have other wishes and fears as well.

Although Giddens (1993) has not been able to overcome completely the dualisms of subject and object, agency and structure and structure and process (Cohen 1989; 1991), his structuration theory offers insights and tools to link individual lives with structural forces. Structure is not external to individual lives; structural properties are both the medium and the outcome of the practices they organise. Actions should be studied and analysed in their situated contexts, showing how they sustain and reproduce structural relations without falling into the functionalistic trap. There are no mechanical forces that guarantee the reproduction of a social system from day to day or from generation to generation, but all social life is generated in and through social praxis. In this sense, structure is internal, embodied; but it also stretches away in time and space, beyond the control of any individual actors. Through this approach, both structure and agency can be included in the analysis. The concept of strategy, for example, is used here to steer a course between giving individuals a sense of agency whilst at the same time retaining a sense of the contextual constraints that shape their lives. It refers to more or less rational principles which authors can articulate and describe, and which form general prescriptions for goal-oriented actions.[1]

The dynamic dimension: Time and space

Unlike the mobility that lies at the origin of their status as migrants, attention to processes of immigrants' dynamics in destination countries has been very limited in the geographical and sociological literature, which is characterised by a static perspective on the position of newly arrived migrants. Time and places, and changes in both dimensions, are not often taken into account (Leman 1997; Pérez 1995). Though both geographical and socio-economic mobility have been shown to be key concepts for immigrants to optimise their opportunities, this topic has not been extensively covered. Migrants move across space (looking for job opportunities in different seasons in different areas), but also across sectors and even across countries, improving their opportunities and blurring academic categories (Knights 1996). In a labour market where their competitive advantages lie largely in their flexibility, in an administrative context that makes it difficult to obtain or maintain work permits, the existing dichotomies of legal versus illegal residence status, and formal versus informal sector employment, are blurred. Within the category of undocumented immigrants, for instance, different degrees of exclusion exist: some are semi-integrated and others live a marginal and isolated existence (Chavez 1992); the movement between these categories by newly arrived migrants has been shown clearly but has not been analysed so far (Massey et al. 1998; Mendoza 1998). Traditional clear-cut definitions of status and work need considerable rethinking to capture the complexity, precariousness and volatility of migrant lives; their movements between existing categories may show relevant dynamics and need therefore closer examination (Kloosterman et al. 1999).

Recently, a wider pledge for a 'new mobility' paradigm has been launched: the movement of people, information and materials that was largely ignored or trivialised in social sciences should be more closely studied (Sheller & Urry 2006). Some empirical work has started to be developed (Gogia 2006). Recently, Schuster has made a first attempt, in distinguishing between 'status' mobility – how and why migrants move across categories such as documented vs. undocumented migrant, labour migrant, family member, asylum-seeker or refugee; and geographic mobility – which factors cause some migrants to move and move again, from one country to another and within countries. She shows convincingly how these are key questions in the daily lives of immigrants (Schuster 2005).

The resulting key questions

Based on these initial considerations, the research question can be narrowed down into a set of subquestions. From an original focus on labour market experiences, the research has evolved to a wider perspective on other dimensions of life. From both the theoretical framework and the interviews, it became clear that housing, social networks and legal status should be taken into account in order to explain possibilities and strategies on the labour market. The study has hence evolved towards a more integrated narrative on migratory experiences, although the central concern remains with employment.
The main question is therefore:
- How do newly arrived uninvited labour migrants find a place in European urban labour markets? How do they get by?

A set of subquestions can be derived from the points of attention outlined above:
- How does the employment situation of migrants develop over time? How can we modify the often static perspective? Can we distinguish certain phases in immigrant trajectories? How do these relate to Piore's three-phase model?

- How do other dimensions of life as an immigrant change over time? What is the role of social support systems, the legal context, the relationship with home and integration schemes? Is there a certain mobility in terms of geography, legal status, improvement of economic conditions?
- How is this trajectory influenced by structural forces such as the needs of the labour market and the state that regulates migration? How does this balance of possibilities and constraints change and evolve in different contexts? As a result, is the migratory experience different in different countries?
- Is the life-course methodology an appropriate instrument to examine the relationship between the agency of individual actors and structural factors? Is it a good tool to map various forms of mobility?

1.2 Research design

In order to answer these questions a research design was elaborated, which will be outlined and explained below. However, rather than testing very specific hypotheses, or measuring outcomes, this study sets out to understand and explain migration dynamics and the variety of mechanisms that are involved. The aim is to see how immigrants cope with conditions at their destination and develop strategies to reach their goal; this implies that individual respondents occupy a central place in the research.

The aim is to reconstruct trajectories over time, to gain an insight into the transitions and choices made by immigrants, and to explore their decisions and motivations within a specific economic and political opportunity structure. The focus on socio-economic and politico-institutional elements inspired the choice for a comparative approach; because of the attention to dynamics over time, a qualitative life-course model was chosen. The migrant group studied are West African immigrants; the particular contexts are Barcelona (Spain) and Antwerp (Belgium) with the explicit aim of comparing them. All these elements will be expanded upon below.

Qualitative life-course interviews

As past events and present thoughts and intentions cannot be observed, the answers to the research question cannot be found in existing statistics. In addition, parts of the group are not included in regular statistics due to their undocumented residence status; others because of the informal character of their employment activities. Motivations and reasons behind decisions cannot be questioned in a survey, pushing us in the direction of qualitative research. Nor is a random survey a possibility, for the targeted group is not represented in administrative databases. Even more important, we could argue that giving out a questionnaire to people living in jurisdictional, social and economic insecurity would not permit the collection of the pertinent information (Adam et al. 2001). Therefore, knowledge has to be based on small-scale studies of selected groups (Engbersen et al. 1999; Mendoza 1998). Particularly for the undocumented migrants that I want to include in the sample, or for the periods in which now regularised workers were illegal, we need to rely on retrospective interviews.

The life-course methodology suits the research questions very well, given that it takes into account changes over time, and employment mobility as well as geographical or administrative shifts of situation. It also corresponds with Giddens' structuration theory (1993), inspiring me to make a strong case for recognising the participants in this study as knowledgeable agents, who can describe what they do and their reasons for doing it with a complexity that often remains completely unexplored in standardised survey approaches. Therefore, evidence from qualitative life-course interviews will be used to get a greater depth of understanding of the strategies of new migrants, and will generate new questions.

The comparative case study

Next to stressing agency, Giddens (1993: 297) puts strong emphasis on the study of the context of behaviour; respondents are mostly geared to the flow of day-to-day conduct, while day-to-day life is also part of the reproduction of institutionalised practices:

> in moving from the analysis of strategic conduct to a recognition of the duality of structure, we have to begin to 'thread outwards' in time and space. That is to say, we have to try to see how the practices followed in a given range of contexts are embedded in wider reaches of time and space – in brief, we have to attempt to discover their relation to institutionalised practices.

As I want to show the political and economic context for understanding immigrant adaptation and integration in the labour market, I choose a comparative research design. It is based on the case study of a single relatively homogeneous group of immigrants in two different cities and countries (Burgess et al. 1994). The case studies provide an opportunity to explore differences between individual life paths as well as collective patterns, put in the context of cross-sectional material. I cannot put it better than Reitz (2002: 1011) when he outlines the need for comparative research, but also mentions 'the complexity involved', saying:

> Most research focused on a single setting. Rather than comparing the impact of different structures, the tendency has been to compare immigrants located differently within the same structure, as well as comparing labor market segments within a given setting (...) However, the research served primarily descriptive purposes because of the uncertain explanatory power of labor market structure, beyond the simpler concepts of discrimination and human capital. In a comparative context, the analytic opportunities increase, but so does the complexity. It is very meaningful to ask whether different labour market structures might lead to different outcomes and, if so, what those differences might be. The answer, however, must take account of two major issues. First, labor markets vary along several dimensions, including not only the size of immigrant segments and niches, but also overall employment regimes and industrial relations processes, earnings dispersions, gender inequalities, career structures and unemployment rates. Because these dimensions are frequently interrelated, the comparative perspective requires that they be considered together and in terms of their joint impact. Second, labor markets also are interrelated with other institutions of society, including education, the welfare state, and even immigration policy.

In Europe, there is varied experience with migration and illegal forms of employment, and covering them all would be impossible. First, comparing more communities in one setting would highlight the differences based on the migration motive, culture or national background, while looking at people from the same group of origin in two settings allows highlighting structural mechanisms of the context. In addition, as Soenen (2003) mentions, detailed information about a group's migration and labour market opportunities is never complete nor at free cost. This means that it would be difficult to develop a satisfactory degree of familiarity with a sample consisting of people from very different origins, each to some extent different in recruitment strategies for migration, ways of entering the country and specialised labour circuits. Second, because the type of analyses proposed implies a good knowledge of the local language and good working relationships with public authorities and other local actors, and due to limited time and resources, just two countries will be compared. This has the advantages of ethnographic richness, as there still can be an adequate familiarity to allow a satisfactory in-depth knowledge of the cases. At the same time, two cases allow us to get a first idea of diversity, and can generate to some extent results that might clarify a bigger picture of life as a newly arrived migrant.

However, international comparative policy research is a very complicated thing to do, and the ways to go about it have their own merits and problems. The extent to which we can control variation in case studies is limited: 'The only way to sustain the view that our cases differ in only a few dimensions is either to know very little about the cases or to willingly disregard most of what we do know' (Bryman & Burgess 1994:34). Rather than trying to argue that our cases represent unique cases or represent dominant groups (Beauregard 2003), it is the fact that they are just one of many ethnic communities having established themselves in just two of many ordinary cities in the last decades that makes them important. Studying them can therefore shed a light on processes that are shared by other immigrant groups in different countries.

Research population

The population will consist of immigrants from West Africa, more specifically from Senegal and Gambia. This choice is motivated by the continuing growth of migration from Africa to Europe in the last twenty years (Castles & Miller 1993): West Africans constitute an important part of the new migration flows into Europe of which little is known (Kaplan 1998; Leman 1997; Mendoza 1997). They also correspond to the category of 'new' migration, as they are arguably part of the increasingly diversified flows, and are relatively new in both Spain and Belgium, with no colonial links between the countries of origin and of destination. Their motivation to migrate is in general not based on the status of political refugee, but rather on the hard economic circumstances in their country of origin; their determination to find work on European labour markets is important for my research. In addition, they tend to be a perfect choice for highlighting the low-skilled niches in the labour market. In addition, they are a highly visible group being black immigrants and largely Muslim, which could potentially attract xenophobic reactions in the host society. A further elaboration of this population's migration characteristics will be provided in chapter four.

Focussing on the Senegambian population automatically means working with a single, relatively homogeneous group with specific characteristics, and giving up claims about this research being representative of wider African migration to Europe. The general dynamics probably are the same, both in the countries they leave as in the countries where they try to build a new life. The fact that Senegambians tend to be economic migrants (Kaplan 2001), for example, has important consequences upon arrival in Europe: they cannot rely on the government support that comes with asylum applications, and therefore depend primarily on each other for financial support and finding work (contrary to refugees). It also implies that their migration project is initially a temporary one, not with the aim of permanent settlement. The specialisation in the labour market, the nature of their solidarity networks, the French language background for Senegalese and English for Gambians, lack of colonial links and timing of migration all make up a specific profile that is (to an unknown extent) different from migrants coming from other parts of Africa. It may however shed light on migration from Mali, Guinea Bissau and Conakry, Burkina Faso and Mauritania.

Research areas

Focussing on cities makes sense because cities have commonly been the first destination of migrants, as they are important transfer points in terms of both mobility and information.[2] Cities continue to be transformed by the presence of new ethnic, racial and religious groupings who sometimes settle in the older cores of cities, or on the periphery in concentrated housing arrays; the city sets the scene for processes of social, economic and cultural integration and exclusion (Body-Gendrot & Martiniello 2000; Bousetta 2000). Large cities are the main gateways and often terminals for newly arriving migrants (Davis 2004). Their urban labour markets in particular have become the primary interfaces between two of the most salient contemporary socio-economic trends discussed above: the post-industrial transition as well as new large-scale immigration flows (Sassen 1991; Pugliese 1993; Kloosterman 1996). The two are interrelated, but the exact way is currently hotly debated throughout a variety of theoretical approaches and in numerous descriptive studies.

This research project will focus on economic change and new migration in European cities; the cases selected are the cities of Antwerp (in Belgium) and Barcelona (in Spain). Both are regionally important port cities with an industrial past, now featuring a changing labour market with a bigger service sector. Barcelona, in the northeastern corner of Spain, is its second largest city, the capital of the autonomous community of Catalonia and the main centre of Catalan economic development. Antwerp, in the north of Flanders, on the river Scheldt, is the second largest city of Belgium, the biggest of the Flemish region, and unmistakably the motor of economic growth in the area. While offering similarities in terms of economic profile (port cities, industrial basis, growing service sector), they differ in terms of institutional and welfare arrangements for immigrants and in the rigidity of the labour market.

Figure 1.1 *Maps of Belgium and Spain*

Source: www.state.gov

Belgium is one of the smaller EU countries and belongs to the core of 'old' Europe; Spain is far bigger and located at the southern border of Europe, forming a direct border with the developing world. In terms of migration history Spain, as other Southern European countries, was itself a supplier of labour migrants until the 1960s, while Belgium has a more long-standing tradition of receiving guest workers (Freeman 1995). The organisation of integration facilities and the legal framework surrounding migration are therefore more developed in Belgium; however, Belgium has moved towards a stricter migration regime, while Spain has been welcoming newly arriving workers. On the political level, Flanders has also seen the rise of an explicitly anti-immigrant political party (Vlaams Belang) that now receives almost 25 per cent of the votes; the socialist party in Spain deals since March 2004 with the migration issues it inherited from eight years conservative rule. The Belgian labour market is one of the most rigid in Europe, with high social protection of employees and heavy taxation on labour, while Spain has a more flexible labour market. The level of welfare provided is very different, with Belgium being quite generous and Spain representing a situation in which the provision of welfare services was aborted before having reached maturity. Therefore, the familial nature of reciprocity networks tends to be stronger in Spain than in Belgium. Comparing two cities that differ significantly can bring to light the differences that are expected to influence the trajectories and decisions of immigrants; they will be developed more systematically in the next chapter.

1.3 Structure of the book

The structure of this book, consisting of eight chapters, follows a relatively simple and classic scheme. This introduction outlines the research as a whole and pays attention to trajectories as the 'dependent' element. It is followed by the second chapter presenting the general analytical framework of the research: it explores central theories and concepts that can help to identify the 'independent variables' relevant to Senegambian immigrants' trajectories. Located in the wider landscape of sociological and geographical literature about new migration and urban labour markets, this framework includes a description of the changing post-industrial labour market, with special attention to the built-in demand for immigrant labour, as well as the state's response to migration flows in the form of immigration regulation processes. These structural factors will guide the analysis: they are illustrated for the two case studies, Antwerp and Barcelona, and allow a better understanding of the ways the ways immigrants enter, find work and live.

In the methods chapter, I focus on the strategies for obtaining and presenting the material collected for this study, from gaining access over sampling to the analysis. I will also deal in more depth with some issues arising specifically from life-course interviews and the challenges in interviewing undocumented migrants. A fourth chapter reflects the importance of migration as a livelihood strategy in Senegal and the Gambia. It argues that migration has become an institution, in at least three ways: the socio-political and economic setting that stimulates people to migrate, the specific migrant 'business' network that allows for networks, information and a fast entry into the informal European labour market, and the crucial role their remittances play on family and national level.

Chapters five to seven constitute the empirical core of this research, presenting the analysis of individual trajectories and the factors influencing them. Respecting the chronology of the life-course approach, I start with a report of the immigrant's life as an undocumented migrant, moving on in the next chapter to the phase of trying to regularise their stay, and in chapter seven I discuss their position as documented migrants. These successive phases run parallel to changing priority to survival strategies in the beginning, documentation strategies later and finally upward mobility strategies. Each of these chapters follows a similar outline, starting with an analysis of the labour market, trying to find patterns in the variety of experiences, and developing a typology of careers in both cities. But I also look for deviant options and the individual characteristics that influence these choices or possibilities. Next, I investigate the wider context in which the labour market trajectories take place, the way migrants try to overcome difficulties in employment situations and the importance of housing, family and community throughout the different steps many migrants take. The aim of these empirical chapters is a comparison of the patterns found in the two cities, and exploring the links to differences in state intervention, or in the functioning of labour markets. I argue that the macro contexts influence the lives of migrants not in a random way or as a side effect, but that the opportunities and constraints for migrants are rather a core element linked to society's structure.

To conclude, I evaluate existing theories in the light of my empirical findings, contradicting, modifying or complementing them with the insights derived from the research.

2 Embarking on an explanatory framework

> In Europe, my brothers, you're black first, citizens incidentally, outsiders permanently, and that's certainly not written in the constitution, but some can read it on your skin. So, you see, it's not enough just to set foot on French soil in order to live the life of those minimum-wage tourists [...]. There's unemployment over there now, too. What assets do you have that'll guarantee you success over there? When you're ambitious, you need a broad back. As illegal immigrants, you'll find it a hard slog if you're lucky enough not to get picked up by the police, who'll bundle you onto the next plane home. (Diome 2006: 124)

In Diome's novel, *The Belly of the Atlantic*, Salie works more than full-time as a cleaning lady to finance her advanced literature studies at a French university. On a return visit to Senegal, she tries to convince her younger brother and his friend – both determined to make it to Europe – that physical strength and determination are not sufficient to succeed, and that structural factors make individual lives difficult. She mentions two elements: the French labour market is not exactly waiting with open arms to receive unskilled migrant workers; and the state has not much consideration for undocumented foreigners. This argument does not impress the teenagers, but her points will be taken up in this chapter.

To explore how the trajectories of newly arriving Senegambian migrants are influenced by structural economic and political factors, this project compares two different cities, Antwerp and Barcelona. A wide range of social theories provides us with a list of elements that might be relevant for how migrant workers try to organise their lives: this ranges from theories about labour markets, over welfare states to migration policies themselves. Once identified, these can be applied to the specific case studies, in order to provide a concrete background against which the empirical analysis of the next chapters can take place. Detailed information on the different opportunity structures will result in concrete questions about the consequences for respondents facing the task of finding their way into two host societies.

2.1 What is new about recent labour migration?

'New' international migration emerged as a global phenomenon at the end of the 20th century; its symbolic starting point is often traced to 1989 and the geo-political and geo-economic changes of that year (Koser & Lutz 1998). The conclusion of the cold war and collapse of communist regimes resulted in the end of Europe's political division and the re-organisation of borders (Castles & Miller 1993). From a historical, conceptual, or philosophical point of view, the label of 'new' migration is arbitrary and debatable (Koser & Lutz 1998)[1]. As a relative and empirical term, it gains in value if one makes clear what is considered the 'old', and in what dimensions the phenomenon is different from earlier. Recent migration can be compared implicitly to the organised guest worker schemes of the 1950s and 1960s, and this juxtaposition may highlight some characteristics that are 'new', such as the changing migrant profile and flows, and the post-industrial labour markets.

The changing migration context

According to IOM (2005: 459), labour migration is the 'movement of persons from their home state to another state for the purpose of employment'[2]. This may sound very clear, but the terminology of immigration is not used with great rigour in daily discourses; to avoid confusion with, for example, asylum, it is necessary to highlight the variation inside the migrant population and to clarify the terms (Carlier & Rea 2001). In fact, when someone is working in another country, a number of legal descriptions might portray their situation.[3] They are likely to be a 'foreigner', a person who is not a national of a given country; they may be 'undocumented', 'clandestine' or 'irregular', all meaning 'migrant workers or members of their families not authorised to enter, to stay or to engage in employment in a state'.[4] However, they are probably not adequately labelled as 'asylum seeker' or 'refugee', terms that are frequently misused. These two concepts are based on the 1951 Refugee Convention (or the Geneva Convention) offering protection to people under a well-founded and proven fear of persecution due to race, religion, nationality, political opinion or membership of a social group.[5] Neither refugees nor asylum seekers can be illegal, given that refugees are granted the permission to stay, and asylum seekers have the right to stay until a decision on their application has been made.

However, we should be aware that the distinctions are not 'natural' but a product of the needs of the political and economic system, or of particular groups within them. The state sets out the administrative and legal conditions, processes and structures for recognition of different 'kinds' of migrants (labour migrants, refugees and permanent residents), and often shapes the political and ideological reactions to them (Bovenkerk et al. 1990). De Genova (2002) draws attention to the fact that social scientists have often uncritically taken over the distinctions, concepts and definitions that follow from migration legislation. It is, for example, quite common to make a distinction between political refugees and economic migrants, a division that coincides with notions of the 'good or deserving' foreigner (meeting the Geneva description) and the 'bad or undeserving' migrant (only looking for a better life).[6] Given that the economic difficulties that developing countries face are a direct result of the political situation of the country, it is difficult to decide if migration is due to political or economic reasons. In addition, the changing definitions in host countries over time show the relativity of these categories (Couper & Santamaria 1984).

The total number of labour migrants in the world is estimated to be 86 million, with 34 million of these in developing regions; in 2000, there were about 52 million migrants among the 465 million workers in high-income countries, making migrants an average twelve percent of their work forces (IOM 2005). They can be skilled workers, seasonal employees, trainees, working holidaymakers, transfers of staff within multinational companies, and cross-border workers. They are bricklayers or nurses, strawberry pickers or IT specialists, prostitutes or cleaners; some of them have contracts as highly paid managers, others live their lives in the margins of society as undocumented migrants. International migration expands its diversity in terms of origins and destinations, as well as social, demographic, and economic characteristics, which differentiates this period from the previous era of guest worker migration (Castles & Miller 1993; Collinson 1994; Massey et al. 1998; Pugliese 1993; Sassen 1994).

In terms of profile, a growing number of different nationalities and ethnic groups participate in the new migratory experience; migrants tend to be younger and more often female, making them different from the ones of other periods of migration in history. Within Europe, the opening of the eastern borders and the war in Yugoslavia initiated flows of migrants from these areas. Migrants also aim for new and different destinations, reflecting the changing poles of economic attraction: the new geography of migration includes the Gulf States, Eastern and Central Europe as well as India and China. In Europe, the Mediterranean countries have become a target for large-scale, spontaneous immigration, despite its rising unemployment and rather low rates of economic growth. New types of migration include intensified short-term and transit migration, as well as clandestine migration. Senegambian migrants in Antwerp and Barcelona are a good illustration of this increasingly mobile and diversified migrant population.

More than a decade has passed since social anthropologists Glick Schiller, Basch and Blank-Szanton (1992) introduced the notion of transnationality to academic discourse, which was soon to become one of the most popular concepts in current migration research. Although migrants have always kept in touch with home, Schiller suggested that an increasing number of immigrants orient their lives to two or more societies. Before, migration between places that were fundamentally distinct is said to have been either circular (with limited attachment to new destination, and migrant returned sooner or later to place of origin) or linear (permanent settlement, reorientation to the place of destination) (Castles 2002). However, the lives of these new migrants cut across national boundaries and bring two societies into a single social field; for some, migration may not be definite or irreversible and even the ones who have settled permanently entertain strong transnational links. The revolution in information and communication technologies has meant that many Africans in Europe are now able to live 'transnationally', maintaining significant social, economic and cultural ties with their countries of origin, and with fellow-migrants living elsewhere. Networks have been a central thematic for understanding the quotidian processes that make up transnationalism 'from below' (Boyd 1989; Portes 1997). Real empirical multi-site research is scarce; one example is Ghana Transnet looking at immigrants in the Netherlands, and tracing back their family members in different sites in Ghana (Mazzucato 2005).

These transnational contacts can result in active involvement in the economic, cultural, social and political life of sending countries; in flows of people, goods, money, and ideas; in the creation of new institutions that cross national boundaries; in short, place has changed to become multifaceted and translocal space. The impact of transnationality on nation-state sovereignty and autonomy, on economic activities as well as the process of migrant belonging, multiple identities, family life and multi-layered citizenship remains an open question (Brettell & Hollifield 2000; Bryceson & Vuorela 2002; Castles 2002; Cohen 1996; Faist 2000; Koser 2003). Although this study will not provide a detailed answer to the issue, the transnational ties will be taken into consideration when trying to understand migrant trajectories: attention will be paid to mobility patterns and community dimensions. At the same time, warnings go up not to exaggerate or presume the weight attributed to transnational ties, nor to assume that every migrant is involved to the same extent (Dahinden 2005).

The changing economic and political context

Economic migration movements towards Europe have existed for a long time, and were sometimes even initiated by industrial countries. The different phases of development that characterise the economic history of capitalism are associated with particular forms of interaction between the production system, the labour market and the state – and therefore with specific forms of migration. At each of the major downturns of the capitalist world-economy there has been a perceived need to restructure the specific mode of production, the state and the organisation of the labour market inflows (Johnston 1993). The combination of post-war economic growth and the inflow of migrant guest workers is well-known.

Recovery from the major downturn in the 1970s has involved a marked shift away from the structures of mass production and the rigid labour markets that typified Fordism, the emergence of 'flexible accumulation', distinguished by a remarkable fluidity of production arrangements, labour markets, financial organisation and consumption (Johnston 1993). The last two decades have seen a simultaneous growth in the complexity of production processes, in the significance of corporate structures of control and international financial systems. This in turn has led to a growing importance of new intermediate or producer services (like advertising, professional services, consultancy, computer services, cleaning, catering and other support services), changes in the pattern of locational advantage and changes in private consumption patterns. This process is generally called post-industrial economic restructuring (Cross & Moore 2002; Pugliese 1993; Sassen 1996) and its consequences for migrants on the labour market will be discussed below.

Another element of the new setting in which migrants arrive, is the ongoing complex debate about whether or not Europe needs migrants to fill the holes left by a shrinking and ageing local work force, and to make the welfare system tenable (UN 2000). The solutions proposed range from increasing the fertility rate, over diversifying the tax bases, to postponing retirement ages and shift to a capitalisation system (in which the present generation saves and capitalises for its own day of retirement), but increasing immigration has also been suggested. The debates between supporters and critics of this idea continue (see, for example, the debate between Harris and Coleman (2003)), but in general, both sides would agree that immigration alone cannot alleviate the ageing of the native population; it can only be a complementary measure and should be subject to practical and political constraints. In any case, these concerns have prompted many countries to consider stepping up immigration; some have already started to facilitate labour market access for skilled immigrant workers: Austria, France, Germany and Switzerland admitted about 15 per cent more immigrants in the last decade (OECD 2006).

Against this background, I will present some theoretical factors that can influence migrants' trajectories in their new home countries. The discussion of these 'independent variables' includes urban labour markets, state regulation of labour markets and migration policies.

2.2 The explanatory structural factors

This chapter explores the structural elements that frame the labour migrant experiences: how do Senegambian immigrants fare after arrival, and how do they make the money they need to realise their goal? In order to structure the answers to this question, I will refer to Polanyi's framework or three 'modes of economic integration'. Households and communities may or may not gain access to resources through either market exchange (market), re-distribution (state) or reciprocity mechanisms (networks), or a combination of those (Polanyi 1944; Harvey 1973; Mingione 1991; Kesteloot et al. 1997).[7] In western advanced economies, access to resources is dominated by 'market exchange', and the most obvious approach for most households is to put their labour on the market. Their wage is the price they get when they succeed in selling this. Others are self-employed and sell goods and services. The law of supply and demand broadly determines what they are paid; as a result, the labour market generates inherent stratification, and unequal access to resources based on strong or weak positions in the labour market. This can be socially destructive. To compensate partly for the structural inequalities generated through market exchange, the state can redistribute when everybody contributes to a common stock of resources that are redistributed according to agreed rules – one of which is the decision about who can access the system. Within the EU the organisation and extent of welfare state provision varies considerably between the different 'welfare regime types'. In this way, the state is also generative of inequalities, and is an important factor in patterns of social exclusion and spatial concentration of poverty. Finally, reciprocity helps people to obtain resources through mutual exchange. Goods and services brought into the system by one participant are given back by the other members, generally in the form of different goods and services, and frequently not at the same time. These features of the exchange process involve mutual trust between the members of an exchange network and binding ties between each participant and their network.

In order to identify the structural elements that will shape the trajectories of immigrants in Antwerp and Barcelona, a first section will deal with economic theories on immigrant incorporation in urban labour markets. Second, the redistribution role of the state in influencing immigrant possibilities and constraints will be discussed, including both its role in regulating the labour market and in defining the conditions for migration itself. Third, the redistribution role of social networks is very important. Immigrants effectively and strategically use social organisation as a resource which assists them in their struggle to live and work (Chavez 1990; Espinosa & Massey 1999; Massey 1999); some groups can fall back on strongly established migrant communities while others cannot do so or only to a limited extent (Engbersen & Van der Leun 2001). Networks can act as a barometer, measuring and comparing changes in the local conditions (Knights 1996), provide solidarity and create an internal market (Engbersen 2001). Hence, the most evident networks are the household, the extended family and sometimes neighbourhood networks or networks within ethnic minority communities. However, as mentioned in the introduction, the ethnic community is considered a constant element in this research and reciprocity strategies are therefore left out at this comparative stage of the overview; they will however be dealth with in the empirical analysis.

Urban labour markets

The past 25 years have seen a transformation of urban economies that is central to an understanding of the way in which migrants are accommodated. Cities used to have a thriving manufacturing economy, serving as staging grounds for unskilled newcomer groups; making a living but also 'integration' happened through the factory floor. In today's post-industrial societies, economic restructuring has changed the nature of labour demand, with both workers and companies responding to the opportunities this transformation presents; the socioeconomic positions of different social groups condition their strategies. However, the links between post-industrial economic restructuring and the labour demand for migrants are hotly debated and have inspired different theoretical attempts to grasp them (Cross & Moore 2002; Cross & Waldinger 2002; Pugliese 1993; Sassen 1996).

According to both neo-classical (Chiswick & Hatton 2002) and dual labour market theories (Cross & Moore 2002; Piore & Sabel 1984; Sassen 1991b; 1996), recent migrants such as the Senegambian population are expected to occupy jobs in remaining industrial sectors minimising labour costs (Kloosterman, Van der Leun & Rath 1999), or in a service sector characterised by polarisation (Rath & Kloosterman 1998), mainly because they are more willing to put up with relatively low wages, long hours and bad conditions (Linton 2002). They may try to escape these conditions by launching their own enterprise (Light 2002;

Kloosterman et al. 1998). Sassen (1991a; 1996) showed how the origin of demand for informally produced or distributed goods and services lies in the structural transformation of the economy. The emergence of downgraded and informal sectors staffed by migrant workers forms part and parcel of advanced capitalist strategies of deregulation and flexibility; it is just one dimension of the wider phenomenon of the 'casualisation' of employment (Pugliese 1993; Schierup 2006). Studies estimate the size of the informal economy as being, on average, between 7 per cent and 16 per cent of the EU's GDP (European Foundation for the Improvement of Living and Working Conditions 2005).

Different theories imply a different view on the time dimension: according to neo-classical approaches, migrants can move up the social ladder rather easily, while many other theories suggest a form of 'blockage' in specific sectors, where individual skills, previous education and work experience do not make any difference for labour market integration. In these fast-changing times, another element is cohort effects, or the time uniqueness of entering in the 1980s or late 1990s. Do labour market entrants of the same period face similar advantages or disadvantages (Clark 1998)? Recent economic developments in Barcelona and Antwerp play a major role in offering chances to newcomers: the degree of post-industrialisation, of economic growth, the presence of informal work, and the sectoral composition of the economy play a role. These elements will be taken into account in the case descriptions below.

State regulation of labour markets

The migrant labour market does not only follow economic laws and evolutions; since the beginning of the welfare state, these processes are mediated by state intervention (May et al. 2007; Schierup 2006). The degree of protection in the labour market, and the rules for redistributing welfare benefits by public or semi-public institutions, are crucial to immigrants' lives, influencing everything from their chances to earn an income, through their geographical mobility decisions to their family lives. A debate about the state is therefore crucial, as it can have influence as a single actor (e.g. in the organisation of welfare systems) or through setting the framework in which other actors perform (e.g. setting minimum incomes per sector); in its prerogative roles as gatekeeper, as provider of welfare and collective consumption, and as preserver of law and order.[8] The structure and institutional framework of the state is therefore critical to an understanding of labour markets. Almost by definition, the rules of the system make this redistributive dynamic explicitly restricted to legal citizens; however, by excluding the undocumented migrants, the state is equally important for them, and the degree of implementation heavily influences this general principle.

A first element is welfare regimes. Although most countries occupy intermediate positions in Esping-Andersen's (1990) ideal-type distinction between liberal, corporate, and social welfare states, it is possible to make a rough comparison between Spain and Belgium. Both countries score relatively high on corporatism, but Belgium has a second tendency more towards the social democratic type, while Spain has many characteristics of the family-oriented group. This would mean that the degree of regulation and protection is higher for Belgian citizens than for Spanish ones; the relative lack of control and the more flexible labour market in Spain might provide more chances for low-skilled and/or undocumented workers.

A second dimension consists of labour market policies. In highly controlled labour market regimes, legal labour is protected by a dense web of state regulations concerning the minimum wages, hours of work, fringe benefits, work environment, health issues, hiring and firing conditions. However, recent trends on post-industrial labour markets have implied a dismantling of labour market regulations, a dramatic increase in the practice of subcontracting, smaller companies, informalisation, flexibilisation and 'casualisation' (Cross & Waldinger 2002; Gordon & Sassen 1992; Held et al. 1999; Jordan & Düvell 2002; Van der Leun & Kloosterman 2006). It has been argued that strict approaches to labour market regulation (like Belgium) have tempered this deregularisation of the labour market. In general, countries with less comprehensive regulation of labour markets and less elaborated systems of social insurance (like Spain), went furthest in increasing flexibility and mobility in the labour market (Jordan & Düvell 2002). On the importance of the informal labour market there seem to be different hypotheses. A high degree of casualisation (Spain) might raise the level of informality, but so might a high level of labour market regulation (Belgium) by unintendedly pricing out many jobs of the formal market through high minimum wages and other regulations that drive up the labour costs above the level of labour productivity (Cross & Moore 2002; Van der Leun & Kloosterman 2006).

A third difference can be found in social policies. When the labour market does not supply an income, the welfare state may provide via the availability of a number of safety nets, in terms of unemployment benefits, health insurance etc., at least for national citizens (Vink 2005). In order to understand which social policies play a role in migrant lives, Baldwin-Edwards (2004: from p. 326 onwards) identifies a number of different phases in the life cycle of a migrant and his relationship with welfare regimes. First, in the case of undocumented migrants, his hypothesis is that they are likely to exist completely outside of the system under conservative regimes, owing to the high degree of regulation. Limited evidence in southern Europe suggests that they are more part of the system. In the phase of long-term residency and bringing over family, southern Europe would represent the most socially unprotected geographical area for migrants, because of the temporality of residence permits and the highly skewed welfare systems. By contrast, the conservative state is perceived to present more rights after substantial periods of employment and residence. In the last phase, the establishment of ethnic communities exhibit high unemployment rates along with low participation rates, and raises questions about integration and include anti-discrimination policies to guarantee competitive and fair labour markets rules. In spite of the growing similarity of basic principles among European states, discrepancies remain in the rights each country grants to foreigners, including social protection, access to work and to citizenship (Geddes 2003; Withol de Wenden 2004).

Migration policies

De Genova's plea (2002) for a scientific 'problematisation' of the history of immigration law shows the production over time of a set of legislative interventions on labour migration, linked with economic needs, and previous experiences with migration. As an answer to the crisis of the 1970s, European countries imposed the principle of closed borders. The creation of the common monetary and economic European market reinforced this trend towards protecting internal labour markets, with more restrictive immigration policies for non-EU workers, except for high-skilled professionals (Awad 2004; Geddes 2003). Border control against uninvited workers became a priority everywhere, as well as the strengthening of public authorities' powers over matters relating to entry and stay. Governments of destination countries have tried to fight against abuse of the remaining channels, by making the procedures for family reunification, students, asylum seekers and tourists with visas increasingly difficult and controlled. In this context, and for the first time maybe in migration history, although they were present before, 'illegality' has become increasingly a pressing policy issue at the core of the migration debate.[9] Undocumented migrants are usually bracketed by public opinion and by political initiatives and racist and extreme nationalist movements into a single category with very negative connotations (Arango & Baldwin-Edwards 1998). By definition and because of hardship, they challenge the system, they break laws and rules, compete with legal migrants and citizens for job opportunities. At the same time, they also live in the core of our society, on the expensive square meters of rack-renters, clean our houses, plaster our walls, pick our tomatoes and wash our dishes, representing unprecedented challenges to policymakers.

In the face of similar problems of undocumented migration, the basis for a common immigration policy has been negotiated in the EU, from the 1986 Single European Act over the Schengen Convention (1990) to Treaties of Maastricht (1992) and Amsterdam (1998). Despite these attempts to harmonisation of immigration policies, the bulk of legislation is still national and discrepancies remain in their approaches to migration policy (Boswell 2003; Favell & Geddes 1999; Stalker 2002). Owing to the distinctive histories and geographies of European states, as well as to pressure from national public opinion, policies differ in the right to enter as refugee and asylum seeker, the length of residence card validity or access to citizenship and the priorities for managing illegal migration (Withol de Wenden 2004). The national immigration and asylum legislation generally acts on the matter according to current political interests and needs, and lack a prospective vision. The mix between these policy elements can be different between countries; in addition, the configuration of and between welfare state and labour market may differ. Freeman (1995) distinguishes three different types of immigration policies and traditions in liberal democracies. The most expansionist and inclusive are the traditional English-speaking settler communities, which are of less interest here.

Belgium belongs to the group of Western European states that as fully developed national states faced labour shortages after WWII, mounted temporary labour programmes for workers from Southern Europe, Morocco and Turkey. After the oil crisis of the early 1970s, all of them declared migration stops; they were faced with the fact that many guest workers did not return but stayed in the country, and that the state was unable to cope with this group. The general public was mildly sceptical, later more outspokenly negative, and nowadays overt conflict and extremist parties can be found in many countries. Politicians try to reassure voters with restrictionist policies while they often lack the capacity and probably also the political will to stop the migration flows. Policies in these countries are still haunted by 'the mistakes, failures, and unforeseen consequences of the guest worker era and by the social conflicts associated with the new ethnic minorities' (Freeman 1995: 890).

Spain, on the contrary, but like other Southern European states, has only recently gone from being a labour exporter and has only in the last two decades become a net immigration country, with specific characteristics (King 2000; King et al. 1997). Spanish immigration policy was marked by the near complete absence of any institutional mechanisms or administrative experience as to planning, regulating or controlling migration; and by the external pressure by the EU to impose them (Awad 2004). This has resulted in a series of new laws imposing visas, work and residence permits, social and political rights, in a partial and ineffective attempt to organise legal entry, curtail illegal entry and regularise those already inside (Freeman 1995).

This discussion has raised a number of variables that can influence the trajectories of migrants in Barcelona and Antwerp. We can see the image of a 'differential opportunity structure' in both cities emerging, based on different limits and opportunities. This image will now be more concrete with a description of the case studies.

2.3 The two case studies

In order to highlight the structural factors influencing migrant trajectories, this study proposes a comparative analysis of two case studies, Antwerp and Barcelona. The functioning of labour markets, welfare policies and immigration politics will be elaborated for the two localities in a detailed and consistent context setting, embedding them in a historical perspective and with attention to the national and the local levels, in a modest attempt to follow Schierup's description of the immense variety of Europe's social and political landscape (2006). The aim is not to test the above theories empirically, but to show the relevance of the elements listed for the variety of immigrants' conditions of social insertion or exclusion in the daily urban life, representing limits, rights, and possibilities in different urban settings.

More than the theory, the actual implementation of the institutional framework is very important for it can differ considerably from the discourse, the principles and even the letter of the law. This requires looking at more decentralised levels of decision-making, where the policies are interpreted and tested against reality. Migrant settlement creates specifically local problems that local authorities must cope with, affecting a broad range of local policy areas, often in the absence of clear or effective national policy (Alexander 2004).

Antwerp

With 461,000 inhabitants,[10] Antwerp is the second largest city of Belgium, a country that counts about ten million inhabitants; it is also an important harbour city and centre for industrial labour, making it a key area for the economic dynamic in Flanders. By the same dynamics, it has long been a stronghold of Catholicism and socialism, since it contained a wealthy trading class next to a massive industrial proletariat: for seven decades, the power was in the hands of socialists and Christian Democrats. The important economic dynamic in Antwerp has attracted immigration since the end of WWII; later foreign workers also engaged in tertiary niches of the urban labour market; this early presence of guest workers differentiates Antwerp from Barcelona (Adriaenssens and Geldof 1997; Eggerickx et al. 1999). More than 150 nationalities live in the territory, making up 13 per cent of the population, with the Moroccans and the Turks as largest non-EU groups (Vermorgen 2002).[11] Many live in the 19th century belt around the medieval centre of the city, an area that was abandoned by its original population in the 1950s and 1960s who moved towards suburban areas. There, 40 per cent of the population is from foreign origin, and unemployment stands at 16 per cent.[12]

In terms of local politics, the politicisation of the migrant question in the decaying 19th-century neighbourhoods of the city, police inefficiency in the face of increased petty crime, the lack of adequate and sufficient social housing projects and the dirtiness of the streets have made Antwerp since 1988 the breeding ground of the Flemish extreme-right, incarnated by the Vlaams Blok party (Blommaert & Martiniello 1996). Next to favouring Flemish independence, the family as social cornerstone and tougher combating of crime, the Vlaams Blok holds radical views on issues such as migrant workers, political refugees and the status of Islam (Govaert 1995).[13] The party is today not only successful in deprived areas, but also in middle-class and well-to-do neighbourhoods; steadily winning elections, they became the largest party in the city with over 30 per cent of the votes and could therefore be viewed as the single most influential element in local politics, as well as at the Flemish and federal level. The fear of the continuing growth of the extreme-right in Flanders[14] motivated government efforts to control and limit these flows and excesses, and to present an image of toughness and strictness, without actually developing a coherent migration policy (Deslé 1997). On the political level, all 'democratic' parties (as opposed to the undemocratic Vlaams Blok) had to join the coalition in 1994 (and again in 2000) in order to construct a political 'cordon sanitaire'. A difficult coalition between Christian-democrats, socialists, liberals, green party and Flemish nationalists had to be assembled through protracted and difficult negotiations; difference of viewpoints and the parties' urge to profile themselves did not favour efficient policymaking. The new mayor, Patrick Janssens, managed to change the dynamics and perceptions; in the October 2006 local elections, Vlaams Belang kept its 33 per cent of votes, but the Socialist party of the mayor took the first position with 35 per cent.

Concerning the discussion of migration, economy and social policies, not only the appropriate municipal authorities are involved and responsible, but also the regional and the national level. Before 1970, Belgium was a highly centralised unitary state including three levels of power: the state, the provinces, and the communities. However, a series of constitutional reforms have fundamentally reshuffled the institutional landscape and resulted in the federalisation of Belgium, bringing about a gradual and complex devolution of powers from the federal level to the Communities and Regions[15] (Blommaert & Martiniello 1996).

Economy and labour market
As suggested above, the evolution of the economy in general and the labour market in particular, are crucial to an understanding of migrant trajectories. Since the end of the coal mining in the late 1970s, Belgium has few natural resources and needs to capitalise on its central geographic location in Europe, highly developed transport network, and diversified industrial and commercial base. The main exports are machinery and equipment, chemicals, diamonds, metals and metal products, as well as foodstuffs. The gross domestic product per head is $29,360; agriculture contributes one per cent, industry 18 per cent, construction 5 per cent, and services 76 per cent to the total GDP (OECD 2005). The disparities in economic performance take a geographical form (Estevão 2002): while heavy industries made the south historically richer and more dynamic than the north, economic growth and employment in Flanders have now surpassed those in Wallonia thanks to a post-industrial modern, late-capitalist private-enterprise economy. Despite a high level of unemployment, some enterprises or sectors in Flemish community have serious problems in finding appropriate personnel. This is the result of a gap between the low level of education of the job seekers and the quality requirements that the employers demand, as well as the sometimes unattractive labour conditions. Despite this demand, populations of migrant origin face high unemployment rates, particularly people with non-OECD nationalities; within the wide variation, the Africans and Turkish are least successful (OECD 2005). In the city of Antwerp specifically, the economy turns around trade, with the seaport at the heart of economic life; another important economic activity is the diamond trade, with a worldwide leading position. Industrial activities have declined since 1970s, resulting in increased unemployment (WAV 2000).

The most recent OECD employment report sketches the situation of the Belgian labour market, as presented in Table 2.1. Compared to the other countries, economic growth is slower; this weak economic growth is translated into a low rate of employment growth. Unemployment is higher than the OECD average, and concerns exist that long term and high unemployment benefits have an adverse effect on labour market performance (OECD 2006). The demand for temporary workers has been growing steadily over the last three years, reaching 90,000 on an average working day (*De Standaard* 10 January 2007); they are often an introduction into fixed work. The costs to employ a person permanently are high. For the informal labour market, the Belgian government estimated undeclared work at 20 per cent in 2004, concentrated in the sectors of construction, hotels and restaurants, cleaning, agriculture, and domestic services (Schneider 2006). The economic crisis has led to an increase in undeclared work, due to the potential cost savings that it allows to employers, as well as to workers, such as savings on tax and social security contributions both employers and workers (European Foundation for the Improvement of Living and Working Conditions 2005). For the growing group of undocumented migrants, such as part of the respondents in this research, gaining access to this informal work is their only option.

Table 2.1 *Key labour market indicators for Belgium and OECD countries*

	1993-2003	2004	2005	Average OECD 2005
Growth of real GDP, percentage change from previous period	2.2	2.4	1.5	2.8
Employment and labour force growth, percentage change from previous period	0.7	0.6	0.9	1.1
Unemployment rate	8.5	8.4	8.4	6.4
Ratio of employer's labour costs for minimum wage workers relative to median wage workers in the 21 OECD countries with statutory minima, 2004	-	0.45	-	-

Source: OECD Employment Outlook 2006

Migration policies
Belgium has a relatively long tradition of migration, attracting a variety of spontaneous migrants because of its central position (Caestecker 2000; Deslé 1997; Lennert & Decroly 2002; Martiniello 1997). The official migration stop in 1974 put an end to active recruitment policies of Italian, Moroccan and Turkish guest workers for the industries of heavy steel, construction, textile and harbours that were hit by a major economic crisis, stagnation and decline (Ouali 1997).[16] Since then and until very recently, the doctrine of zero-immigration has dominated; the admission, entry, visit, and settling of foreigners have been based on more and more restrictive legislative and statutory provisions, partly reinforced by the process of European integration. The 15 December 1980 law constitutes the basic text on questions of foreigners' administrative status; it limited family reunion, study permits and work permits for non-EU foreigners, and proposed voluntary return schemes to foreigners (Caestecker 2000). The law has been modified more than twenty times, centring around three major points but always pointing

to more limitations (Bribosia & Rea 2002; Vuylsteke 2006). First, making the conditions for entry to the country more difficult; second, restricting the procedures for recognition of refugee status, making it rapid and clear; third, hardening the rules for residence, settling, deportation, social protection and foreigners' access to the labour market.

In fact, this migration stop was never fully implemented and Belgium has always remained a country of immigration, with never less than 35,000 entries per year (Lennert & Decroly 2002; Vlaamse Gemeenschap 2003), though never in a pro-active planned way. Free circulation of EU citizens remained possible, and the guest worker population have, instead of returning home, brought their families over in family reunion schemes (in 2004, this figure mounted to 31,342, more than double the number of asylum seekers (*De Standaard* 21 October 2006). There were legal admissions for foreign students for the length of their studies, and work permits for specific categories of highly qualified workers (Wets 2001). Belgium also became a country of passage for people on the way to the UK (Demets 2003), shown by the relatively large numbers of people caught around the harbour and train stations.[17] The right of asylum has continued, and other people choose to reach the country as undocumented migrants, illustrating the theoretical trend explained above. As an asylum application seemed to be the only way left to hope for a residence permit, the system with its various competent authorities had to cope with a flood of improper asylum demands.[18] In the early 1990s, the number of asylum applications was around 5,200 per year, but in the later 1990s, it reached on average 18,000.[19] The government claims that their decision to give asylum seekers only material support instead of money has resulted in a decline to 11,600 applications in 2006 (*De Standaard* 3 January 2007).[20] The accompanying regularisation in 2000 gave residence to about 40,000 people, out of 50,000 applications (OECD 2005; Wets 2001). Migration is an important phenomenon for Belgium and numbers are above the average for the EU. Over 8 per cent of the population, or some 850,000 people out of 10.4 million, do not have Belgian nationality; around 70 per cent of these are EU nationals (OECD 2005). Recently, a system has been opened in which Eastern European workers can migrate to Belgium in the framework of specific job contracts that fill gaps in the labour market.

However, politics seem unable to control totally such a complex social process as migration (Caestecker 2000). In addition to legal migration, Engbersen estimates that between 100,000 to 150,000 people live as undocumented migrants in Belgium (*De Standaard* 20 January 2007). Their only hope for regularising their stay is marriage or article 9.3 of the law, providing the exceptional opportunity to demand a visa when already in Belgium, for humanitarian reasons. This case by case procedure has now become a standard step, but a very small number of people are regularised (Wets 2001). Although the repatriation capacity of the state is limited and the presence of undocumented migrants is sometimes tolerated, an active detention and repatriation policy exists (Wets 2001). Many of them seek shelter in the immigration concentration neighbourhoods of large cities: in Antwerp-North, some schools have 40 per cent undocumented children, 75 per cent of the patients of *Medecins Sans Frontières* and 70 per cent of the non-Belgian victims of rack-renters are people without papers. All aid organisations have seen their stock of clients grow so strongly that they have had to close the door to a queue of waiting people – although only an estimated 20 per cent asks for help (Frederix 2005).

More recently, the demographic and economic need for migration were the subject of strong discussion; despite the external and internal pressures to open the borders, there is no political consensus within Belgium (Martiniello 2003; Ouali 1997). In the framework of migration from the new EU member states, Belgium chose to close its borders; however, it facilitated the procedure for work permits from Belgian companies needing extra labour force in specific niches confronted with a shortage ('bottleneck professions'). In 2006, some 6,800 migrant workers entered, of which 85 per cent work in agriculture and horticulture; the construction, catering and transport sectors also took several hundreds of workers each.

The Belgian nationality code, which was adopted in June 1984, has also been modified on several occasions, resulting in progressively easier access to citizenship. The so-called 'quickly Belgian law' of 1 May 2000, put Belgium on the avant-garde in the field of acquiring nationality. On simple declaration in the municipal administration, every resident staying legally for three years in Belgium can become Belgian in one month, after being interviewed by the Public Prosecutor about their conduct, but not about their willingness to integrate as before (or automatically for third generation). In 2000 this resulted in about 54,950 applications, mostly from Moroccan, Turkish and Congolese residents.[21]

Social policies
In Belgium, the gradual construction of the welfare state since the end of the 19th century has resulted in a system of significant and relatively adequate income redistribution, financed through taxes and social security contributions (Vranken et al., 2001). Gross public expenditure in Belgium consistutes 28 per cent of GDP at factor cost in 2001; after direct and indirect taxation of public transfer incomes, the total net social spending stands at 26.3 per cent (OECD 2005:32). According to Esping-Andersen (1990), the Belgian welfare state belongs to the continental conservative type; conservative because it is still based on the tra-

ditional family model, preserves the social hierarchy determined by the market, and participation in the system of redistribution is defined by one's position in the labour market. The risks covered include pensions, unemployment benefit, sickness and disability benefits, industrial accidents, occupational diseases, family allowance and sickness insurance. In addition, thanks to an additional redistribution scheme in 1974, a subsistence income is available to everyone, including those who do not participate in the labour market, which means the level of social protection can more or less be compared to the Scandinavian social-democratic countries (Dewilde 2004). However, for undocumented migrants there is only a basic right to some emergency health services, some social services, and education (Desmarez et al. 2004; Wets 2001).

At the same time, the system is labelled 'corporate'. This means that the social partners are closely involved in policy determination and in the management of the social security system. Collective negotiations, in which employers, the state, and the unions take part, determine the labour market agreements, resulting in a more regulated labour market, where labour protection and conditions are subordinate to the aim of flexibility. The high labour costs and strict regulation of the labour market are said to stand in the way of active job creation policies in the private sector, and the welfare state is strongly biased against the expansion of government social services as an alternative strategy for employment promotion. To meet these changed circumstances, consensus has grown about the 'active welfare state approach' in the second half of the 1990s. The relationship between social security and assistance has changed and is still changing by the introduction of other distribution principles than need, such as merit or moral arguments.

Specific integration policies for immigrants developed quite late throughout the 1980s and 1990s, because of the hidden consensus on the provisional character of guest worker migration (Martiniello 2003). The existing and expanding foreign and ethnic minority population left Belgian society facing never-anticipated integration problems, particularly regarding education and labour market incorporation. Many smaller private initiatives had started to support former migrants and their children, and in 1981 a first law against racism was introduced. It was only after the first breakthrough of the rightwing Vlaams Blok party in the 1988 local elections that a Royal Commissariat for Migrant Policies was erected, to be replaced in 1993 with a permanent institute 'Centre for Equal Opportunities and the Fight Against Racism'. Phases of progress have often been inspired by three elements: the electoral success of extreme-right, Islamic fundamentalism and urban violence (such as the May 1991 urban revolts in Vorst) (Deslé 1997). The separate actions and projects, financed privately and by different public authorities, were gradually brought together and are now coordinated by the city.

The DIA (Integration Service Antwerp) coordinates the city council's policy on minorities in three fields (Vermorgen 2002): the support of the services in their contacts with the population of a different cultural background and the introduction of diversity management in the whole of the city; the reception and the settling down of new residents; and the fostering of contacts with and participation of the established ethnic minority communities in the city (Blommaert & Martiniello 1996).

As the design of integration policies belongs to the authority of the communities, integration policies have traditionally taken different shapes in the different regions. Flanders, inspired by the Dutch multicultural model, focused on cultural and linguistic integration. This has been criticised because the concept of integration is transformed into a purely voluntaristic concept, controlled by Belgians, centred on vague notions of a culturally homogeneous nation-state, and finally the responsibility of migrants alone (Blommaert & Verschueren 1991). The policies developed in the Walloon part followed the French republican model with a general focus on relieving socio-economic inequalities (Blommaert & Martiniello 1996). Now, policies seem to converge as there is more attention to general social and economic considerations in Flanders, and for cultural diversity in Wallonia (Martiniello 2003). Overall, the tendency has been to move away from a target group policy towards a diversity policy and one of equal opportunities, horizontally represented over all departments of the city. Since 2004, some groups of newcomers (non-European, unemployed) are obligated to take an 'integration course', including language courses and an offer of intensive labour market guidance (Desmarez et al. 2004).

Barcelona

Barcelona is considerably bigger than Antwerp, with 1.5 million citizens; Spain outsizes Belgium fivefold with 42 million inhabitants. The percentage of immigrants used to be considerably lower, with two to three per cent, constituted mainly of Moroccans, Peruvians and EU citizens.[22] However, Spain is now the country with one of the highest rhythms of immigration in Europe, even only looking at legal entries, with an increase of 24 per cent in 2003 (Pajares 2004). A socio-historical approach to the Spanish state, political culture and civil society reminds us that Spain has a fairly young local democracy dating from 1979, when the first local democratic elections took place. The first local democratic elections in 1979 were won by the main Social democratic party with large majorities. In Barcelona the local branch PSC (Partit dels Socialistas de Catalunya) has remained in power until today through different coalitions with other leftwing parties like the ex-communists, and the left oriented nationalists. At the national level, the socialists won the elections in 1982 and stayed in power until 1996, when the Popular Party ruled for eight years, until the socialists took over again days after the Madrid bombings that left 191 people dead in March 2004.

Somewhat parallel to Belgium, the Spanish 'State of the Autonomous Governments' since the early 80's has gradually been giving increasing jurisdiction to the regional governments, making Spain today one of the most decentralised countries in the EU.[23] Local governments as well have gained in jurisdiction and have become the closest institutional level to the citizen. Because of limits in terms of financial resources, and restricted political power, most policies necessarily need the collaboration of both levels. In issues of migration, the region of Catalonia does not have the authority to manage autonomously immigration from abroad, and has to comply with the general lines of Spanish state policies in relation to work and residence permits; the different powers will be discussed where relevant.

Economy and labour market
In the 1980s, the opening of the Spanish economy to foreign capital and firms implied economic restructuring and a changing post-industrial labour demand (as described in theory above). The administration advocated liberalisation, privatisation and deregulation of the economy of the predominantly family-based small firms and introduced some tax reforms to that end. The low productivity sectors (intensive agriculture, tourism, the construction trades and small industries) faced reduced percentage gains due to the end of the internal rural exodus, while the need to keep being competitive in a European market made it unaffordable to raise salaries. The types of jobs involved implied hard manual labour, low-status and flexible work in the service sector or casual and often seasonal labour, increasingly rejected by the Spanish population. While these often entered unemployment, Spain turned to immigrant workers from poor countries. However, critics argue the attention to flexibilisation of the labour markets has lead to a neglect of the necessary structural reforms of sectors (Magone 2004): Spain has still inefficient agricultural and industrial sectors, often small scale, with some forms of production struggling to keep up technologically with the more advanced economies. The rapid economic growth has led to the development of segmented labour markets with large informal sectors generating a demand for workers. Catalonia in particular has experienced in the 1980s and early 1990s powerful economic developments linked to a combination of more-or-less standard post-Fordist economic restructuring and more regional tendencies, inspired amongst others by the new strategic geographical position in the EU, and the 1992 Olympic Games

in Barcelona (King & Rodríguez-Melguizo 1999), attracting flows of international immigrant workers.

Gross Domestic Product per head stands at $19,869, considerably lower than Belgium, with agriculture contributing 4 per cent, industry 18 per cent, construction 11 per cent and services 67 per cent (OECD 2003). The main industries include textiles, transport equipment, metal manufactures and agricultural products. The Spanish economy records relatively strong growth compared to the other EU countries, as seen in Table 2.2, with five percent annual growth on average. It also belongs to the highest group for employment and labour force growth. Very sharp cuts in unemployment rates were recorded in Spain, though they are still above the OECD average; more importantly, the report notices that this 'went hand in hand with a marked slow-down in the growth of output' (p. 34). This 'productivity-poor' growth has been most visible in Italy and Spain, with productivity growth falling to very low levels, and it is linked to the increase in employment of less-educated workers.

Table 2.2 *Key labour market indicators for Spain and OECD countries*

	1993-2003	2004	2005	Average OECD 2005
Growth of real GDP, percentage change from previous period	3.5	3.1	3.4	2.8
Employment and labour force growth, percentage change from previous period	3.5	3.9	4.8	1.1
Unemployment rate	14.4	10.4	9.2	6.4
Ratio of employer's labour costs for minimum wage workers relative to median wage workers in the 21 OECD countries with statutory minima, 2004		0.3		

Source: OECD Employment Outlook 2006

A particular characteristic of the Mediterranean economies is their dual nature: a technologically advanced primary sector, with high degrees of unionisation and state-regulation alongside an extensive underground economy of localised networks of smaller handicraft and industrial workshops, often family-based, which have now expanded to sectors that are integral parts of Spanish industrial economy (Calavita 1998; for Italy, see Schierup et al. 2006). The relatively large informal sector is historically linked with the presence of self-employed workers, micro-enterprises and subsistence economies, while subsequently the policies of work flexibility have contributed to its existence (Quassoli 1999). An EU study in 2000 calculated that the underground economy in Spain represented 22 per cent of the total (European Foundation for the Improvement of Living and Working Conditions 2005).

Another form of segmentation is shown in the proliferation of temporary and part-time jobs, which are in excess of 30 per cent according to the most recent Employment Outlook. Many workers are trapped in temporary/non-employment cycles that represent as much as 11 per cent of total employment in Spain (OECD 2006). The labour force is increasingly split between older, long-term workers who enjoy indefinite contracts and high levels of protection, and contingent employees with fixed-term contracts (Calavita 1998).

The role of immigrants in the economic picture is aptly summarised by Schierup and his colleagues in some of the subtitles of their most recent book: *The Shifting Role of Migrant Labour: Between 'Primitive Accumulation' and 'Flexibilization'* and *From 'Irregularity' to 'Atypical Jobs'* (Schierup, Hansen & Castles 2006). This points at the fact that immigrants, many of them undocumented, used to be a residual factor boosting flexibility in sectors under heavy global competition; while nowadays, many of them are regular workers and a central structural component of the economy. The jobs they occupy still tend to be marginal, as seen in the temporary and part-time contracts, linked to employers' drive for flexibility and diminished working conditions and labour costs.

The economic growth is directly linked to the arrival of migrants, and this relationship had become widely acknowledged by Spanish public opinion (*El País* 22 March 2007), labour unions, employers, and authorities. It is estimated that its contribution to the GDP in the decade 1995-2005 has been 3.2 per cent annually (Caixa Catalunya 2006). On a regular basis, reports are commissioned stating that Spain will need more migrants to meet the labour demands of its growing economy.

Migration policies
Spain was traditionally a country of emigration, and continued to be so for the biggest part of the 20th century. Its economy after 1950 was, and to some extent continues to be, characterised by the coexistence of economic sectors of high and low productivity. This lead to the rapid movement of many workers to other regions within Spain as well as to other European countries, leaving some rural areas depopulated in the 1970s (King, Fielding & Black 1997). However, the 1973 oil crisis represented the closure of Western European countries to further labour migration and with it, the end of the cycle of mass emigration of Spanish workers. During the later 1970s and early 1980s, Spain started to receive considerable flows of return migration, consisting of workers and their dependants, although large numbers of Spanish continue to live abroad (Cachón 1999; King 2000). However, the development has

been accelerating and the increase in migration has sharpened after 1995 and even more after 2000, as seen in Figure 2.1.

Figure 2.1 *Foreign residents in Spain, evolution 1955-2008*

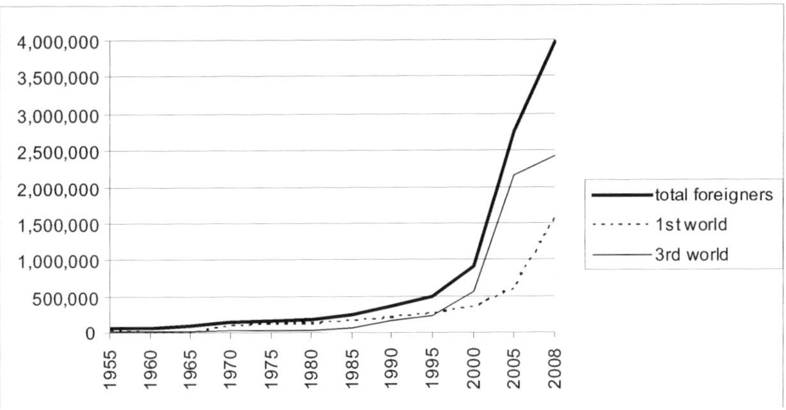

Source: www.ine.es, www.mir.es

In response to these growing numbers of immigrants, the first Spanish law set up to regulate immigration, the 'Foreigners Act', was passed in 1985. From the early start until today, Spanish public authorities clearly try to reconcile two opposite logics when designing migration legislation (Escrivá 1997). One is compliance with strict policies of border control as demanded by the EU (to which Spain was incorporated in 1986), and the other the fulfilment of certain needs for unskilled workers in agriculture, industry and services. Early laws clearly fell short of what a comprehensive immigration regulation should have been: they were perceived as very controversial, restrictive and discriminatory[24] (Gortázar 2002). What is more, the policy agenda of the Foreigners' Act did not correspond to regional situations and 'over time this conflict resulted in the gradual development of a more sophisticated set of policies that increased the autonomy of Spanish authorities in this area' (Moreno Fuentes 2000:2). Regularisation of undocumented immigrants, extension of social rights, or the development of special bilateral agreements for the import of temporary and seasonal workers would represent the other side of the coin of Spanish immigration policies. A new 'Foreigners Act' was passed by the government of the PP in 2000, after winning the general election with an absolute majority. It modified an earlier pro-immigrant law, hardening considerably many conditions, and increasing the period of required residence for individual regularisation from two to five years. The aim was to encourage measures for integration when legal, but restrict access to these rights for the majority of the aliens (Gortázar 2002). The socialist government modified the law again in November 2003, softening some of the sharp edges without changing the bottom lines.

Politicians took and continue to take a low-profile stance on migration policy, which reflects both a lack of confidence in dealing with such a new issue, and the ambivalence about the immigration question (King & Rodríguez-Melguizo 1999). Public attention to migration issues was very low, but Zapata-Barrero (2004) points out that in 2000 an important qualitative change took place, with immigration passing from being a technical and administrative matter to being a topic of social and political importance, often mentioned as first or second worry in public opinion surveys.

The contradiction to the widely communicated border controls and policy of toughness is a practice where immigrants continue to arrive on a daily basis despite investing considerable amounts of money and resources to build an effective system of closed borders.[25] This means that the implementation of a strict control of migratory flows is often softer in reality than on paper. Once inside, the *laissez-faire* approach of the Spanish authorities in terms of the enforcement of the law provided an optimum environment for the community. Therefore, the regularisation campaigns have been a powerful tool in immigration policy (Mendoza 1998) and represent one of its more pragmatic aspects. Although they raise criticisms for providing strong incentives for further undocumented immigration, the Spanish government has used them on six occasions (1986, 1991, 1996, 2000, 2001, 2005) to try solve problems of exploitation and marginalisation. By legalising all immigrants they give the migrants living in Spain without a working permit or residence permit access to a legal and administrative status and facilitate their access to markets (labour, housing, banking, etc.), and public services (social security, education, health, personal social services, etc.). In addition, as early as 1993 Spain adopted a quota system officially presented as a tool to promote active immigration. It was designed to distribute work permits for specific regions and economic sectors in Spain to potential immigrants abroad (through Spanish embassies and consulates). In practice though, instead of attracting new workers, the quota system is functioning as a concealed regularisation mechanism for irregular immigrants already present in Spain; issuing an annual average of 30,000 work permits mostly to migrants form Latin America (Favell & Hansen 2002). Making the addition, Carvajal (2004) sees that between 1986 and 2001 at least between 600,000 and 700,000 people have been regularised, plus 140,000 of the contingent between 1993 and 2000 (and other channels left out here). This leads Gortázar (2002) to ask how many legal immigrants are in Spain thanks to special regularisation and how few immigrants entered and remained in Spain in a regularised situation.

Social policies
The Franco regime expanded an existing series of basic schemes for social protection in the areas of pensions and health care, although selective and particularistic, following in general terms the conservative-continental model described by Esping-Andersen (1990). However, the violent suppression of protest against exploitation and deprivation of the popular classes partly explains the weakness and characteristics of the Spanish welfare system, which is to date not as all-embracing as welfare systems elsewhere in Western Europe. The democratically elected governments have made considerable efforts to increase public expenditure through the universalisation and modernisation of the health system, and increasing the level of pensions and other benefits; at the same time, the macro-economic logic has come to stress flexibility of labour markets and limited government intervention (Magone 2004: 183; Moreno 2006). Gross public spending lies considerably lower than in Belgium at 21.7 per cent, but the difference becomes even larger in the net social spending, where it goes down to 18.9 (OECD 2005: 32). Because of the lower level of welfare benefits, largely compensated by the still important role of family networks, Spain has also been qualified as a fourth type of welfare state, the family-oriented Southern European type.

Since the 2000 law, legal immigrants have the same civil and social rights as Spanish nationals, and undocumented immigrants have the right to basic social rights such as free access to public healthcare services, free compulsory education (three to sixteen years) and the very scarce public housing. This is based on the criterion of residence, explaining why even undocumented immigrants inscribe in the census. With regard to specific policies focused on the integration of ethnic minorities, there seems to be a lack of a clear policy paradigm framing the development of an incorporation policy. When a specific policy targeting the immigrant population is launched it generally has a short-term focus and it is aimed to tackle problems as they appear, not really planning in advance to meet future needs (Agrela 2003). Many migrants rely on third-sector organisations and social services that help undocumented immigrants, often with support from state administrations (Domingo, Kaplan et al. 2000). King (1999) qualifies this Spanish model of integration as close to 'differential exclusion' (going back to Castles): migrants are incorporated into certain areas of society, but denied access to others, based on the belief that their admission is only a temporary phenomenon.

Zapata (2004) summarises the Catalonian plan of immigration policies as very advanced, with reference to principles as integrated policies, intergovernmental relations, social participation, equality of rights and duties, access to services and sectors, and codevelopment. Associations and NGOs have a strong say in the debate, together with public administration and interest organisations, although political participation is strongest at the city level. The extent of inclusion depends in large part on the town where the immigrant lives and on the civil servant asked for support and services. In Barcelona, there are municipalities like Vic and Mataró, where various measures towards social inclusion of immigrants have been taken regardless of their documentation (Domingo et al. 2000). King (1999) argues that the Catalan government has a stronger commitment to the integration of migrants than does the national government, which can be linked to several factors. Not only has the region a longer history of incorporating migrants from other parts of Spain (Morén Alegret 2002; Pascual de Sans et al. 2000). They also face the risk of the gradual dilution of their own specific identity by the arrival of culturally and ethnically different groups which may feel tempted to embrace a general Spanish (Castilian speaking) umbrella identity, instead of a combination of a regional Catalan plus the general Spanish one (Moreno Fuentes 2004). Some of the distinctive Catalan features can thus be found in the reliance on the concept of 'jus solis', while Spanish law is based on 'jus sanguinis'; and in the fact that language represents an emblematic instrument of social integration. The general attitude towards integration policies is trying to avoid different treatment between social groups of different cultural or geographical origin; migration-related questions are channelled through general services if at all possible (Morén Alegret 2002; Pascual de Sans, Cardelús & Solana Solana 2000; Rigau i Oliver 2003). However, diverse services of attention specifically dedicated to foreign immigrants have been developed, and some important specific programs in education, health and protection of minors have been taken. The government of Catalonia has contracted-out their social services provision to migrants to NGOs and supports their task by means of public subsidies (Roque 2003).

2.4 Conclusion: Summarising hypotheses

The available openings or limits for immigrants are to some extent a consequence of elements of the theoretical framework: the economy and resulting labour markets, different degrees of control and regulation and different welfare states and immigration policies. In terms of labour markets, some low-skilled jobs have disappeared due to technology, increasing productivity and progress, but others have been created, mostly in the service sector or in activities that cannot be substituted by relocation and subsequent imports where production needs to be organised close to the consumption market. Some of these jobs in the lower steps of the labour market have become vacant because of higher expectations of the original workforce; others are linked to the changing economy stimulating the demand for low-skilled workers. This seems to be the employment context in which Senegambian migrants will have to find their way. The juxtaposition of economic and welfare state dynamics regarding labour migration makes it clear that the global labour market and the system of welfare states described above have competing logics. Several authors mention the contradiction between contemporary forces of globalisation, the dismantling of economic borders and the demand for cheap labour on one hand, and the restrictionist stance of western capitalist democracies regarding immigration in the other (Massey 1999: 312; Van der Leun & Kloosterman 2006).

Comparing both cities in terms of migration in Table 2.3, the percentage of residents of immigrant background is still larger in Belgium as an old immigration country, but numbers have been growing constantly in Spain, and immigrant workers nowadays represent a substantial proportion of the total workforce. The earlier experience of Belgium translates in a better-equipped institutional framework, although Spain has rapidly caught up over the last decade. Economic trends show the growing structural dependency of the Spanish economy on migrant labour, and the reliance on sectors that attract low-skilled workers (tourism, agriculture, small-scale industries). Migrants in Belgium arrive in a more regulated post-industrial labour market, with less space for low-skilled jobs, and a context of a solid set of welfare provisions, while redistribution through the state is more residual in Spain.

Table 2.3 *Theoretical elements of comparison, as background for different migrant trajectories in Antwerp and Barcelona*

	Antwerp	Barcelona
Urban labour markets	More post-industrial	Industrial moving towards services
	Stagnating labour market with high regulation	Growing economy needing flexible and cheap workers
	Service-based economy	Tourism, agriculture
	Large informal labour market	Large informal labour market
State regulation of labour markets	Corporatist welfare state	Mediterranean welfare state
	Very regulated labour market	Relatively flexible labour market
	High social protection	Limited social security
Migration policies	Previous guestworker schemes	Relatively new and fast migration
	Larger foreign population	Relatively small but fast-growing foreign population
	Restrictive migration policy	Changing + regularisations
	Rightwing party Vlaams Belang	Not political until recently

In what follows, we will see whether and how the trajectories and strategies of Senegambian migrants are shaped by these features of the cities, by the resources offered and the constraints imposed by the local contexts. Given the life-course method of the research, the analysis of the empirical material will follow and respect the time dimension as suggested by an apparent sequence built into the migration project. Three stages will be distinguished[26], each presented in a separate chapter: 'survival strategies' apply mostly to migrants who arrive in Europe without the necessary documents; afterwards, many of them may try to regularise their stay, developing 'documentation strategies'; and finally, they may start to consider strategies for upward or geographical mobility.[27]

The combination of these three phases with the structural elements discussed above, results in a series of hypotheses that will guide the empirical research. To start with, in the phase of survival as an undocumented migrant, I expect:
– More informal work in the booming Spanish economy than in Belgium

Subsequently, in the area of documentation strategies:
– More rigid implementation of migration legislation in Antwerp than in Barcelona
– More chances for obtaining papers in Spain than in Belgium

Finally, in terms of mobility strategies:
– Easier to find work in the growing Spanish labour market than in Belgium
– more social protection in Belgium than in Spain
– Less special services for migrants in Spain than in Belgium.

Before answering these questions, the methods with which the data were collected will be explicitated in the next chapter.

3 Data collection: Interviews and participant observation in a hidden population

> To tell or not to tell? How to tell? Do I spell it out or not? So what do I do? A few lines appear on the ceiling. Narrator, your memory is a needle that weaves time into lace. And supposing the holes were more mysterious than the patterns you make? (Diome 2006: 97)

The aim of this research is to gain a better understanding of employment patterns and survival strategies, family situations and mobility decisions of newly arrived migrants. I want to obtain not only information about personal characteristics (such as education, work experience, legal status, social networks, time spent in the country) as well as an image of these processes, but also an idea of the way they are experienced, how choices are motivated. What is more, it is important that the variety of trajectories be represented in the data. This implies that there is a need for in depth, qualitative information, which was gathered through interviews and participant observation, both of which will be discussed below. This argument for qualitative research is even more relevant as the topics included phases in which people resided illegally in the country, or who at some stage performed informal work.

While the interviews and participant observations will be valuable in giving a detailed account of the Senegambian migrants entering Barcelona and Antwerp and the sectors of employment they seem to occupy, this research aims to go beyond a specific ethnography. In order to set these data in a more general context of the operation of local labour markets, and the role of immigrants in them, multiple sources of extra information were relied on. These included statistics as well as the collection of a wide range of policy documents on the cases, and a selection of newspaper articles from two main newspapers (*De Standaard* in Belgium, *El País* in Spain) to cover more recent trends and debates. This information will serve to frame the results from the interviews; it allows situating the research sample within the broader pool of migrant experiences in both cities; in short, this may allow avoiding the trap of localism. Next, I interviewed 28 key informants from labour unions, NGOs working with immigrants and municipal immigrant services in both cities (see list in appendix B); this provides the essential background information to legislation, history, the specificities of the research group, the comparison with other migrant communities. They were very useful in giving vivid and summarised accounts of information that can sometimes be found in books, but also in providing an insight in the day-to-day challenges, power struggles or choices made in the different spheres of migration policy. Although the empirical analysis presented later is based on migrant experiences mainly, all other information informed my understanding of the background and underlying mechanisms.

3.1 A new world opening up

The difficulty of building contacts, trust and sample frames within hidden communities are well known; in the case of immigrants, problems are likely to be magnified in cases where migrants have moved illegally and fear to reveal their identity to researchers. I will explain below how a new world, that of Senegambian immigrants in Barcelona and Antwerp, opened up for me in a complex interaction between the community, me, and chance. In their respective articles about researching undocumented migrants and homeless youth, both Cornelius (1982) and Ensign (2003) have discussed methodological challenges that have to be considered when planning, doing or disseminating research with hidden populations. I refer to them heavily in the following discussion of the points of special attention that cover my fieldwork experiences and strategies.

Gaining access

As I was looking for Senegambian migrants only, who are numerous but not a majority in both cities, and not visibly different from other black groups, gaining access was not easy. I therefore decided to rely on individuals in the community who then introduced me further.[1] I also invested considerable amounts of time in 'being around' in the community, participating in parties, meals, and discussions, joining people for shopping or going out. From a methodological perspective, being around was necessary in order to do the very interviews: because of different cultural interpretations of time and the precariousness that characterises their lives, fixing appointments ahead turned out to be frustrating, and often interviews were done instantaneously when running into someone, or finding him or her at home. In addition, being available for the unexpected meeting or opportunity facilitated numerous new contacts. However, participant observation and the resulting friendships can also have a negative influence on the recruiting procedure. Without knowing or realising, one can get associated with cliques and social groups that do not get along, influencing the search for more respondents; or people can feel left behind or even cheated if you start contacting other groups of which they have negative images. On the level of the information obtained, participant observation enables the researcher to understand better what is said in interviews, which is particularly relevant in the case of research with relatively 'different' populations in terms of culture, living conditions and experiences (Soenen 2003). It increases the familiarity with the culture of respondents, as well as the degree of trust; it allows asking for additional explanations, double-checking, and triangulation of information, thereby bringing advantages in interpretation or abstractions. Moreover, sometimes the observations give you information that completes the interviews – or sometimes contradicts it.

Sampling

The population I am targeting (part of which is undocumented) cannot be sampled through any strict randomisation procedure; samples that include undocumented migrants are usually not representative, and it is impossible to arrive at credible generalisations for the whole population (Cornelius 1982).[2] Usually, a rather small set of initial contacts is asked for assistance in making contacts with other members of the social network, and the researcher should always start from several independent sources that tap into the population one is trying to get at. This 'snowball method' tends to keep refusal rates relatively low and it is therefore widely recognised as almost a prerequisite for meaningful surveys in this field.[3]

Within the limits of snowball-methods, my sample was inspired by the concepts of theoretical sampling, constant comparison, and saturation from the Grounded Theory Approach (Glaser & Strauss 1967). The individuals in the research should represent the main variety of phenomena that are conceptually important when assessing the relationships between core variables; some of these variations can be derived from theory, others will emerge from the research itself (Rubin & Rubin 1995). This involves a process of progressive focusing throughout the fieldwork, driven by feedback of the analysis into the data collection: these are not strictly separated phases in qualitative research. Based on the analysis of a small number of interviews, and with the necessary theoretical background information and knowledge, the researcher is able to take decisions about the selection of more data sources according to their ability to add to or challenge emerging theory. Indeed, 'theoretical sampling' is very important to help generate the theoretical equivalent of a statistically representative sample. However, I would prefer to call my sampling procedure 'purposeful' rather than theoretical (Holkup et al. 2004; Patton 1990), given that my final aim was not the construction, from the ground up, of a new theory. Another matching term could be Maximum Variation Sampling (Ensign 2003; Tilly 1996). I wanted to cover the diversity of working experiences and strategies (sectors, contracts, levels of specialisation), which might be a result of many other differences: age, sex, and ethnicity, socio-economic backgrounds, varying education, length of time in the host country and so forth.

The process of data collection is ended when the 'theoretical saturation point' is reached; for serious practitioners of the grounded theory approach, this term refers specifically to the development of theory. Frequent use within multiple bodies of literature has resulted in its meaning becoming diffuse and vague, and following Guest et al. (2006), I rely on a more general notion of data saturation when little new data or information is revealed by additional interviews. Using data from a study involving sixty in-depth interviews with women in two West African countries, these authors found that saturation of the codebook occurred within the first twelve interviews, although basic elements for metathemes were present as early as after six interviews; variability within the data followed similar patterns. Anyhow, in this kind of research, it is not so much the sample size that needs to be justified but rather the sampling strategy:

> The validity, meaningfulness, and insights generated from qualitative inquiry have more to do with the information-richness of the cases selected and the observational or analytical capabilities of the researcher than with sample size. (Patton 1990: 185)

Given the time and energy invested in establishing a first set of contacts, it was tempting to stick to these groups. However, with uncritical snowball sampling there is a clear bias towards well-connected individuals, long-stayers or permanent settlers, because they have larger networks, are easier to locate and more recruitment paths lead to them. Most people refer to those whom they resemble, meaning a particular sub-group might be over-sampled when relying solely on peer recruitment.

The most challenging issue was therefore to keep the diversity mentioned above in mind, and make the effort to go out in search of new entry points in order to find individuals that are more difficult to reach. The background information from statistics and key informants guided the sampling process, by pointing to the diverse characteristics to cover. From the participant observation, I obtained even more knowledge necessary to do purposeful sampling. I knew people with families were around before I interviewed a married person with children, I heard that rasta-men are perceived as distinct from the main population, that artists have their own experiences; that there are different specialisations in hawking, that I would need to find self-employed workers. I then contacted people with a good knowledge of the community (elderly men, religious leaders, owner of a phone shop) to find people with these specific profiles; I urged respondents to think of those groups; I moved areas in Spain during fieldwork; everything to diversify networks and entry points.

3.2 The interviews

I was able to conduct 35 interviews in Belgium, and 46 in Spain, between October 2005 and September 2006. The interviewees represent the different situations, generations, backgrounds that I thought might be important. The smaller number in Antwerp is due to the fact that the experiences in Belgium seem to be less varied than in Spain (see chapters 5 to 7). A more detailed discussion of the sample in relation to the population as a whole will form part of chapter 4. Here, more attention will be paid to the particularities of the interviewing process, from the informed consent, to the qualitative life-course approach.

Informed consent and anonymity

Informed consent of the participants is of crucial importance for all research, but in this case, both parts of the term proved problematic, sometimes because of respondents' undocumented status, sometimes because of a profile of low education. First, it is hard to 'inform' people who have difficulties reading and writing about the possible impact of my work; living in a world far away from academia or any written sources, it was never clear to me if explaining the concept of a study, research project or book made any sense to part of the group I was interviewing. Second, the standard written consent sheet was problematic for people who come from an almost exclusively oral culture, who try to live invisibly and may not even want to give their real names. Attempting to obtain written consent in these cases would be cumbersome at best and could jeopardise the safety and well-being of the undocumented people. Therefore, in my research oral consent is used instead of written consent (Byron 1994: 12; Ensign 2003).

As Sin (2005) mentions, a narrow interpretation of approval as a 'ritualistic enactment of consent-seeking' (passing the research ethics committees or the signing of a consent form by respondents) does not absolve researchers of further need to engage in ethical concerns and reflexive practice; consent seeking should not be thought of merely as an event. When doing research, I often noticed that the negotiations about ensuring informed consent continued before, during and after the act of research; people asked again about my work, my links with the government or writing a book throughout the interview, or during time spent together. This illustrates that there is a certain amount of power for the respondent to participate or not, and to decide what to tell or not; many possible respondents refused to participate in the interview in their own indirect ways. Others disclose only partially by withholding information or refusing to answer specific questions. Still others turn the interview situation around, and decide how much they want to tell me as the rapport with the researcher developed. However, it is important to remember that the research relationship is inherently an unequal one, even in cases where attempts are made to share power (Holkup et al. 2004).

When guaranteeing anonymity in the introduction of an interview, we usually refer to an academic technique of covering identities in scientific publications by using pseudonyms – the same was applied in this study. However, especially with narrative, in-depth, or life histories, the specifics of such things as the job strategies, the migration history, and the family situation, can make it impossible to hide completely the identity of an informant (Ensign 2003); it is usually impossible to assure complete confidentiality of data with just the convention of using fake names. This is probably even more pertinent for small groups or close communities like the ones who participated in this research: someone familiar with the group could put all information linked to a pseudonym together and complete the puzzle of a concrete individual. This invasion of privacy would represent a breach of confidentiality and might result in a risk of psychological or social harm. Great care was taken in writing up and reporting the information to ensure that names, locations and other data that might reveal identities or residences are kept anonymous. In order to avoid insiders from completing the puzzle of a specific person based on different fragments, sometimes pseudonyms are left out.

However, for undocumented people the more relevant anonymity is their well-guarded invisibility to police and government institutions; it might be the shame for other members of the community when facing difficulties; or the relative ignorance of the general public vis-à-vis illegitimate strategies. The traditional 'protection' does not mean so much when their main worry is if the interview will somehow be communicated to the police or the labour inspection.[4] A considerable number of respondents asked questions to ensure their safety; however, a considerable number of people wanted me to skip these explanations. They expressed complete trust, as I was introduced to them by a good friend; their safety was in the person that linked us, not in my academic procedures.

Interview methods: Qualitative life-course approach

Social research perspectives have recently paid more attention to the intrinsic longitudinal character of research topics and longitudinal analysis would be necessary to understand the dynamics that lead to a specific (migration, labour market) decision or outcome at a specific point in time. An appropriate alternative to successive survey waves can be found in life-course analysis, characterised by its aim to understand the causes, processes and consequences of change over the life course, and to assess the interaction of different influences (and for its specific use in migration studies, see Criado 1997; Hareven 2000; Harris 1987; Mayer and Tuma 1987; Tang 2002). Within this framework, individual behaviour is always regarded as a sequence of outcomes, some due to structural conditions in society, and others to the individual's initial characteristics or subsequent experiences. The life course is defined as a set of inter-related trajectories: in this case a combination of educational, labour market, legal status, and migration trajectories. A trajectory is the course followed as the subject ages, and each one comprises a number of transitions: more or less sudden or radical changes of status. Studying the life course means reconstructing all the trajectories and transitions and analysing them coherently as a unit.

Many different approaches exist within this broad field of research (Miller 2000); a more quantitative and cross-sectional one would imply collecting the same data for everyone, and base the analysis on general relationships among a great number of variables. However, different people may have experienced entirely different events, or they may have entirely different reactions to similar events, which may lead to different outcomes; therefore each individual may have his/her own individual set of relevant variables. As I am interested in how respondents define processes and motivate decisions, how they live the events in life that form the process; as I hope to understand the interaction between these processes and the socio-economic conditions, I resort to an in-depth approach. The more qualitative life-course interviews I carried out allowed tracing a variety of interactions between variables, although by its nature only in a limited interval of time and space. To quote Byron, I also believe that insight into these daily life issues reveals more about the system behind migration, and that they need not be purely descriptive:

> The anthropological tendency to focus on a single case in the study of migration and migrants groups has been heavily criticised (...). Yet the issue of how people cope with the material and organisational problems of their lives is a very important part of a comprehensive perspective on the migration process. (Byron 1994: 12)

Life-course analysis in its qualitative form is usually carried out through open or semi-structured interviews in which the respondent intends to reconstruct his own biography, within the borders delimitated by the interviewer. My aim was not to stimulate exhaustive oral histories but rather to obtain contextualised cases that are structured and influenced by arguments and debates produced from pre-existing guided questions. The interviews consisted of a semi-structured approach, in which I tried to complement subjective impressions and explanations with detailed factual information about particular events, that would allow a link to larger societal and historical processes (Hareven 2000; Jovchelovitch & Bauer 2000). The agenda of topics covered derived from the theoretical framework developed above: the field of migration history, social networks, skills in the labour market, and legislative impact. I used the technique of 'participatory diagramming' (Mikkelsen 1995: 78), drawing a time line with the respondent while running through the different experiences. This helped to go back to the chronology, providing a form of 'hard' information, and presenting it in a condensed and readily understandable visual form. This tool made communication more effective and reliable and has a corrective function. However, this preconceived categorisation was flexible enough to leave space for the individuals' own accounts of how and why their situations had changed throughout their lives. As the population was very varied and maybe rather exotic to me, open interviews revealed unanticipated topics; also, many respondents were highly creative, articulate, and eager to contribute their ideas and the input of their subjectivity and agency should be acknowledged (Ensign 2003). In my case, the entire fieldwork was cumulative: all of the information generated by previous interviews was brought to bear in formulating questions for each successive interview, therefore altering the very layout of the interview scheme.

A number of choices were left for the respondent to make, with the underlying goal of making them feel comfortable and thereby optimise the flow of information (Tang 2002). The first strategy was to make them more comfortable by letting them choose the place of the interview, as it can influence the power dynamics between the interviewer and interviewee: settings included their home, my home, a bar, or the office of an organisation. Second, whether the interview was recorded or not was also left to them; if they disapproved, I would take written notes and type out the interview from memory immediately upon arriving home. Moreover, I took care in question wording to minimise the sensitivity of certain topics that must be discussed in interviews. The most obvious example is the question about the respondent's immigration status, but also the question whether they ever worked with someone else's papers; or committed other kinds of fraud.[5] To relax the atmosphere around these topics, I would sometimes explicitly express my sympathy for necessary informal strategies; this often made them talk more easily. With Jordan, I noted that 'many irregular migrants were quite willing to say that they broke the rules in order to earn, and that they felt justified in doing so because the rules were unreasonable and unfair' (Jordan & Düvell 2002:98). Interviews took between half an hour and three hours, but the standard was slightly more than an hour. I also paid attention not to rush home; the post-interview period often proved to be very interesting; in talking informally people can open up and give more details on a wide variety of topics, as well as ask questions. These data were typed out upon arrival at home and then added to the interview document.

Another important point concerns languages. I do not master the main Senegalese language, Wolof, enough to conduct interviews; nor do I speak Mandingo, the official language of the Gambia. Without any doubts, those languages would have led to a more trusting relationship with the participants; they would have expressed their thoughts and feelings more precisely in their mother tongue, which would possibly have resulted in quite different data. Notwithstanding, given that official languages of those countries include French and English respectively, and that participants had lived for varying times in Spain and Belgium, all of them were able to express themselves in one of the languages offered for the research: French, English, Spanish or Dutch. Their language skills varied considerably, and there was often quite a lot of language switching going on, shifting to a native or foreign word depending on the topic of conversation.

3.3 Conclusion: Limits and advantages of the data

In-depth life-course interviews in two cities were chosen as a way to find answers to research questions that are longitudinal, comparative and that link individual experiences with the socio-economic context. The strategies for obtaining and presenting the material collected for this study were presented above, and some issues arising specifically from interviewing a hidden and vulnerable population were explored. Next to considerable amounts of participant observation, a total of 81 interviews were carried out, aiming to highlight very different profiles and histories. The evaluation of this material is mainly positive: the interviews are dense and information is abundant in different fields.

However, some critical remarks and comments should be made about the method itself. A first major problem with life-course analysis is related to the fact that life histories as told by an individual migrant are narratives that both interpret the past and make it acceptable, understandable, and important in the specific interview setting. This 'distortion' is a necessary correlate of the method; on the other hand, this information allows us to see how things fit together in the minds of the respondent or how people make sense of their world (Anderson et al. 1991). A related issue is linked to the reliance on memory in life-course analysis: the weakness in chronology is one of the greatest limitations of all oral memories. How feasible is it to reconstruct long detailed lifelines in a highly mobile group? However, Thompson (2000) describes how the initial selection by the brain is by far the most drastic, affecting any kind of contemporary witness. In addition, memory depends upon social interest and need; migration may be an experience relevant enough to store. An alternative way to correct subjective and collective myths and impressions is to ask detailed questions about particular facts and accounts of everyday life. The cultural dimension composes another difficulty. In the end, we have few other possibilities when interpreting other cultural groups than starting from our own experience; Mikkelsen (1995) points out that we should be aware of the limitations of ethnocentric interpretations. Briggs (1983) shows how the intersection of two or more sets of conversational norms (in different cultures) can cause problems, and how for instance nonverbal forms of communication as found in participant observation can allow better interpretations. Finally, the active participation of the interviewer means that his/her own biases, fears and enthusiasms influence the questioning style and interpretation (Adepoju 2004). More than that: interviews are not about scooping up the facts from the informant's talk in some unproblematic way; interviews are social interactions and therefore part of the social world (Flick 2002).

Second, my own characteristics influenced without any doubt the processes of gaining access and sampling. On the one hand, the gender dimension clearly played a role: the fact of being a young female researcher raised at least sympathy and sometimes outspoken interest from a predominantly male research population.[6] This sometimes facilitated agreement to carry out the interview, although the information obtained may sometimes have been presented in a way that was designed to impress me. Although the profile of Senegambian migration is predominantly a male one, I wanted to interview some women as well, but contacting them proved to be extremely difficult for me. I can enumerate a variety of reasons why this may have been the case, but have no answer to which one was conclusive. Maybe because women tend to speak less foreign languages. Maybe because they generally studied less and consider themselves as less interesting sources of information. Maybe because they are busier with organising the day-to-day lives of their families and have less time. Maybe because the setting of an interview is too formal for them. Maybe because they saw my hanging around with Senegambian men as a possible threat. Even when agreeing, the interviews tended to be shorter and less informative, as also noticed by Pérez (1995). On the other hand, being Belgian also seemed to play a role: in Spain, I was a foreigner like them, and the 'outsider solidarity' meant that a good introduction, open attitude and empathy towards migrants were enough to obtain consent. It took considerably more effort to convince people to do the interview in Belgium, in particular for undocumented migrants; even the ones who became friends would avoid participation. The main reason for the reluctance in Belgium might lie in the more harsh control upon undocumented migrants. Potential respondents probably linked me to the power of the state and its reputation of hostility, control, and repatriation; this affected my ability to establish a confident and informal relationship with participants – basically taking a lot more time (Martín Pérez 2006). As one central figure in the Senegalese community in Belgium told me when I discussed this issue with him: 'maybe that is because your country scares people more than Spain?'

If there is a way to cope with these shortcomings, it seems to lie in a very good understanding of the context of the interview and the respondent, theoretically, statistically, as well as socially. The dialogue and closer contact during semi-structured interviews allow for a more precise process of presentation and analysis; in addition, participant observation offers the opportunity to share ideas, review the data and test the interpretation, having time to unravel the surprising and at first incomprehensible. Another rule of thumb is to be reflexive about one's own role in the research, not only by writing one's own social and cultural position into the research, but by exploring in depth whether any or all of these aspects of self identity lead to bias. An ethnographic research diary that captures the flux and uncertainty of the process can provide rich and crucial insights (Mauthner & Doucet 2003). In addition, more general data such as key person interviews and available statistics can serve to put specific experiences in context. However, as a researcher who worked only in two sites, with migrants from one source region only, I cannot easily extrapolate to speak of experiences in other sites, persons from other source countries, other specialised strategies or labour market sectors.

4 How migration from Senegal and the Gambia became an institution

> Ndogou nodded agreement, took out her notebook and added to the long list of outstanding payments. Everyone who runs a business in the village has a notebook like hers. The island's overflowing with old men who can no longer fish or plough their fields – productive in the old days, now reclaimed by forest – and with migrants' wives, surrounded by their broods, who consume on credit, on the strength of a promised money order. (Diome 2006: 20)

A first step in order to understand the possibilities Senegambian migrants have in the labour market of their host country, is to take a closer look into the nature of their migration project, the background of the country of origin, and the specificity of the expatriate community. The characteristics of migrant flows are often tied with the economic and/or political situation at home, and even the destinations they choose are influenced by historical links between both areas. Africa is a region of considerable, essentially intra-continental migration, consisting of regional movement by refugees, undocumented migrants, and seasonal labour migrants. Emigrants to northern countries include skilled workers, students, semi-skilled and unskilled workers, and recently autonomous female migrants (Adepoju 2004). Knowing about the country of origin might help to understand who they are, what they know, their motivation, their personal aims in terms of economic and social progress, and the determination to succeed, all of which are most important in terms of the background to the book. Most of the local patterns described below are not necessarily specific to Senegal and the Gambia; they form part of a global socio-economic system, and are to be found in different patterns throughout emigration countries everywhere in the world.

In this chapter, I will explore the driving forces behind continuing migration from Senegal and the Gambia to Europe over time. What is more, I hope to show how emigration has evolved from being an occasional survival strategy in rural areas to becoming the most widespread perception of opportunity for youngsters, a support network spanning a wide area involved in economic activities, and an indispensable source of income for families at home. First, I will show how economic activities in Senegal and the Gambia have narrowed due to ecological and political factors, resulting in limited possibilities for subsistence. This will be based on how Senegambian economies and populations fit into the global economic system. Second, I will examine more closely the routes into Europe, Spain and Belgium in particular, highlighting the importance of the existing community in attracting and supporting more newcomers. Third, I will explain the Senegambian migrant 'business' concept that functions as an ethnic niche for employment. Finally, I will discuss the relationship migrants keep with their homeland and the family, the importance of remittances, and the consequences for the original migration project.

4.1 Why leave Senegal or the Gambia?

The theoretical reasons for migration listed in the introduction have taken specific concrete shapes in different episodes of the migration story from Senegal and the Gambia (Barros et al. 2002; Guilmoto 1997; Tall 2002). An overview of chronological patterns will be given below, based on developments in the region of origin, changes in the host countries, and the cycles of migration. This shows that there is no real discontinuity between traditional forms of migration and more modern waves (Traore 1994); at the same time, my argument would be that the scale and weight have increased considerably, turning an occasional temporary solution into a continuous pressure valve.

The research population is based in a region of origin, West Africa, the reasons for which have been explained in the introduction. Senegal and the Gambia stretch along the West African coast from the Sahel desert region in the north to a moist, tropical south (see Figure 4.1). As the Gambia is actually an enclave in Senegalese territory, formed by British colonisation of the otherwise French territory, there are similarities in geography, environment, population groups, and history. The main religion is Islam, and similar ethnic groups are found: Wolof, Fula, Serer, Jola and Mandinka represent the largest groups.

With a joint population of thirteen million people, both countries have enjoyed long spells of political stability and democracy since independence in 1960[1] (Jettinger 2005), but this stability has not translated into economic prosperity, as an economic analysis by the OECD shows (2005). Because of limited natural resources, poor soil quality in most of the region, and colonial pressure, the economy is based on cultivation of one cash crop, peanuts, predominantly for export of vegetable oil; this makes them hostage to fluctuations in the world production and prices of the crop. Senegal is a model pupil of the IMF and WB, but small poor peasants continue to be disadvantaged in the competition on the global market. Consequently, both countries rely on foreign aid to fill gaps in their balance of payments (Conteh-Morgan 1997), as well as on cash remittances from citizens living abroad.

Figure 4.1 *Map of Senegal and the Gambia*

Source: www.columbia.edu

Table 4.1 below summarises some key data for both countries. With a life expectancy of 56, an illiteracy rate approaching 60 per cent and school enrolment ratios of 38 and 50, respectively, Senegal and the Gambia belong to the 25 least developed countries: they are 156th and 155th out of 177 countries in the UN Human Development Index (UNDP 2006). GDP stands at about $1,800 while a considerable part of the population lives on less than one dollar per day; life with less than two dollar per day is a daily challenge for 63 to up to 82 per cent of the population. Total fertility is still relatively high, resulting in a large young population: 40 per cent are aged under fifteen. Both countries participate in the Heavily Indebted Poor Countries Debt Initiative of the World Bank.

Table 4.1 *Most recent key data for Senegal and the Gambia, 2004*

	Senegal	The Gambia
Total population (millions)	11.4	1.5
Life expectancy at birth (years)	56.0	56.1
Adult literacy rate (% ages 15 and older)	39.3	38.0 (est)
Combined primary, secondary and tertiary gross enrolment ratio (%)	38.1	50.3
Gross Domestic Product per capita (PPP US$)	1,713	1,991
Population living below $1 a day (%)	22.3	59.3
Population living below $2 a day (%)	63.0	82.9
Total fertility rate (births per woman)	5.0	4.7
Population under age 15 (% of total)	43.0	40.3
Urban population (% of total)	41.3	53.0

Source: UNDP Human Development Report 2006

Before the 1960s: Colonialism

The history of Africa does not start with colonisation, of course; in a rich past with empires and conquests, religious wars and economic crises, temporary or seasonal migration networks between empires and kingdoms have been an important part of regional livelihood strategies for many centuries. Aderanti Adepoju points out that African history is deeply rooted in migration, with the most important mobility patterns determined by the long distance trans-Saharan trade of salt, gold, slaves, skins, gum, ivory and spices starting as early as the 10th century (2004). During the era of colonial occupation from the 17th and 18th centuries onwards, these goods were exported from the coasts towards Europe; in the case of the cruel transatlantic slave trade an estimated ten to twelve million people were transported to the American continent. Internally, workers would move towards mines and plantations for export crops as cotton or peanuts, or to the cities as colonial education encouraged people to abandon rural life. This disruption, the theft of natural resources and the cultural stereotypes established under colonial rule, lie at the base of the continent's backward position today, and are therefore linked to contemporary migration.

In the case of Senegal and the Gambia, these colonial links expressed themselves in a variety of migration patterns (Barou 1987; Tall 2002). Facilitated by the fact that all colonial citizens at the time had both local and colonial citizenship, local troops joined the respective French and English armies across the world in the two world wars. Some workers were employed in administration or as sailors on boats (for a fascinating overview of their links to Marseille, see Bertoncello 2000). Some individuals worked temporarily in France or England in blue-collar positions. Others studied in French colleges and universities and some diamond traders settled in Europe (Bredeloup 1993). As a

French colony, Senegal even had representatives in the French parliament. Sometimes these people preferred to remain in France or England, rather than returning to Africa; they would normally work in sectors where other guest workers were found, in manufacturing industries and construction.

The 1960s and 1970s: Agricultural crisis

In the 1960s, most people lived from subsistence agriculture; however, migration was already beginning to form part of the livelihoods of the countryside. Garnier (1990) illustrates the general process very well, based on an intensive study of one specific village. In the traditional system, food self-support formed the basic goal of agriculture; on the side, some cotton or other commercial crops would be grown, in order to raise money for the limited monetary needs. However, the need to survive was complemented by the aim of creating some wealth; at the same time, the situation on the global market for raw materials turned negative; and it became impossible to cover the increasing monetary needs inside the village. In the beginning, farmers would rely on traditional solutions in times of crisis: they sold part of the harvest or cattle herd, or one male family member migrated seasonally to work in nearby towns or cities (Camara 2002).

The start of serious Sahelian droughts that affected the peanut-growing area in the second half of the 1960s, and particularly in the 1970s, exhausted the villages' reserves, and left only migration as a solution (Tall 2002). The population increase in this period, combined with old methods of agriculture contributed to this dynamic. The migration of youngsters (including women) from the rural community into the cities to join a wage economy became a common goal; those who did not find employment in one city migrated to another, often ending up in the capital Dakar. In an illustrative anthropological account of life in the Casamance region, Lambert (2002) found that most elderly men had worked in the city before, demonstrating a circular movement of people and a cyclical experience of families, with young people earning money in Dakar for the maintenance of the family and to construct the family house, previous to returning to marry. The population movement shook the existing balance, by sucking part of the labour force away from the fields, and by creating new needs for socially necessary goods; in fact, it drastically changed the system from subsistence economies into monetary capitalism. Inside Senegal, the international dependency relationship between centre and periphery was reproduced (Gonin & Lassailly-Jacob 2002), and migration came to represent the promise of marital stability, economic security, and social prestige.

Others found their ways to neighbouring countries, or the more successful African regions such as Gabon and Ivory Coast.

A small proportion of these migrants found employment in Europe; for historical and linguistic reasons (French is the second language), Senegalese migration was initially oriented towards France. This was not an adventurous enterprise, but a well-prepared long-term project supported and financed by the extended family. Parallel with previous internal forms of migration, the survival of the village and security of the community was the central aim, expressed in a rotation system: youngsters were sent abroad for some years, marriages and children in the home country guaranteed remittances for family and village and made their homecoming more likely (Barou 2001; Bodin & Quiminal 1991; Quiminal 1995). They returned afterwards to let someone else take their place; in the absence of visa requirements in France, this did not present a problem. The celibate young men would usually live in hostels, often relying on existing social networks, and being integrated in French industries confronted with a lack of workers. This specific form of migration first affected the Soninke and Fula from the valley of the Senegal River (Ndiaye 1996; Traore 1994). After 1973, this system changed considerably because of the economic crisis in Europe and the subsequent closure of borders for migrant workers (Barou 1987; Bredeloup 1993; Diatta & Mbow 1999; Traore 1994). Because of the Fordist crisis in the industrial and construction sectors, migrants started to work as entrepreneurs and in businesses.

The 1980s and 1990s: Structural adjustment

In a next phase, the failure of several policies of national development would add to the livelihood problems, while problems of continuing desertification and globalisation of the economy deepened the crisis in the traditional agricultural system (Camara 2002; Diop 2002; Gonin & Lassailly-Jacob 2002). Foreign debt increased,[2] and finally led to the ill-planned structural adjustment programme (1982-1992) devised and sponsored by the World Bank and the International Monetary Fund. The conditions of the loans imposed privatisation, cutbacks in the public service sector, and opening of markets by removing subsidies; this led to tremendous economic burdens and austerity measures in education and health systems, diminishing salaries in the public sector, and reduced access to education, health, food, and social services (Conteh-Morgan 1997). The disengagement of the Senegalese state resulted in a combination of economic growth with greater poverty: the unconditional opening of markets meant the progressive destruction of vulnerable sectors and the population grew faster than the economy. A 50 per cent currency devaluation in 1994 made life more expensive because of the rise in cost of necessary imported items. The opening up of the country also meant giving up the need for a permit to leave the country and, at the same time, the devaluation increased the importance of remittances from migrants abroad. The 'old' migrants continued to display the small wealth that they managed to acquire, and make a strong impression on youngsters during their short visits in their home country.

Rural migrants were funnelled from the hinterland to Dakar looking for work and income: the city grew from just 100,000 people after WWII, to more than three million inhabitants today. The consequences of the ongoing economic crisis became visible in the urban labour markets: because of employment stagnation and cuts in services, jobs were more difficult to find, and even well educated people faced high unemployment rates (Diatta & Mbow 1999). In addition, incomes in the city decreased because of the mounting competition from newly arrived rural migrants (annual migration rates of 6 to 8 per cent) used to even lower incomes (Adepoju 2004; Fall 2003). As a result of the failure of the state, and the government's abandonment in 1986 of the policy of protecting products manufactured in Senegal, they find themselves at a dead end, not having found what they were in search of, nor being able to return (Lambert 2002). Only the informal urban sectors grew (Barou 1987), particularly around the Dakar Sandaga market where foreign goods were sold.

Propelled by the globalisation of the economy and accelerated pauperisation, more families invested in an international migrant, widening the strategy to other regions of the country and other ethnicities (Adepoju 2004: 73).

> Thus, migration is commonly used by Africans to ensure the survival of their families or to pursue economic mobility to supplement dwindling household resources. Households generally select and invest in a family member who is viewed to have the greatest potential for generating migrant earnings and sending remittances.

Despite the new restrictive immigration acts and the economic crisis, people still attempted to enter France in search of badly paid or informal employment as the economic conditions in the poorer African countries had deteriorated even more than in France[3]. But the orientation shifted from France to an exploration of a variety of other countries; Italy and Spain became increasingly popular (Pugliese 2004; Robin 1996b), although they reached out for New York (Ebin 1990; Fall 2002; Stoller 2002) and almost everywhere in the developed world (Schmidt di Friedberg 2000). In the cases where they were unable to find salaried work in the shadow segments of mainstream industries, they integrated in the 'business' network of the Islamic brotherhood as explained below. Notwithstanding the West European protectionist policies, migration intensified throughout Europe. As return and rotation became impossible, the men tended to settle and engage in family reunion while they had often not been able to access decent living conditions. Most women were therefore coming in an induced way, through family reunion with their husbands.

The most recent trend: globalisation

The 40-year rule of Senegal's Socialist Party came to a peaceful democratic end in 2000, when Abdoulaye Wade, a lawyer and a veteran opposition politician took power. The atmosphere was one of optimism, even euphoria (Vengroff & Magala 2001), as he promised democratisation, economic recovery, and good governance reforms; however, Wade did not live up to the high expectations in his home base (Dahou & Foucher 2004). There have been frequent changes in ministerial posts, a lack of transparency in budgetary management, and bombastic but unrealistic infrastructural project proposals. These various debates underpinned the legislative and presidential election campaigns in 2007, but on 25 February, Abdoulaye Wade was re-elected with 55.7 per cent of the votes (*De Standaard* 28 Februay 2007).

Economically speaking, the situation has become more hopeless. In agriculture, productivity went down 50 per cent in 30 years – in 2001, farmers were able to increase production, but due to international falling prices, heaps of peanuts remain unsold, and incomes fell even more. Traditional grains like millet fell out of use because people started to eat bread made from subsidised wheat imported from Europe; the same applies to local milk production being replaced by imported milk powder, or onions and tomatoes. Despite structural problems of insufficient diversification, inappropriate land laws, desertification and merciless global competition, the primary sector (also including livestock, forestry and fisheries) still employs about two-thirds of the active population. A study measuring the incidence of poverty in Senegal in February 2001 found 48.5 per cent to be concentrated in rural areas (cited in: OECD 2005). The dramatically declining stocks in traditionally rich fishing grounds is also leading to dwindling incomes among fishermen; they blame overfishing by massive European and Japanese trawlers, which are no match for their wooden vessels. The secondary sector (concentrated in food processing, construction materials, chemicals and textiles, 23 per cent of GDP in 2003) faces a lack of foreign investment, a limited domestic market, and insufficient institutional support for small and medium enterprises. In terms of infrastructure, moving goods and people is difficult, costly and slow; Dakar currently sees traffic jams at all times of the day, at all days of the week. The modest tertiary sector is slowly growing, particularly the branches of tourism, telecommunications and transport, with the harbour of Dakar benefiting from an excellent geographic position and the civil war in Ivory Coast. In a comparative report about shadow economies worldwide, Schneider shows that the share of shadow economy in African nations has increased between 1999 and 2003, in the case of Senegal from 45.1 to 47.5 per cent of official GDP. The limited local economy means that citizens are often unable to earn a living wage in a legitimate manner. Working in the shadow economy is often the only way of achieving a minimal standard of living (Schneider 2006).

A 2002 survey of the labour market in Dakar sheds a light on the problems faced (OECD 2005). Unemployment in the strict sense of the word was estimated at 11.7 per cent of the active population. However, if the number of those working less than the official working hours and those working for less than the minimum wage is added to the number of unemployed, underemployment hits nearly 72.5 per cent of the active population in Dakar. Some 7.5 per cent had relatively stable jobs in the public sector, where average income was around $283 per month. The proportion of workers in the formal private sector was 16 per cent, with monthly salaries averaging $214. The informal sector was by far the largest one, accounting for 76.4 per cent of workers, bringing home about $74 per month, still below the minimum wage, despite longer working hours and the absence of social security benefits. Many families survive by combining several micro-businesses, varying according to seasons, occasions, and time of the day: selling in the market in the morning, selling on the streets in the afternoon, sell cold drinks or snacks from home, day-labour in construction, helping out friends with shops, braiding hair, carrying water. A high proportion of families can provide for the daily needs by putting incomes together; however, any accumulation is impossible, ruling out housing improvements or investment in higher education, and any misfortune (illness, handicap, death, fire, loss of harvest) leads immediately to disaster. Senegal, despite its stability and relatively good position, cannot offer improved economic prospects to its population, whether it is on the level of survival, welfare or social promotion.[4]

In the meantime, about three million out of eleven million Senegalese are living abroad and sending home millions of dollars in official remittances each year. On their return visits, even if only after five or eight years, they bring back a minimum of goods that are unachievable for their comrades: mobile phones, clothes, radios or TVs, jewellery; they may have saved to bring over a car, or start the construction of a house (Kaplan 1998). Those migrants often pretend to be better off than they actually are, leading to distorted information that serves as a strong incentive to migration. However, even if they try to explain the difficulties of life in Europe, their material condition contradicts their words. This parade of prosperity is irresistible for the curious, creative, adventurous, and ambitious young men who do not understand anti-immigration policies, bureaucracy, and crisis in the European economies or racism (Kaplan 1998). Respondents in the research mention all these elements as factors in the migration decision: from dire poverty over ambition and curiosity to being pushed by family members.

Whereas up until the 1980s the educated civil servant was the symbol of success and the point of reference, the emigrant has nowadays taken his place as role model (Tall 2002). For a whole generation of young people, education no longer represents social mobility; with just courage and perseverance, the migrant is able to support his family and make investments. Migration is at this point seen as the only way to survive economically and, more importantly, to be someone. This ideal has affected very diverse groups: the recruitment base in Senegal and The Gambia currently covers the whole population, all ethnicities, all brotherhoods, including the higher educated,[5] middle classes, people with jobs, single women and underage children (Bertoncello & Bredeloup 2000a; Tall 2002). With diversification of profiles and destinations, more clandestine and spontaneous migration, the Senegambian migrants illustrate the general trends developed in the introduction. Migration turns into a dream and a furious obsession: they are determined to leave, even if it has become a path fraught with administrative obstacles. It is hard to imagine the extent to which migration has become a feature of life: young people plan to leave, they work to leave, they talk about leaving, and they move around in order to leave.[6] They spend their time on the internet chatting with foreigners, flirting with tourists, working hard to save, nagging parents and family for permission and money to leave, queuing endlessly in front of different embassies. Once the decision to migrate is taken, families often pool their economic resources (including remittances) to send one member into the world to improve their fate back home; an intricate network of recruiters, employers, immigration authorities, relatives, and friends abroad makes the rest of the process possible.

It is sometimes suggested that the migration flow will slow down when current migrants would give correct information about the hardship awaiting adventurers. This is, by the way, an underlying reason for governments' tough stand of migration and repatriation, as a means of deterring new migrants. One fieldworker in Barcelona told me that stories from Gambian migrants have had a regularising effect on the most recent inflow, because their fellow countrymen tell them that there is no work in Spain. Another one, himself a migrant, explains that honest information does not discourage them:[7]

> If you explain things, look, nothing is easy there, there is no work, no papers, not this, not that, people are suffering there, some people want to come back... you get the impression that they do not believe you. They have in their head this migration project, which they want to realise, a dream in fact, and they see you as somebody who is putting limits. They don't like it. They say 'yes, yes'. But you know perfectly well that he thinks he will succeed. He will do better, work harder and realise his project.

The dominant perception of migration is still one of limited character, a temporary move in order to make some money that would allow them to invest in Senegal and generate an income for themselves and their family (Black & King 2004). But inside the communities in Europe, one now finds settled migrants at retirement age next to newly arrived undocumented youngsters, students as well as international business women, highly skilled specialists recruited by international companies next to women who came for family reunification, some restless adventurers crossing numerous countries and second generation children of the diaspora. This changes the organisation of families and communities, the meaning of social control, the relationship between generations, and the links with the home country (Epstein & Gang 2004).

4.2 Making it to Europe

In the face of Europe's closed doors, immigrants engage in an interaction with the rules, developing strategies to circumvent migration law, limit the consequences of breaking it, or creatively trying to match conditions. Legal and bureaucratic obstacles to migration and settlement are seen not as absolute barriers, but as factors to be taken into account in personal strategies, migration networks and community infrastructures (Castles 2002). The migration trajectory itself can take a variety of forms, characterised in the first place by legal or illegal entry, and then by the direct or indirect nature of the trip, by the means to travel and so on. Legal entry is the most straightforward, but simultaneously the most difficult to organise: it requires the standard necessary documents, ranging from a valid passport, a visa, a sum of cash money, three month salary slips, a considerable sum of money in a bank account, proof of health insurance and an invitation or guarantee in the host country. Another legal way to enter is in the framework of family reunification, which implies a different set of conditions to be fulfilled by the person in the host country. Many migrants come with a tourist, business, diplomatic or student visa as part of legal or diplomatic missions, musician or sports delegations;[8] sometimes this document covers a real aim, very often it is used strategically with the goal of migration (Adam et al. 2001; Black et al. 2006). A surprising number put their hope on illegitimate visas, false passports, borrowed passports, fake identities, bribing migration officers, or buying the necessary documents; and some succeed. Most people become undocumented when the visa expires or when they travel to a third country. Travelling by plane with a visa is the main entrance route for respondents: 31 out of 35 interviewees in Belgium entered this way, and 33 out of 46 in Barcelona; improper visa use applied to 24 and 22 of them respectively. Despite this fact, making the visa requirements for tourism and business ever stricter could damage the very engine of western economy, as this freedom of movement forms a crucial part of the open global system.

Parallel with the implementation of more restrictive politics in the field of legal migration, we can note the evolution in clandestine strategies. Those without the connections or budget necessary for a visa have resorted to long and frequently dangerous journeys as a way of circumventing migration controls: hiding in or under trucks or crammed in boats they risk their lives to enter Europe. Since the beginning of the 1990s the most common trajectory for Senegambian migrants, as explained by seventeen respondents, involves leaving from home, moving north by plane, public transport or just walking until reaching a Maghreb country, most often Morocco (Barros et al. 2002; Bouhdiba 2006; Collyer 2006; IOM 2005). On the way they regroup by nationality, religious group or ethnicity, sharing support and information; some gather in Libya to earn the money needed for continuing the trip (Tarrius 2002). Once in Morocco they try to enter the Spanish enclaves of Ceuta and Melilla, or they attempt to cross the Strait of Gibraltar by small boats and rafts; recently the Canary Islands have become an alternative destination. In principle the whole enterprise could be completed in a couple of months, but some respondents travelled three or four years in transit, and two made exceptionally long trips (eight and twelve years) (Collyer 2006). The very fact of making it to Europe is also an achievement and a source of status and pride, as many don't make it or die in the challenging trip; it has almost become a 'rite de passage'. After being chased by the police and mafias, deported, locked up in prisons or detention centres, losing money, seeing people drown in dangerous nighttime trips across the Mediterranean, and being scared to death, they are determined not to give up easily.

The participants' travelling histories reveal a much more complex picture than is captured by statistics. The route is often indirect: some may have travelled to another African country before going to Europe; others have lived in one or more other countries; still others come and go more than once; and many end up in completely different countries than planned. Out of 81 respondents found in Spain and Belgium, thirteen started their career elsewhere in Europe (Poland, Russia and Switzerland one migrant each; Italy and Germany three each; France four). This shows how migration cannot be considered as a simple change in place of settlement, and even less as a one-time departure and clear moment of arrival: it creates a set of movements between territories where the limits cannot be defined once and for all.

Networks are a crucial element in all the steps of a migration project (Ajibewa & Akinrinade 2003; Boyd 1989). Epstein and Gang (2004) analyse the influence of others on migration decisions, and show how both the personal network as well as the 'herd' influence the decision and the choice of location through advice and information. But the network is also important for funding the trip: apart from personal savings or borrowed money, many have received support from family members, who sometimes sell everything or take on debts to complete the necessary sum (Herman 2006). Networks later help during the trip and, as explained in chapter 5, provide support on arrival in the host country. As a specific form of networks, the role of brokers, smugglers or human traffickers and their organisation should be mentioned (Black et al. 2006; Koser 2000). As shown by the terminology, variation exists in the degree of organisation, commercialisation, and exploitation displayed in assisting migrants on their trip. Beyond the help from family members, friends or unknown people, most migrants have to rely on the paid services of intermediaries for forged documents, assistance for crossing borders and the practical organisation of the trip (Adepoju 2005; Salt and Stein 1997). Increasingly the existence of large organisations looking like travel agencies is noted on the market: they recruit clients and offer them a complete package, with a network of local agents responsible for part of the trajectory; these organisations often control the migrant after arriving in the host country, to make sure he pays his debt. *El País* cites a secret report by the UN Regional Office for West and Central Africa (ROSEN), saying that 300,000 Africans enter the EU every year, and that 80 per cent of them use the services of traffickers' organisations, which have a yearly trade of 237 million euro (*El País* 28 August 2006). In addition, Krissman suggests that studies of international migration networks should include not only labour-sending hometowns and border smugglers, but also employers that demand new immigrant workers (Krissman 2005).

The route to Belgium

For Senegalese migrants, Antwerp is not an obvious choice of destination, as it is not so established in the mind-set of the migrants in the same way as France, Italy or the US. Ending up in Belgium is sometimes less of a conscious choice but rather the outcome of random circumstances, networks or chance encounters. They mostly come with a tourist visa and an airplane ticket (Adam et al. 2001; Geets et al. 2006). Some of the earliest migrants in my sample, and a second-generation Senegalese key informant, described the history of the community in Antwerp. Senegalese workers and students in France sometimes spent weekends in Antwerp to party, and in order to have some pocket money, they would sell African art objects in bars. A couple of Senegalese diamond traders were also present from the start. For professional hawkers Antwerp was a transit zone when travelling to or from Italy, France and Germany, to buy or store goods and to take a rest. Afterwards some found a new job or a wife, or otherwise preferred to settle in the city, mainly around the train station; this small community attracted compatriots. During the economic crisis after 1973, hawking became the only option for both newly arriving migrants as well as workers losing their jobs; the 1990s formed the heydays in this sector. In the regularisation of 2000, a considerable number of them were regularised and entered the mainstream.

Today, the registered West African community in Antwerp amounts to some 600 inhabitants (in 2005) but it is a well-known fact that this does not include a large illegal population. The city centre is clearly the centre of the community (450 people), based on their hawking tradition, the closeness to transport and supply infrastructure, cheap housing, but also through the attraction of African shops and bars (Planningscel Antwerpen 2004). These are mostly owned by Nigerians and Ghanaians who represent a larger and earlier African presence in Antwerp. Some older migrants or individuals who married Belgian women also live outside the city, in the periphery of satellite towns.

The route to Spain

History
Spain has only recently become a destination country for Senegambian migrants: it used to be a place of transition. According to several key witnesses, a small Senegambian community existed in the Barcelona region at the end of the 1970s, consisting of former students who had become undocumented in France and sought a more relaxed life, and others who had been blocked on their way to France when labour migration recruitment stopped (Kaplan 1998). Throughout the 1980s,

small numbers of new migrants came in, while the 1990s saw an acceleration of new arrivals, which even increased after 2000; simultaneously, family reunion started to consolidate the community and increase the numbers. Next to the factor of geographical proximity, the presence of family or friends was the first reason for migrants to choose Spain as a destination; the successive regularisation campaigns and the clandestine work possibilities without much risk of being deported, were other reasons mentioned (Pérez 1995). Catalonia seems to be particularly attractive because of its vibrant economy. In Barcelona city, the public records (including many undocumented immigrants) show about 700 residents from West Africa. At closer look, a remarkable difference with Antwerp emerges: a more significant community of Senegambians actually lives in satellite towns around Barcelona (like Mataró, Sabadell, Terrassa and Granollers), taking the number up to 4,300 in the 2001 census.[9] Economically speaking, these municipalities and Barcelona form a functional unit, in which many industries are decentralised to the peripheral towns and coordination and management functions are concentrated in the capital. This coherence is reflected in the institution of the Barcelona Metropolitan Area, defined by the Regional Planning Laws of the Catalan Parliament in 1987. The geographical configuration of employment possibilities and the cheaper housing motivate Senegambian migrants to settle outside the city centre, contrasting sharply with the pattern in Antwerp as will be shown in the empirical chapters. This confirms that the location of workers is determined by the spatial structures of the economic activities in which they work, as well as the provision of housing.

Recent trends
Increasingly in recent years, the determination and desperation of African migrants trying to reach Spanish territories has captured the headlines of local and international press:[10] over the summer of 2006, they adopted the motto 'Barca ou Barzakh', 'Barcelona or the afterlife'. The 'patera' (a small precarious boat) and later 'cayuco' (wooden open fishing boat) arriving on the Southern or Canarian coasts filled with black immigrants has become the symbol of illegal migration, creating the image of an invasion, and serving to justify tightening of the laws. However, the problem with sub-Saharan migration is not the numbers or the volume, as they compose only 5 per cent of the total number of immigrants in Spain, but the often tragic circumstances that show perhaps the bitterest face of migration.[11] It is estimated (*El País* 16 April 2006) that between 1989 and 2002 almost 10,000 people have died or disappeared attempting to enter the Spanish territory from Morocco; in the first six months of 2006, 490 bodies were found on African and Spanish coasts and between two to 3,000 went missing. A closer analy-

sis of the evolution of this phenomenon between autumn 2005 and December 2006 reveals the concrete interplay between the determination of the migrants, Spain's policies preventing migration, and the quick adaptations of traffickers (*El País* 3 June 2006). A map of key migrant routes (Firgure 4.2) shows main entryways from north to south, which runs parallel to chronology: the most northern strategies have been replaced recently with longer trips starting in the south.

Figure 4.2 *Key migrant routes from Africa to Europe*

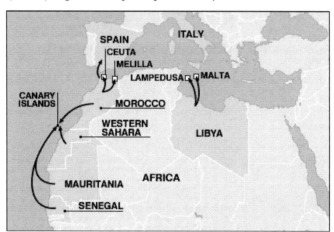

Source: news.bbc.co.uk

Spain started to work on a European subsidised integral control system and invested in collaboration with Moroccan authorities, in order to prevent illegal crossings of the Strait of Gibraltar and from the Western Sahara to the Canary Islands. When these measures became effective[12], thousands of migrants regrouped in the bushes around Ceuta and Melilla in autumn 2005 and jumped the fences in a series of massive raids. After thirteen deaths, hundreds of deportations and the decision to increase the height of the fence from three to six meters, migrants discovered another route to arrive at the Spanish shores via Nuadibou, a Mauritanian border city. More than 1000 migrants in three days and a couple of diplomatic missions later (*El País* 14 May 2006), a repatriation agreement was negotiated. Just days later boats started to depart from Saint-Louis, the most northern city of Senegal, making the trip nowadays 1,200 km and eight to thirteen days long; later, departure points in Dakar and Southern Casamance were also identified, up to Guinea Bissau. Summits, presidential visits, the promise of 35 million euro in development aid as well as 4,000 openings for legal migration to Spain, convinced the Senegalese president to collaborate in controlling the sea and to accept the repatriation of about 5,000 citizens (*El País* 17 October 2006).[13] The Senegalese government hoped that by using smaller regional airports this would pass unnoticed and avoid losing public credit in the face of elections in 2007. Throughout the summer ever increasing records of arrivals were announced per day, weekend or week; at the end of December, the counter was just below 31,000 arrivals on the Canary Islands (equalling the numbers of the last four years together – *El País* 27 December 2006)[14]. The most common profile was revealed by Red Cross research amongst 667 immigrants detained in Mauritania in the summer of 2006: they were mainly Senegalese between eighteen and 30, with primary education and previously working in business or agriculture. And despite wounds and infections from the first trip, more than half were determined to have another try (*El País* 11 September 2006). Over the year, the traffickers have adapted routes responding to the changing police vigilance; the market is very profitable, with an endless demand and prices between 500 and 1,000 euro per person.[15]

4.3 Senegalese business tradition

When asked about actual or previous activities, respondents mostly mention 'business'. In western minds this concept evokes connotations with bookkeeping, marketing, business plans and cash flows; but there is another 'business world', one of nomadic entrepreneurs, animating an underground economy of global reach, raising respectable profits (Peraldi 2001; Tarrius 2002). It is based on trust, verbal promises, close networks spanning different ethnicities and cultures, mutual support and collaboration, but also on exploitation and criminal activities. It involves masters and 'ants' (Tarrius 1992), a wide range of formal as well as informal activities and transactions, often essentially occasional and not necessarily professional. Snatches from my fieldwork include the following: I brought the first copy of the new Youssou N'Dour CD to Belgium in December 2005; the next day, somebody made 30 copies of it and sold them at four euro each: 120 euro profit. Another person buys twenty pairs of shoes from a Pakistani friend and sells them for a ten-euro profit. In the centre of Barcelona, phone cards cost only 3.8 euro, while they are sold in Mataró for six, creating a small-scale traffic. Someone hears about a truck full of T-shirts with a production fault, and he sells them to a garage that uses them as rags. A woman visiting Barcelona brings the new fashion in fabrics from Paris and sells them during her visit. There is no clear delineation between the occasional hawker and the one who fills three containers every two months, between the one who has no papers and the one travelling back and forth for many years; some activities generate only pocket money; others are real international businessmen... (Marfaing 2003b). Business represents an accessible opportunity that inscribes itself in the informal economy, so familiar in Africa (Torres Perez 2004); at the same time, the commercial activity is a way of life rather than a job (Barry 1992; Harding 1992). In this way, business is everywhere all the time, everybody is always on the watch for an interesting deal, and every Senegalese is a potential businessman.[16]

In the specific Senegalese context, hawking, selling, peddling, import-export and business are partly overlapping concepts, and a term that respondents themselves use frequently is '*modu-modu*'[17]. This wide variety of activities will be explored below, as well as the particular network underpinning the most recent trade diaspora – showing how it becomes an institution that supports migrants and links them to their home country.

A wide spectrum of activities

The first and most common method of commerce is hawking or mobile selling, a Senegalese specialisation[18] (Diop 1990; Sow 2004; Stoller 2002; Torres Perez 2004; Vargas Llovera 1997). In Spain and Italy, the tourist beaches and squares are the most popular and lucrative places. In Belgium hawkers prefer to sell inside bars where they are more hidden from the eye of the police; the summertime, when people are out on the terraces, is therefore more dangerous. Some hawkers use this difference in location to make a seasonal tour of Europe: going south during the tourist season, back to Belgium during the winter. Hawking without a permit is forbidden and many of them have no residence permit. This combination makes them vulnerable not only to police checks but to abuse from bar owners or clients, ranging from racist remarks over stealing goods to physical aggression. To avoid this, some migrants have specialised in ambulant selling within their own community, visiting private houses with merchandise targeted at their colleagues and friends. Finally, a limited number of hawkers have formalised their business and sell in markets and summer festivals throughout Europe.

The goods they sell vary, not in the least with the budget they can invest, but they also adapt the merchandise to the place, the weather, and the latest fashion. The offer can range from umbrellas to leather coats, ethnic musical instruments, belts, or sunglasses; from reproductions of famous paintings to stilettos, from towels to strings and from African masks to cheap electric toys. A more recent trend in Barcelona is selling copied CDs and DVDs in restaurants and bars. The profit margins depend on the goods (and on the days); and incomes range accordingly from most precarious to comfortable: two or three euro profit per CD or DVD, 99 cents per cotton bracelet. However, the really good business lies in counterfeiting of elite brands: the goods are in high demand and the profit is high.[19] A well-done fake Breitling watch requires an investment of 75 euro, but can be sold at 500; although one is not that lucky every day, it is a chance not to miss. The negative sides are the higher investment and the more severe penalties when caught. The most profitable and most dangerous are criminal activities based on this principle: next to the famous diamond shops in Antwerp, they sometimes offer fake but identical looking jewellery to clients. And some people have a role higher up the hierarchy, as the person producing the pirate CDs and DVDs, or as the broker for counterfeit goods. The production of this merchandise links into a global economy, with commercial networks bringing it from China, Pakistan, Spain and Italy down to the hawkers (Tarrius 2002).

A second kind of business is based on larger scale import-export transactions in the informal sector, based on existing price differences. The economic divide between Europe and Africa (but also the US and Middle East) guarantees interesting profits for those who can cross borders without paying duties (Sow 2004; Tarrius 2002). In this profession, mobility in all its forms organises the activities and structures the trajectories (Bava 2000). Travelling through the country on the most modest level, moving to other countries in Europe as part of business deals; and the most international businessmen hold itinerant trading in high regard, linking the US, Europe, the Middle East and Africa (Bertoncello & Bredeloup 2000 a; Diouf 2000). Some places represent central functions like Dakar and Paris, and others are flexible, depending on local seasonal opportunities. In fact, there are an increasing number of very successful businesswomen. The new information technologies make this global network possible (Tall 2003). Although being a successful international businessman is almost everyone's dream, becoming one requires more means than most migrants can ever bring together. The starting capital represents just the beginning; the supporting network is another crucial factor, and a small role as link in the profitable chain is a more realistic expectation than being at the very top.

The goods being traded cover a wide range, following the level of specialisation and investment: import from Senegal and the Gambia includes African beauty products, hair extensions, art, cloth, food, spices, musical video's, cereals, sweets and incense. Surprisingly, the product lines show the interpenetration of the commercial networks of Africans and Asians: braids, for example, are produced and traded in China or Pakistan in quantity (Bava 2000; Sow 2001; Tellegen 2000). African businessmen go to buy there, or stock up in wholesale centres in Paris or import personally from the home country to distribute everywhere in Europe. Also exported to Africa are new electronic devices like mobile phones and watches, trendy clothes and sport shoes, underwear and perfume, toys and household appliances, but also second hand clothes, fridges and computers. The most booming niche of the last two decades is the trade in second hand cars and spare parts (Beuving 2006; Gambaracci 2001; Nwolisa Okanga 1995): most second hand European cars look new in Africa, and as they are not used for private transport but to serve as taxis, relatively high prices are paid. With more imports coming in, returns have been diminishing and the high profits have become a myth and an illusion (Beuving 2006).

Thirdly, for all mainstream self-employed jobs, a parallel informal system exists. Some women have a fully furnished informal shop at home; some men act as travel agents for air companies and get a free flight when they bring in a certain number of clients. Others act as informal car mechanics or exchange brokers. I got a nice idea of the extent of economic activity inside the community at a baptism that I assisted at in Barcelona:

> The hostess wears four or five different dresses during the night, all the ladies look like queens with embroidered African fabrics, and with hair styles so complicated that they require days of work. The men and children are freshly shaven and wear new cloths. Those fabrics must have been imported, sold, sewed; all the guests went to a hairdresser and women had their make-up done. In addition, an army of women must have cooked today to provide food and drinks for over 80 people, and during the evening, two photographers and one cameraman record everything for the family back home... And then the entertainers of the evening: three traditional singers, two men for music and light, and two different percussionists' bands. (field notes)

Sometimes the commercial character is difficult to define: the same woman may braid the hair of a friend for free at one point and serve as a beauty parlour at another; at the weekly gatherings in Business Street dinner would be cooked for more than fifteen people, yet it was not one of the existing informal restaurants.

To conclude, the business model developed by migrants shows their flexibility, in not only registers of commercial practices, choices of products, definitions of markets, modes of financing but also profit margins:

> They have thus appropriated the most important reflex of contemporary liberal cosmopolitanism, taking advantage of economic opportunity: sell whatever is in demand a lower price, always respond to demand, and acquire captive markets. (Diouf 2000: 696)

While they are busy, we can think whether they represent ethnic entrepreneurship, a bazaar economy or whether they are the lowest echelons of an innovative worldwide business.

The Murid connection

A special note should go to the well-documented role of the Murid brotherhood in recent Senegalese migration (Bava 2002; Copans 2000; Diouf 2000; Fall 2002; Harding 1992). The Murid brotherhood is a Senegalese religious group founded in the 19th century by a charismatic leader (*marabout*) named Amadou Bamba, preaching hard work, solidarity, and absolute submission to the marabout. Their economic involvement and diversification has been aptly summarised by Copans (2000) in the title of his article 'Murids of the Fields, Murids of the Cities, Murids of the Mobile Phone and the Internet'. Each of these three phases corresponds to specific modes of inscription in space, formulas of financial accumulation, relationships with the wider world, as well as new representations of their community over time (Diouf 2000; Lacomba 2000). In a first stage starting at the end of 19th century, the Murid brotherhood successfully carved out a space for itself within the colonial system and its economy of peanuts; the money they accumulated allowed them to become a powerful organisation with a large political and economic influence in Senegal. Second, some Murid merchants were involved in peanut trading in cities and colonial ports; later, the rural migrants became involved in the rapidly developing informal import-export sector. Afterwards, in the age of international migration in the 1990s, the brotherhood managed to almost seize the monopoly of the informal trade diaspora. This shows how Muridism adapted flexibly to economic change, not as a planned strategy, 'surfing' on the *modu-modu* link the same way they did on peanuts earlier (Copans 2000).

Although the brotherhood itself does not organise 'business', the trust and common identity facilitate the creation of global connections, with a Murid contact in every city, who has established privileged relations with local intermediaries, enabling them to obtain products at prices that other merchants cannot match; they also provide accommodation and informal lending systems. It offers a personal project for youngsters, a support network upon arrival, and prevents them partly from engaging in deviant activities (Lacomba 2000; Schmidt di Friedberg 1994). Its network of local *dahira*'s (circle of disciples) links back to Senegal and to the global community, with Serigne Mamor Mbacké, the figurehead of the nomad marabout, guaranteeing continuity and legitimacy by his trips and advice (Bava 2002; Guèye 2002). In addition, the grandchildren of the Mbacké family travel around Europe or the US to solve spiritual problems and at the same time make some money for a couple of months. Both in Senegal and abroad, Muridism is a popular movement attracting a wide population of young, urban, mobile Senegalese because of the international linkages and entrepreneurial style of leadership, its emphasis on adaptation to western-oriented consumption styles while being faithful to religious traditions. This shows the brotherhood as an illustration of both the fluid and adaptable process of globalisation and the multiplicity of cultural identities.

4.4 The importance of migration back home

Migration, or perhaps it is better to say remittances, have also become a cornerstone element of Senegalese society. For most Senegambian migrants the decision to leave was often a family decision; if not, loved ones and friends are likely to become interested once the immigrant is able to send money home. In general, migrants show a strong solidarity and persisting relationships with relatives left behind,[20] as well as a maintained attachment to their country (De Jong et al. 2002). As soon as a migrant arrives and finds an odd job, he will start to send money home; for most migrants this continues throughout their whole life, and this relationship may influence important decisions during their trajectory. People that cut the links with their family after migration are badly regarded and none of my respondents even considers this option.

> All the Africans in Europe, they did not come for themselves, they came for their family. If it was only me, I could stay in Africa; I know I will be fine. But maybe you have brothers, sisters, they have problems, they want you to help them. (Sadani, 28, in Barcelona since 2003, undocumented, garbage collection)

Remittances are a hot topic (Taylor 2004): in political conferences and academic publications all over the world their aim and effect is discussed, focussing on 'productive' versus 'consumption' uses, two points taken up below. Negative critiques point at the unsustainable forms of dependency they create if only providing consumption goods. These have been mitigated by a broad recognition of the positive roles of remittances as they affect the social and economic development of numerous countries around the world, if only by sheer scale. There are different ways to send money, thanks to modern information technology: a transfer between bank accounts if both parties have one, or alternatively by expensive transfers with Western Union. However, the most common way is to consign the money to a friend who is travelling back or a broker; during return visits, many gifts and donations are redistributed, and money is both spent and invested (Asiedu 2005). In most statistics these informal transfers are not included, nor are the 'in kind' transfers (sending cars or containers filled with goods) leading to imprecision and underestimation of the flow (Fall 2003).

This section will sketch the important relationship with home, the money sent there and the future planned there, illustrating how vital migration has become on both the level of the family and the country.

Remittances and consumption

Research in France in 1998 showed that 174 out of 201 West African respondents sent money home, 108 on a regular basis (Blion & Witeska 1998). The regularity can vary as well as the amount (a small sum monthly, an extra budget for festivities or emergencies, presents and investment during return visits) (Robin 1996a), but in this study it added to about 10 to 15 per cent of the annual income. A recent study in the municipality of Madrid revealed that 70 per cent of the migrants sent money home, with an average of 24 per cent of their salary (*El País* 12 February 2007). When an immigrant starts sending money home, often between 50 and 150 euro a month in my sample and in other research (Diatta & Mbow 1999), it is sent for day to day maintenance.

For many families, regular remittances are a lifeline and the dominant source of income to pay for rent, medical expenses, school fees, bills or food expenses as well as clothes (Jettinger 2005). A household budget survey in Senegal in 1994 revealed that between 30 and 70 per cent of family needs are covered by remittances (Adepoju 2004). The money is sent to someone the migrant trusts, in order to redistribute it to the wife and children, parents, other relatives who are living at home, a second wife and her children, or more distant family in the village (Garnier 1990). These 'expenditure linkages' transmit remittance impacts to other households, including ones that may not send migrants abroad (Taylor 2004).

> The problem in Africa is that there is no social security. The social security is the immigrants. We are the OCMW for a whole family and many more. Me, personally, I have more than 500 euro of costs every month to pay my family, my children back there, et cetera. (Sheikh, in Antwerp since 2004, undocumented, import-export)

Next to its economic necessity, migration is also bestowed with the complex cultural meaning of representing success, and remittances become a powerful social activity, accelerating the consumption spiral. Whether the help is only enough to help with daily expenses of food and housing, or is invested in education for children, assistance with health problems, a trip to Mecca for the parents, a second wife for the father, or a house with garage on a beach in Dakar, a whole community is aware of the rising standard of living. At this stage the person who left is already a hero, probably reinforcing the image of previous migrants and compelling new ones to migrate in search of funds to meet 'these newly established consumption levels and therefore, social requirements' (Romaniszyn 2000: 140). The spending priorities of the family back home do not always correspond to what the hard-working migrant had planned, leading to painful discussions and misunderstandings. In many cases the migrant actually pays the orders at a local grocery store immediately instead of sending the money to the family (Diop 1990; Ndiaye 1996; Tall 2003).

Remittances and investment in development

Transfers from overseas Senegalese were estimated at $421 million in 2003, representing six per cent of GDP (Dahou & Foucher 2004; OECD 2005). This figure has risen strongly since 1999 when it stood at 88.8 million dollars. As in many other countries, remittances are currently higher than development aid and foreign investments from industrialised countries together.[21] The 'export' of migrants and what they send back represents one of the biggest sectors of economic growth, accounting for a considerable source of national income. Diatta and Mbow and others (Ba 1997; 1999) have optimistic views of the development potential of remittances: Senegalese living abroad increase substantially the revenues of families living in the village, and they foster the development of these localities. Through their savings, investment and knowledge, they contribute in a significant manner to the economic and social development of their country. The fruits of migrants' labour enable other villagers to remain at home and consequently not feel constrained to join the exodus. This view is shared by a respondent:

> If every family could have one immigrant, ten years from now Senegal will be different, a lot of people will not even want to come to Europe. (Sadani, 28, in Barcelona since 2003, undocumented, garbage collection)

As a consequence, remittances are becoming a political factor and emigrants are increasingly considered as important agents in the economic and social development of their country as they actively fill some of the holes left by the state (Adepoju 2005; Diatta & Mbow 1999; Tall 2002). The AU's Vision and Strategic Plan for 2004-2007 also places the diaspora at the centre of its aspirations to maximise the benefits of migration for development in Africa. A ministry for the Senegalese abroad was created to manage this phenomenon, encourage migrants to become more actively involved agents in investments, and to reinsert them back in their country's economy, sometimes in cooperation with IOM. However, the reality is more complicated, and the effect seems to be limited (IOM 2005).

A first investment commonly made is in a plot of land, and later in the construction of a house (Marfaing 2003b; Tall 1994), often a new family house in the village, later a house in the capital. Housing has become a very popular investment as it covers many functions: it is a way of saving, a productive investment when rented or sold, it may one day provide accommodation for parents. In the urban environment of a city like Dakar, Thiès or Touba, it softens the housing crisis, but on the other hand it leads to wild urbanisation, permanent construction sites and rapidly rising prises due to speculation (Marfaing 2003a; Tall 1994). Next, the migrant will try to think about a small profitable activity for family members, such as a car that they can use as a taxi, a stall with second hand import goods, a sewing machine to be a tailor, a hi-fi installation to be a DJ (Grillo & Riccio 2003). Finally, the final intention of almost every migrant is to invest in a big profit-making project (Marfaing 2003a) that would allow him to return home as a successful individual. But many also want to contribute to the development of their country by applying the knowledge and experience they gained through the migration experience.

> Sooner or later I would like to go back to my country. I think my country needs me, I did not come to stay here. I am waiting to have a lot of money, that is what I wait for. But not to keep my millions in the bank, that makes no sense. I need money to invest, to give work to the fellow countrymen who don't have a job, to help them, that is how I see the development of my country. Because if I have my money here and I stay here, I help to develop Spain, not my country (Pape, in Barcelona since 2000, regular status, shopkeeper).

In the early days, a grocery shop would at least allow the migrant himself to come back and even carry some status; small-scale regional tourist accommodation ('campement') was a popular investment for a while. Later on, communication centres with phones and computers became attractive, and most recently the people who managed to construct a number of apartments in Dakar are able to realise the comfortable return they always imagined. Following the general trend in the Senegambian economy, most migrants nowadays dream about a business, often in import-export. Despite this generalised intention, Blion (1998) finds that only 30 out of 201 respondents in his study reported productive investments in the home country – and it is important to ask why.

A number of obstacles stand in between the vague dream and its successful realisation. A first element is the unfavourable climate for investment in the home country, with the unpredictable administration and infrastructure leading to a lack of trust. Second, with the increasing competition of other migrants, only a very specific plan in a promising sector can really make a difference: possibilities are specialised informatics' services, renewable energy, or industrial waste dealing. However, thirdly, most migrants are not in a position to be capitalist entrepreneurs or create a rentable economic structure because of a lack of business background. Finally, the sum of money needed for a successful return home is often considerably higher than expected; people without a background in informal business often misjudge the budget for even a modest project. Given the generally low migrant incomes in Europe, the periods of unemployment, and unexpected costs for the family at home, it takes longer to save that amount.

In addition, the early migrants to France organised themselves in associations based on ethnicity, brotherhood, or region of origin, who would gather monthly contributions and invest them in community provisions: sanitation, a small hospital, an ambulance, a school or a mosque (Daum 1993; Grillo & Riccio 2003; Kane 2002; Marfaing 2003a; Ndiaye 1996; Quiminal 1993). These translocal development organisations were seen as vectors of development, and they did very good jobs, but they suffered from similar critiques as western development aid, including increasing dependency. In Catalonia a more advanced vision of co-development is heavily supported by the local government, explicitly linking cooperation with the migrant groups present on the territory (Diao 2004; Giménez Romero 1997).

One can easily note that the contribution of remittances to development in terms of job creation or innovative entrepreneurship is rather limited. There is a clear impact on construction and commerce, but many products are imported and are thus not pure added value for the home country. In order to seek to leverage more remittances into economic development, common recommendations include the strengthening and speeding up of formal transfer mechanisms at lower prices, the involvement of migrants' associations to stimulate collective remittances for community development, and support for credit unions and other micro-finance institutions (Diatta & Mbow 1999).

4.5 The sample

This background information provided the starting point for a sampling procedure. The aim of the sample was not, as explained above, to be representative of the whole Senegambian population, but to cover a variety of groups and migration experiences. An overview of the sample sheds some light on the composition of the flow, as presented in Table 4.2. In the first place, it illustrates how economic migration is a factor of selection in itself: the ones who leave are not the ill or elderly, not even the poorest and hungriest, if only because you need a minimum of money to be able to leave. Instead, migrants tend to be the strong and healthy youngsters with capacities, motivated and well prepared. Given the male tradition of migration in this population, and the relatively early stages of migration to Spain and Belgium, it comes as no surprise that the profile is one of young single men: the majority of the respondents are bachelor males under the age of 35.[22] As for previous education and work experience, the general image is one of lower educated people, at least from a European perspective, and of people leaving the insecure informal employment discussed above.

Table 4.2 *Overview of respondents by key categories*

		Antwerp N=35	Barcelona N=46
Gender	Men	32	35
	Women	3	10
Age group	Younger than 35	18	29
	35-50	14	15
	Older than 50	3	2
Ethnicity	Wolof	21	6
	Peul	5	12
	Others	9	30
Family situation	Single	17	23
	Married, family in Africa	5	11
	Married, family in Europe	13	12
Legal situation	Documented	23	30
	Undocumented	12	16
Arrival in Europe	After 2000	10	22
	In the 1990s	13	17
	Before 1990s	2	7
Level of previous education	Only Koranic school[23]	1	14
	Primary education finished	13	21
	Secondary education finished	15	9
	Higher education finished	6	2
Previous work experience	Fixed formal job	8	3
	Informal job	13	33
	No job	14	10

The group does include, however, a smaller but considerable group of people with higher degrees and fixed formal jobs prior to leaving; many of whom left out of ambition or curiosity.[24] The profiles as shown in the figures repeat the main categories found by other research, and confirm that I covered the most important groups

(Anguiano Téllez 2001; Kaplan 1998; Marfaing 2003b; Pajares 2005; Pérez 1995; Vargas Llovera 1997).

The moment of arrival in Spain and Belgium shows some very early migrants in the 1970s and 1980s; they were the exception, because France was a more common destination at that time. However, the 1990s saw a large increase, continuing in Spain after 2000. In terms of legal status, the majority had a residence permit at the time of the interview, but most had previously been undocumented; a considerable number of undocumented migrants were interviewed as well. I had no problem finding people from all Senegambian ethnicities in Spain, representing the most isolated rural corners of the country. In Belgium, however, I found respondents mainly from the Wolof and Peul groups; in addition I noticed that they tended to come from the capitals Dakar or Banjul, or Thiès, Senegal's second city. Closely linked to this is the fact that respondents' educational level in Antwerp is generally slightly higher than in Barcelona. If the migrant is married, another interesting difference is reflected in the numbers: in Antwerp, the majority of migrants has their family living with them, while in Barcelona, half of the families live in Africa. These differences will be developed in more detail and linked to other parts of the research in chapter 7.

4.6 Conclusion: Senegambian migration

This chapter discusses why and how contemporary Senegal and the Gambia, like many countries in Africa and around the world, are marked by disequilibrium between the available resources and the needs and hopes of the population. The crisis of the traditional agricultural system, the lack of perspective in industrial or service sectors and the problems deriving from global competition are the main reasons why people emigrate. Because of this push-dimension and the subsequent dynamics of chain migration, the flows no longer correspond to Europe's labour needs; far from being an invasion, we should remember that most migrants just move to neighbouring countries inside Africa. However, when they manage to arrive in Europe, the Senegambian community carved out a niche in the informal business sector that enables immigrants to jumpstart a career. The networks provide support, goods to sell, as well as information; all these elements facilitate integration. Thirdly, for the families at home, the remittances have become a structural and indispensable source of income; the country as a whole is also adapting to this structural dimension. In short, migration has been a permanent part of history and tradition of the people, but the transcontinental option has nowadays become a structural institution, a shared dynamic of survival on the level of the individual, the family, the brotherhood and the country. However, precisely because migration is used as a means of crisis management, it is not necessarily the best solution for all problems (Adepoju 2004):

> The sending country does receive big flows of money, but the money is atomised in many ways: the number of people sending it, the sporadic nature over time that it is sent, and the different sectors in which it is used, for distribution and consumption only, not so much for investment or business. It is me and my friend sending home 200 when we can, used to buy a fridge and to refurbish the house and send somebody to school and cure somebody in hospital. But at no point it provides an income for the government with which things for the common good can be organised or a project can be launched (François, in Antwerp since 2003, regular status, in training).

This chapter also showed how the world is interconnected in continuous and complex ways, and how changes in politics or consumption patterns in one place evoke 'answers' or adaptations elsewhere, how dynamics transcend geographical borders in short spans of time. Migration, development, and international relations are closely linked. Many respondents mentioned that migration is unavoidable under the present circumstances; the only long-term perspective to limit the immigration flow is development in the countries of origin. This should not be based on help, but on transformations of the economy: the economy must be modernised, diversified, and decentralised in order to make it a tool for reducing poverty. Beyond this, it is necessary to improve public policy and to modernise social relations and the institutional environment, stressing coherence and efficiency and transparency. Without Afro pessimism, one can only start to imagine the amounts of money, energy, and effort that should be put inside. In the meantime, the migration pressure is likely to continue.

The next three chapters will present the empirical material on the experiences of migrants once they arrive in Europe. They will describe in depth the trajectories and strategies of Senegambian migrants, both in the labour market and on a more general level, in the specific context of Antwerp and Barcelona. An ideal-type chronological approach will be developed, starting with life as an undocumented migrant, without suggesting that all migrants will necessarily follow the steps in this order. The mainstream experiences shared by many respondents will be represented first; next to this, there will be substantial room to show alternatives or atypical routes that other individuals develop, or to stress changes over time for different cohorts of arrival. The relevant differences found in experiences of the interviewees will be explicitly linked to a comparison of the macro characteristics of both cities.

5 Survival strategies as an undocumented migrant

> Look at Wagane; now, he's a real role model, a worthy son of our village. He's been to the ends of the earth to make his fortune; now he's spreading it around. Leave, go where you can, but seek success instead of just staying here [...]. Go and look for work, and don't forget, my sons, every scrap of life must serve to win dignity! (Diome 2006: 84)

The example of previous successful migrants is the manual for the newcomers in Europe: the old fisherman in Diome's novel encourages the youngsters idly playing football to migrate, work hard, earn money, and do all of that with dignity. Little does he know about the reality of life and work as an undocumented migrant... The shared aim and ambition of Senegambian migrants is to build a better life for themselves and their families back home, to raise the family income as well as to ameliorate their future prospects. Given the agency-focus of this study, the central theme in this chapter will be on the strategies people adopt to reach that goal in the host societies, the resulting trajectories, and how far they get. There is a consensus that the rather extreme term 'survival strategies' is not appropriate for most groups in Western European welfare states; however, in the case of new migrants, particularly those arriving without residence permit, one might consider using it. The uncertainty and the insecurity of their existence justify the notion of survival strategy.

The full spectrum of survival strategies includes undocumented as well as formal work, periods of unemployment or support by transfers from governments. Van der Leun and Kloosterman (2006) stress how a wide interpretation of 'labour' is necessary to understand migrant labour market trajectories, and developed the schematic representation below.

It shows the different spheres of the economy where migrants can work, based on the degree of regulation by a government. The most strongly regulated domains are the ones of governmental positions. At the other extreme non-monetary transactions are located, based in an exchange- and gift-economy by family and friends. In the middle, we find monetary relationships as in salary or self-employed positions, which can be subdivided into a formal and informal economy, and a criminal and non-criminal one. Policies differ from country to country, and from theory to practice. For undocumented migrants only the left side is accessible, unless false or borrowed papers allow them to pass on to the right side. I make a distinction between the formal or informal economy but this does not overlap completely with people being undocumented or not, which makes it difficult to classify people or jobs. A migrant without papers (undocumented) can do formal work with another's papers; documented migrants can do informal work.

Figure 5.1   *Domains of economic help*

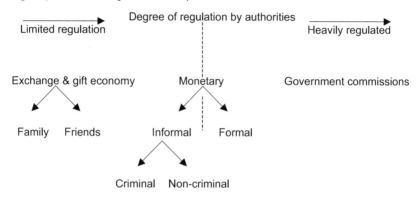

Source: Van der Leun and Kloosterman (1999: 121)

In this chapter, the labour market experiences of undocumented migrants will be the primary topic; I will look at entry jobs and the development of later trajectories, with special attention to the different cohorts of arrival. Subsequently, I will present additional survival strategies; as undocumented migrants are not entitled to state redistribution, these will be located in the reciprocity sphere.

5.1   Work experiences of undocumented migrants

A majority of respondents, 60 out of 81, have entered the countries of destination illegally, or became undocumented a few months after their arrival; either way, they went through phases where they did not possess the necessary documents that allow a normal entry into the labour market. According to Soenen, legal status influences labour market trajectories in three ways: through exploitation by employers, by concentration in lower wage jobs because of difficulties to maximise returns to their human capital, and because of a lower reservation wage. This means that undocumented migrants are ready to accept lower wages (or worse conditions) due to a lack of other support systems such as social welfare, or due to precarious positions (Soenen 2003; Van der

Leun & Kloosterman 1999). Below, I will sketch how these elements lead to specific trajectories in the two cities. By definition, they have to rely on alternative circuits of information, and they can only access the informal jobs, often concentrated in specific sectors. However, undocumented migrants can sometimes participate in the official labour market, by working with someone else's work permit. At that point, their trajectories will form the subject of formal labour market behaviour – showing that there is no absolute correlation between being undocumented and working informally.[1]

In Antwerp

Upon arrival in Europe, migrants follow the traces of friends or family from home, and they may arrive in Antwerp, be it planned or by coincidence. The path often leads to a shared apartment such as Business Street number 13,[2] a house known for hosting Senegalese hawkers:

> In Business Street, the first three months, the accommodation and the food were free. In the meantime, the friends explain a bit how the business works, I borrowed some money from different people, I learned about the police and the good addresses, and I started to go selling myself. Business Street is almost a business-school. Afterwards I started paying 100 euro per month for the rent, and then contributing for the food. I started and it worked very well, I could even send money home. At first, business was very good, I could send home about 100 euro per month. (Bakeba, in Antwerp since 1993, regular status, unemployed)

A more vivid picture of this existence, together with the changes in this sector over time, will be given next, as well as some examples of respondents developing alternative strategies in the world of informal labour.

The hawking sector as an entry into the labour market

For the overwhelming majority of respondents informally arriving in Belgium (nineteen out of 27), hawking was the start of their labour market career, and most continued doing this until the moment they were able to obtain a residence permit by marriage or regularisation. Not only active members of the Murid brotherhood participated, illustrating the centrality of business networks for Senegalese migration in general, as discussed in chapter 4. Hawking is a rather evident path to take upon arrival as an undocumented migrant when the social context pushes in that direction.

Many did not have any previous experience in business or selling in Senegal – and more than one was very surprised to discover the way the legendary migrants, portraying themselves so successfully and rich back home, actually try to make a living. However, after a couple of days or weeks, they accept that there is no other way, other than criminal activities; instead, they prefer hawking as an honourable and honest way of earning some money.

> When I came to Antwerp I saw the people leaving with the bags, and I was surprised and later shocked. I did not understand in the beginning; but when I heard about the selling in bars, I was shocked. You know, I lived very well in Senegal; I had everything I wanted, and I could not imagine doing this for a living. You loose your dignity in selling: the goods are not good, you lie to people, and you make them pay more when you discuss the price. Also, in selling you will never get any respect, people feel pity or despise but never anything good. But I also had to do it, there was no other way; I had to eat and pay the rent and live. But I was so ashamed; I had never done anything like business and I did not like it. But also I don't want to steal. (Youssou, in Antwerp since 2000, undocumented, working in horticulture)

Previous education, work experience, or diplomas do not play any role: hawking absorbs both the immigrant who only went to Koranic school, and the one who studied in university, as explained by a former mathematics student:

> The *modu-modu* they live in their own universe, they don't go out to understand, to learn, they don't know. In my case, in Brussels, as they speak French, maybe even without papers I could do something there, they have organisations for that, to continue studying. But when I arrived here, the modu-modu they think only about money, and they contaminated me, I forgot my studies. The people don't even believe that I am a university student, so much I was completely contaminated. Even my wife when she arrived she asked me why do you live like this? You speak French, you have studied; you could have had a different life in Brussels or Liège, I told her she was right but it was too late to change (Aziz, in Antwerp since 1994, regularised, shopkeeper).

To avoid being caught by the authorities, they cover their merchandise (and intentions) in supermarket bags, university labelled back packs or laptop cases; to avoid being seen or caught with large quantities of goods, some have a network of distribution points where they leave the stock, taking only samples on their journey. They are not only afraid of the police; they are often confronted with abuse, racism and threats from barkeepers or customers. Because of their undocumented status, it is difficult for them to rely on protection by the law, leading to a de facto impunity for those who want to attack them.

> But it is not a nice job, sometimes people say bad things, or they can even beat you, or take things without paying, and you cannot do anything because if the police comes it will be you who has the problems. Therefore, you have to tolerate it. (Bakeba, in Antwerp since 1993, regular status, unemployed)

As explained by Bakeba above, the immigrant network is central in the whole process, from the early days' subsistence support in accommodation and food, over possibilities to borrow money for an initial set of goods to sell, to more experienced hawkers sharing experiences about the police or bar owners. Their working day starts in the early evening, at about 6 or 7pm, and can continue until late at night, particularly in weekends. With the unsafe climate of the 1990s, they were pretty much confined to the environment of the shared house for the rest of the day, spending their time cooking, eating, talking, and watching TV together. These particular characteristics of this hawking life lead some people to muse nostalgically now that they have moved on.

The level of income depends on the period, the skills, the experience, the range of articles for sale and respective profit margins, the presence of a fixed run of customers, the amount of time and energy spent in going around, but is in any case variable. It is difficult to estimate, but it can range from almost nothing on bad days to about 1,500 euro or more a month (in the heydays of the 1990s). People have to plan and distribute their income over longer periods, covering the days or weeks when they do not sell anything with savings from the good days.

Since 2000, life has become more difficult for new cohorts arriving, and income for the hawkers has diminished, due to a combination of policy elements showing increasingly strict controls. The Antwerp police started a persistent campaign of heavy scrutiny against the numerous counterfeit shops and businesses at Falconplein, the main supply centre in Belgium; the subsequent controls, arrests and fines for all kinds of breaches of the law caused the shops to close over a couple of months and (probably) move elsewhere. To show a firm attitude against criminal activities, symbolic and highly visible police actions are undertaken in well-known immigrant areas such as North and De Coninckplein[3]. After the 2000 regularisation, police currently target their identity checks in different ways, focussing more on specific activities (like hawking) and places (like communication centres) rather than people walking on the street. A third element making life difficult is the proliferation of cheap shops selling Chinese import goods at very low prices, undermining the competitive edge of the hawkers, as explained by Malick:

> The situation has changed a lot; the business is not working as well any more. Now every street almost has a cheap Pakistani shop where you can buy sunglasses and t-shirts, the very things that we used to sell in the bars. The cheap prices have arrived everywhere, also in the markets every week you can find them. (Malick, in Antwerp since 1989, regularised, industrial cleaning)

Alternatives and further trajectories
As mentioned before, the majority of hawkers remained in their business until the moment they obtained legal residence status; two of them started a larger business filling containers. However, a small number of respondents managed to find alternatives outside hawking. Two musicians came from Senegal to France and the Netherlands respectively with temporary permits linked to their profession, and because of prospects for next concerts or unexpected travelling to third countries, became undocumented; they just continued their music activities. A married undocumented woman worked informally as a hairdresser, while one of the rare women who came to Europe on her own initiative to earn money, found a job as a waitress, showing how the African neighbourhood in Antwerp creates networks of employment:

> One day there was a festival in De Coninckplein, and I assisted, I was sitting in a Gambian bar. The woman had seen me a couple of times before, and I saw her very busy, lots of clients. As I used to be a waitress before in Gambia, I asked her if I could help her out that day... and I did, I worked there the whole day. Later in the evening, she asked if I needed a job, and I worked in this bar from the next day for a couple of months. (Ndeye, in Antwerp since 1996, regularised, unemployed)

Some people really hate the hawking and try to escape; two of them managed to do so with links to the wider Belgian community, finding work in construction and renovation:

> I had no papers, so I started selling as well, but I always tried to talk a lot to the people in the bars, so I got to know many people and they would buy me drinks and discuss. Like this I got to know a man who took me for a job in construction; well actually,

in demolition, of a very old building. I was very happy because I hate the bag and the selling, I prefer every kind of job to selling, I prefer a job. And for that I was very motivated and working very hard; so the man liked me. Afterwards a friend of his took me and I was working in construction with him for eight months. (Youssou, in Antwerp since 2000, undocumented, working in horticulture)

Two other respondents have taken up work in horticulture, mostly picking tomatoes and chicory. When looking closer into their employment situation, a strange contradiction arises: they need papers in order to work informally. Employers fear the labour inspection, and prefer a legal worker to an undocumented one, even for informal work, as the fines are lower. The undocumented migrant borrows papers from someone else, is hired officially for a couple of hours a day, but then works many more hours at informal conditions and without contract.

Personal problems occur frequently: conflicts with a boss or colleagues, misunderstandings, gossip, jealousy; it is difficult to make the difference between an interpersonal conflict and a racist attitude. However, the process that is described in the case of undocumented workers quite often goes as follows:

You know, when you have no papers, you feel you have to take every chance and not spoil it, so you work very hard, harder than everybody else, and you are more flexible, you want to work all the hours that are possible. So sometimes, the boss needs somebody in the evening or in the weekend, or one week not everybody needs to come as there is not enough work to do. He will choose you because you work very hard. This will create jealousy in the people who were there before you and are not picked. If they know you have a different name in reality, or you have told them before about the false paper, they will tell the boss and you will have to go (Musa, in Antwerp since 2004, undocumented, import-export)

Another observation is that undocumented migrants can only very rarely mobilise their human capital or professional experience, and they do not have higher salaries than those without qualifications (Adam et al. 2001). A migrant with an English graduate degree has no better chances and is picking tomatoes all the same, as his borrowed paper does not show his real qualifications. Undocumented migrants have to accept socio-professional downgrading.

In Barcelona

After the first days with friends or family, a different pattern tends to develop in Barcelona:

> My first job was in the first week, after three days, it was the boss of one of my cousins, and he said he needed someone for one week. It was in a flower field, the ones we call chrysanthemum. I was disillusioned very quickly, because it was painful, and it was so different. In Senegal, we talk and we don't control ourselves during work, but even my cousin, when I want to talk to him, he told me not to talk during work, when the boss can see us, so me too I shut up. So, we work, I don't know at what time we will stop; when we take a break to eat, I thought we would stop, they tell me 'you, where are you going with your bag, we are only taking breakfast'. We ate, and we spent the whole day there; from 8 to 10 am, then till 1 pm, then we have lunch and everyone is talking. At the end, we went home at 7 pm. For me it was very cold, the month of April, and I was wearing my coat. I told everyone I was very cold. The boss also knew that I just arrived: when he speaks to me, I just look because I don't understand what he's saying, he just asked my name. That is how I spent the first week working. [...] He paid me in pesetas, many notes in red and green; the others when they received their envelopes they were smiling, but me I don't know how much I earned, I don't know, I asked another one, how much is it, he told me this one, the 1,000 pesetas note, is 3,500 CFA in Senegal. I counted how many notes of 1,000 I have... it was a lot, a lot. For this first week they paid me 27,000 pesetas. I was very happy as well. Afterwards my cousin told me to go to the market to buy a chicken, but I told him I will not eat, I want to keep the money (Thierno, in Barcelona since 1999, regularised, construction).

This quote sheds early light on some dimensions of employment as an undocumented worker in Barcelona: the generally poor knowledge upon arrival, the difficulty of adapting to the work rhythm and ethic, the difficulties in different language and climate, but it also shows how rewarding the first payment was (approaching a month's salary for educated people in Senegal). More importantly, it brings up two points that need further elaboration: job-hunting strategies are located within the migrant community; and agriculture is the main sector for first entry to the labour market. Subsequently, I will explore how careers develop after this first occupational experience.

Job searching strategies

In the informal sector, there are by definition no mainstream institutions involved in job hunting, although the process can be rather well organised, as will be shown below. A very common start for respondents in Barcelona is to ask friends and relatives whether their bosses need extra workers; indeed, the employers often take the initiative by asking workers they trust to bring friends for jobs. A variation of this can be found in construction, where subcontractors tend to call at migrants' houses to find workers. All undocumented immigrants in the sample combine this 'searching through friends' with the 'asking' strategy: this implies going round workplaces checking if vacancies are available. In the municipalities around Barcelona, this is a tradition mainly in agriculture; people walk around in the fields and around glass houses to ask employers for a job; 'walking' can be used also in industry, but is not as popular or efficient. This shows a general knowledge of job locations and eagerness to work, particularly as many Africans have just arrived and have limited knowledge of Spanish (Mendoza, 1998).

> When I arrive, I go to look for work, on my own; my cousin did not help me. Of course, I don't speak Spanish, but my brother tells me, if you know 'hello', you will learn something every day, with strength, with the necessity and with the hardship, and after one week I knew enough to find a job. I saw a man in a field, I day, "hello sir, I look for work if you have it"; some say yes, some say no, like this. (Amadou, in Barcelona since 1983, regular status, plastic industry)

In major agricultural regions, such as the south of Spain, a day-labour system exists for seasonal work; Brussels has some similar sites as well. Men and women, mostly of migrant origin, look for employment in open-air markets by the side of the road, at busy intersections, in front of home improvement stores and in other public spaces (for an extensive overview in the US, see Valenzuela et al. 2006).

These are illustrations of collective networks, in which the community as a whole channels and is channelled into a specific sector of the informal economy; in contrast, some people have a more individual network without much community backing, but often based on particular skills (Geets et al. 2006). The next respondent is an illustration of this difference. He was a carpenter in Senegal, acquired skills in construction in Portugal, and built an informal employment network:

> So when I come here, the things go a little bit well, I have no papers but I am working with so many bosses. Sometimes in a

workshop, because I have many skills, sometimes also in construction, welder... this kind of things. Also assembly, where my brother is working, so as I can understand this kind of work, I am doing it for him: also I work here in cleaning; here in Spain, to clean the train lines. Sometimes someone sends me to Barcelona to work, constructing grids in gardens, tennis fields; swimming pools, you know. But always for limited time, and without contracts, always by people who know me, but without contracts. (Bara, in Barcelona since 2002, undocumented, construction)

The agricultural sector as an entry into the labour market
From early on, there has been a substantial presence of the hawking tradition in Spain amongst Senegalese migrants (Sow 2004; Torres Perez 2004; Vargas Llovera 1997), as in any other country, and six of them were interviewed.

But a more significant number of respondents (thirteen) started their informal career in Spanish agriculture, a sector mentioned in the economic analysis of Spain before. The importance of this sector for black immigrants is confirmed by key informants in the employment sector and in other publications (Bell 2003; Hoggart & Mendoza 1999; Kaplan 1998; Mendoza 1997; Pérez 1995). Some of them work in rather small family-based enterprises, other in ultra-modern highly computerised glasshouses, but the jobs are generally unskilled in nature. Possible previous experience in farming in Africa is not useful as the techniques and crops are very dissimilar. Specific skills used by African workers (like pruning, driving machines, etc.) have mainly been learned after leaving their home country. Key informants agree that agriculture has some of the worst labour conditions in the informal sector, because it operates in a sector under global competition. Agricultural workers need to be available (often staying at the farm, or get to work early in the morning), flexible (ready for overtime, long days of up to eleven hours and weekends in peak times, but sometimes there is no work at all), and hard-working (physically hard conditions, in different weather conditions, often in stooped positions, often carrying heavy loads). Salaries are low: common incomes in agriculture approximate three euro per hour; employment is never long-term or secure, as an early autumn storm or late frost can lead to massive unemployment; many positions are part-time, short-term, seasonal, or even casual. In conclusion, Martínez Veiga (1999) argues that the Spanish agricultural sector is almost entirely secondary in nature if we exclude proprietors and their family: almost all work is temporary, with clear wage discrimination and housing discrimination. Mendoza (1997) concludes that the competitive advantage of African workers in agriculture lies in physical endurance and job flexibility.

A very particular example of temporary farmer work flexibility is shown by people following the pattern of subsequent agricultural campaigns of olives, asparagus, potatoes, strawberries and fruit picking over different regions across Spain (Martínez Veiga 1999). Each peak period of employment in specific crops attracts workers from all over the area and even abroad. This system is informal and badly organised, resulting in conflicts when more workers show up than work is available (Santana 2000).

Over time, the time people spend searching prior to encountering their first job in agriculture has changed, probably due to increasing competition and control. Migrant cohorts entering the labour market in the 1980s until the end of the 1990s mention found a job in a matter of days or weeks, and were often guaranteed an income over a longer period of time: employment lasted for over a year up to ten years. For the cohorts entering after 2000, the situation has become a lot more difficult: new laws impose heavy fines on employers hiring clandestine workers and even many family enterprises are scared off. Respondents mention more casual work than before, or indicate that they need to work with someone else's papers.

> For a long time I did not work. Oh yes, very short jobs, maybe two or three days, or one week, and then finished. Then I stay one or two weeks without anything, no work. It is always in the fields, never in factories, but gardens, flowers. I look and search, but I cannot work. You know, I look for money, it is my goal. But nowadays it is very difficult. So difficult. There is no work, many people, a lot of harassments. Maybe tomorrow there are possibilities, but now I cannot find them. Every day I leave for searching, but they always ask papers, if you reply 'no', it is finished. If you have no papers, it is difficult. You have to work to get papers, but the work is easier to find with papers. If you have papers you can start tomorrow. (Sadani, in Barcelona since 2003, undocumented, casual work)

Alternatives and further strategies

Several respondents found informal entry to the labour market through other sectors: mainly in construction sites (six) and textile workshops (three). But, what is more important, several of those who started in agriculture changed sectors and started working in small industries, in slaughterhouses, and hotels later on in their undocumented career (relatively similar results in Alicante (see Vargas Llovera 1997)). Some can stay several months; others combine odd jobs, like distributing publicity, parking cars or being night guards in construction sites or on a private holiday compound. A divorced mother of three who left her children in Senegal while preparing a better life for them started cleaning informally in a hotel. Oli is doing an unpaid 'internship' in a textile workshop, hoping the employer will hire her later. In addition, one respondent was hired to work in a Gambian phone centre, where his university degree with some computer experience proved to be useful. Undocumented migrants cannot access self-employment, but they often do provide the cheap labour necessary in this ethnic niche.

Commuting times are often long, two hours is not exceptional, because construction sites change regularly, and because people change jobs so often that they cannot move houses every time. Most work in small enterprises, without contracts and cash payment, and as they do not generally specialise in one type of job, but go from one sector to another, they are not able to climb the socio-economic ladder (Engbersen & Van der Leun 2001). As in agriculture, those who entered these sectors after 2000 often mention working with someone else's papers, as employers are not prepared to take the risk of control. In order to avoid checks from work inspection, several respondents mention adapting their search strategies and going three or four stops away from the centre of towns, working even more at night or during weekends. Smaller companies as well as the domestic sector are also less likely to be regularly checked by state officials.

It can safely be argued that undocumented migrants are chosen because they are cheap, flexible, and more willing to accept hardship; in other words, their precarious situation is their competitive advantage (Solé et al. 1998). Apart from a few good employers, respondents mention considerable exploitation (Pajares 2005), ranging from impossible working times, no protection in dangerous situations (e.g. in construction, or chemicals in agriculture), to withholding salary. Pay may range between 600 and 750 euro per month in general, for more than full-time hard work. The fact that people do not complain about the exploitation they suffer[4] does not mean that they are not aware of being exploited, but they know that in their circumstances they have no choice. The inequality between undocumented worker and the employer is accepted; both have their place and know it, because the spirit of survival (and the need for a breadwinning) underpins all other considerations. Many respondents face long periods of unemployment, mostly due to the unstable nature of employment in the black labour market.

The recent evolution towards tighter controls implies a cohort effect and has forced people to shift towards hawking, in particular selling copied CDs and DVDs. In recent times, people who did not consider this kind of work feel they are forced into this business:

> To find a job, right after I arrived, I went to the fields, I see that wherever I go, they ask me for papers, but I did not have them. For the laws of Spain, if you don't have papers, you cannot work, and I stayed like this for a long time. When I saw that there is no solution, my friend told me the only thing left to do at this time for people who have no papers is to go out in the streets and bars and sell cds and dvds. It was not at all what I wanted to do, I don't want to be in business, I wanted to work as I did before. But I started selling cds and dvds, and till now that is what I do. I was very disappointed: the stories of Senegalese migrants coming back home are wonderful, and they bring home a lot of money, but nobody tells you how exactly they have earned the money. (Habib, in Barcelona since 2003, undocumented, hawking)

Out of six hawkers, four mentioned that they took this up out of desperation, and all of them arrived in the last three years. In the Spanish context, the control issue is less pronounced than in Belgium, because selling in streets and beaches is not prohibited; however, selling counterfeit objects is. In the centre of Barcelona, a campaign of increased control has been launched to chase the hawkers from the main squares; this has inspired some hawkers to move to the suburbs or neighbouring towns.

In general, the sketch above has shown that for the position of undocumented Africans on the Barcelona labour market it seems to be of little relevance what their experience is in the country of origin. Educational or professional records do not seem to play a role, except for some opportunity windows for technical skills immediately useable in Spanish environments. Some examples include Salif who trained as a welder and worked illegally in France, Italy and Spain; or Segui who learned about construction, painting and decoration in Libya and worked in construction in Spain. Assane wanted to pursue a profession and through his Spanish teacher started training to be an electrician. It was a significant sacrifice, as he needed to pay for the course, study and work at the same time. However, his actual job in a textile workshop is more inspired by the wish for papers than by his knowledge. Some respondents take language classes, as many schools do not check residence permits; however, most postpone investing in education until a later stage.

5.2 The functioning of the informal labour market

Despite the lack of permit to stay and thus to work, and the absence of legal employment, we have seen that living on the margins does not present an absolute obstacle to some form of economic integration. The industrialised countries include an important informal economy relying on undocumented migrants for low-skilled, unattractive and underpaid work. Some respondents have left jobs where they considered the working conditions as unacceptable; hawkers can definitely make more money after building some networks and experience; and people who find longer-term employment can manage to reach a level of stability. This makes some authors suggest the existence of forms of social promotion even without papers, in the US (Borjas & Freeman 1992), but also in Belgium (Soenen 2003): by gaining specific human capital, like fluency in the language or creating larger networks, undocumented migrants can increase their incomes over time. In this research, I see more evidence for the statement of Van der Leun and Kloosterman (1999) in seeing no promotion at all, only short jobs with a low income, both for people of low education and high education. Despite people moving between jobs all the time, calling this a 'career' is impossible at this stage.

What is more, the employment status is sometimes difficult to determine, given that it may change from day to day, or that the income generated is not always linked to the hours of work done. A hawker, for example, may be working full-time (or more), but making only fifteen euro a day; work in agriculture can be casual, temporary, part-time or, often, all such classifications at once. Odd jobs may include everything from helping a couple of hours for unloading a truck, to keeping a friend's shop open when he is travelling. Engbersen (1996: 64) found that 'even when using a broad definition of work, including odd jobs, casual employment and prostitution, I found that about one third of the research group was without work at the time of interviewing'. This number is clearly less pronounced in our sample, but respondents do find themselves regularly in and out of employment and frequently face periods of unemployment in between jobs. The busy employment pattern of other undocumented respondents also suggests that unemployment is simply not an option for illegal migrants (Perez 1995). This stresses the typical characteristics of a reserve or buffer labour force.

Comparing the trajectories in Barcelona and Antwerp, we have seen first a significant difference in the relatively uniform choice for hawking in the case of Belgium, and the wider variety of patterns in Spain where people generally start working in agriculture, but can also be found in other sectors (see Table 5.1). The reasons for this difference will be explored below, be it in a tentative way, taking a closer look at the political and economic configuration influencing the informal labour market. Numbers show that both Belgium and Spain score high on the share of informal work in the total economic production, up to 20 per cent (European Foundation for the Improvement of Living and Working Conditions 2005); for the reasons behind the different employment patterns we will have to dig deeper. One suggestion is raised by Van der Leun and Kloosterman, who mention that the crucial variable in determining the distinctness of undocumented workers is, next to the employment laws, their enforcement regime (Van der Leun & Kloosterman 2006). The particular experience or specialisation of Senegambian migrants on the labour market will also be put in the wider context of migrant employment in both countries, showing differences or similarities in sectors, status, or jobs.

Table 5.1 *Overview of jobs in Antwerp and Barcelona for undocumented migrants in the sample*

	Antwerp			Barcelona		
	First	Later	Now	First	Later	Now
Hawking	19	-	7	6	2	5
Agriculture	-	3	-	13	6	4
Construction	-	1	-	9	9	0
Industries	1	-	-	2	6	3
Services	4	1	1	3	8	2
Unemployed	3	-	2	-	-	2
Total number of undocumented migrants	27	-	10	32	-	16

Sectors

For Spain, one notes the above-mentioned dominance of agriculture as the entry job into the labour market, closely followed, however, by construction and hawking. What is more, a considerable number of people change sectors after their first employment (sometimes several times, explaining why the numbers do not add), with strong presence as unspecialised workers in industries (frequently textiles) and services (Mendoza 1997). These are to a large extent the sectors mentioned in other research in Europe (European Foundation for the Improvement of Living and Working Conditions 2005), heavily subjected to the strategies and practices of post-Fordist flexibilisation described in the theoretical chapter. However, as the numbers show, they are present to different degrees and articulated in significantly different ways in Antwerp and Barcelona, depending on the modes of labour market regulation, and forms of industrial relations.

Santana (2000) sketches the developments in agricultural industries that opened a niche for immigrant employment. Since modernisation took off in the 1960s, Spain has seen traditional agriculture give way to technological innovation in (mainly) small and medium family enterprises. The mechanisation of many areas of the production process led to a decline of the proportion of the population working in agriculture from 22 to 8 per cent between 1976 and 1998, a concentration of companies and more intensive use of smaller areas of land. For the most recent decade, Bell (2004: 43) stresses the 'context of highly intensified, industrial and ferociously competitive form of agriculture, often dominated by supermarket chains, with no attention to the social and environmental conditions in which the production takes place'. In this context, a manual workforce is almost all that is needed for fruit- and vegetable production, and particularly in periods of pruning and harvesting. These activities are affected by climatic uncertainties, come in seasonal peaks, do not guarantee stable (year-long) employment and are characterised as low-skilled, hard work that demands high mobility of workers. Local workers do not accept these conditions any longer because they can 'escape' to other sectors in the growing economy; because the internal Spanish inequalities have softened (previous Spanish workers came from Southern regions), and because they can rely on forms of social welfare support. In intensive family-based agriculture enterprises, the labour demand problem tends to be solved with the temporary employment of foreign workers: between 1990 and 1998 the increase in foreign workers was 1.882 per cent; many temporary schemes have been launched, and many undocumented workers find jobs in this sector. Martínez Veiga concludes that the agricultural sector, with the exception of proprietors and their family, constitutes almost entirely a secondary labour market (Martínez Veiga 1999).

In construction, large companies have over the last twenty years reduced their own workforce and hired subcontractors for the simpler jobs (Honsberg 2004). In addition to the characteristic atomisation of the process and large cyclical economic variations, it creates possibilities for a huge secondary labour market with temporary contracts, low wages, job insecurity, health and safety problems, and on the job training. The fact that undocumented workers have no state support and less negotiation power pushes them more than natives into this sector; private consumers are also ready to employ undocumented workers for renovation. For Spain, Schierup's chapter studying the building industry illustrates this very well (2006: 238); and again, Martínez Veiga concludes that a large share of construction industries is secondary in nature (1999).

The character of industries in Spain and Catalonia also changed during the 1980s: an accelerated and thorough process of industrialisation took place in a context of increasing international competition; this forced plants and companies to close down or to reduce costs. Still, a considerable number of small and medium enterprises, often family based, are fighting for survival. Flexibility and precariousness increased in the absence of a strong welfare state, with the emergence of a shadow economy that was easier for immigrants to enter. This tends to take the shape of 'invisible factories', often found in Catalonia (Magone 2004). The significant share of migrant workers without a residence permit and bad conditions has been documented, for example, in catering and the confectionary industry in the Netherlands (Van Naerssen 2002). Often undocumented work is part of a larger informal share of employment in these sectors, much done by residents or legal foreign workers.

In both the remaining manufacturing and in the new service industries in Spain, there is an ongoing demand for flexible labour and a continuing stream of employment opportunities, which do not require high educational levels, pay low wages and offer little regulation. Sectors that grow in general in the formal labour market, but in an atmosphere of marginalisation of workers, contribute to, if not push, an increased participation of immigrants in informal economic activities (Kloosterman 1996). Immigrants, probably more than other groups, have seized these new opportunities and participate significantly in informal economic activities.

These sectors also exist in Belgium, and very similar processes of casualisation and subcontracting have occurred over the last decades, yet we did not see any Senegambian presence. That does not mean there would be no informal jobs in these economic sectors in Belgium. On the contrary, construction, agriculture and horticulture (particularly glasshouses and the seasonal peaks in fruit picking) and catering reportedly rely heavily on informal and/or undocumented labour. However, Senegambian migrants do not seem to have access to these jobs; the reasons for which will be explored below.

The reasons for differences between Barcelona and Antwerp

A first reason could be the size of the Senegambian community, which is far bigger in Barcelona than in Antwerp. It is generally noted that informal migrant social networks, once established, tend to push newcomers along already mapped trajectories in the labour market, leading to concentration in specific places or enterprises. In these reduced niches, they do low-paid work (Geets et al. 2006; Mendoza 1997; Van der Leun & Kloosterman 2006). In that sense, a larger community may provide more variety of information, with more options to follow. However, the use of social networks may also be a consequence of, rather than a reason for, the segmented nature of labour markets, combined with the particular opportunity structures that arise from peculiarities of national economic circumstances. Observation and statistics reveal an ethnic specialisation, with many Polish women working as cleaners, while Philippines and Ecuadorians work more as internal domestic workers; horticulture attracts male Polish workers, but also Romanians and Moroccans, while construction is the domain of Eastern Europeans (Verbeken 2005: 12). In Spain, Polish are in the sector of renovation, and Moroccans in regular construction sites (Colectivo IOE 1998). This ethnic specialisation explanation holds for the hawking specialisation of Senegambian migrants; but it does not help us to understand the wider variety of job options in Spain.

A second reason might lie in the different size of informal labour markets in both cities. The theories mentioned earlier were not able to give us a decisive answer. For Belgium, it was suggested that higher tax and social security burdens, together with strict labour regulations, might render informal employment more attractive than in the more flexible labour market of Spain. On the other side, the argument goes that the tradition of a dual labour market with a large informal economy provides an ideal setting for the post-Fordist informality. Surprisingly, the informal labour market in both countries is large and about the same size. According to a study by Schneider, Spain and Belgium are at the top of GDP generated by informal economies (along with Greece, Italy and Portugal), with percentages of 21 and 22, when the European average is 16 (2006).[5]

The different rationales behind these comparable figures might be an explanation for the behaviour of undocumented Senegambian migrants. The possibilities in the informal economy may link with the economic structure and development. In the high-skilled and highly regulated formal Belgian labour market, with little economic growth, the logic is one of an inflexible labour market, where undeclared work is relied upon to cut labour costs by tax evasion. Some highly competitive sectors may feel they need to adjust the level of effective workers to the cycle of production, as well as to limit drastically the fixed costs of production by avoiding social contributions. Given the sectoral composition and the degree of specialisation, a large part of informal labour may actually be performed by skilled local or legally foreign workers, and only a smaller share may be left for unskilled work. A recent OECD report based on 5,422 prosecutions for irregular work shows that in all sectors where foreigners do irregular work (agriculture, construction and catering), the share of nationals is far higher, and foreign irregular work constitutes only 23 per cent of the total sum; the part of undocumented migrants must be considerably lower (OECD 2005:137).

The booming Spanish labour market represents a truly dual system, where a relatively regulated labour market and welfare regime protects part of the citizens, while a large traditional informal sector has recently started to harbour (and exploit) mostly immigrants in the quest to enhance post-Fordist flexibility (Schierup, Hansen & Castles 2006). The main economic sectors, like agriculture, construction and tourism, and their structure (the predominance of small companies) lend themselves more to these developments. In these lower segments of the deregulated labour market, productivity is relatively low, and may provide much better opportunities for undocumented migrants, which function more as a reserve labour army. A careful hypothesis could be that informal work is done mostly by locals in Belgium, and by undocumented workers in Spain. Therefore, a wider range of options might be available to undocumented immigrants in Barcelona than in Antwerp.

A third element is variations in implementation and enforcement of the law. In a recent report about undeclared work in Europe, the European Foundation for the Improvement of Living and Working Conditions concludes that the frequency and extent of controls of the implementation of tax, labour and social security provisions are inadequate in most European countries. The lack of determination in the fight against undeclared work may be linked to the positive effects that employers benefit from, but also to the indirect advantages for (middle-class) individuals that make governments and labour unions reluctant to fight it (European Foundation for the Improvement of Living and Working Conditions 2005). To change this, the European Commission is currently considering a new directive that might result in employers of undocumented migrants facing jail in the near future. For the moment, differences remain in the priorities given to measures to reduce undeclared employment in different member states. Research by Le Voy et al. (2004) suggests that the governmental priority in combating undocumented labour is higher in Belgium than in Spain where it ranges from medium on the national level, to low on the local level.

Belgium has over the last decade made consistent efforts to fight undeclared work (European Foundation for the Improvement of Living and Working Conditions 2005), firstly by getting a grip on the domestic service through a system of 'service cheques', which provide a relatively cheap official alternative for childcare, ironing or cleaning.[6] In addition, the chances to identify undeclared work administratively have been increased through a system whereby all new employment must be declared immediately to the authorities, and through administrative checks of the files of tax authorities and other governmental bodies. Another strategy is inspections by specialised teams, often in alleged high-risk sectors, coordinated by a permanent unit, with legislative measures to prosecute cases of social/employment fraud. Employers risk fines when they employ undocumented immigrants, while the latter will be deported when caught. The head of inspection services complains that 800 people controling all the sectors in Belgium are not enough for a large-scale systematic offensive, and the probabilities of being caught are relatively low. The strategy is therefore one of well chosen actions to make employers think about the risks (Verbeken 2005).

In Spain, the government embraced a relatively lax attitude in controlling and imposing sanctions on those employers who hired undocumented immigrants. 'Politicians are not keen on intervening in the informal economy which is often of crucial importance in some parts of the country and specific areas of activity, as the business involved are often struggling to survive in an increasingly internationally competitive environment, or the targeted families have hired people to fill gaps left by the welfare state (care for children and elderly)' (Moreno Fuentes 2000: 18). In the dual economy sketched above, undeclared work is almost an accepted and approved social practice, a structural feature of the national, regional or sectoral economy and employment (OECD 2003). Labour inspections are relatively rare; the government relies most on inadequate tax authorities. There is also a long tradition, consolidated by the Franco regime, whereby the state carries out only a moderate supervision of private activities. When illegally employed workers are discovered in companies, it is difficult to prove how long they have been working and the penalties are therefore small (European Foundation for the Improvement of Living and Working Conditions 2005). Even the OECD suggests that strengthening labour inspections (if necessary), would be a cost-effective complement to border controls (OECD 2003: 18).

The fact that the informal economy is more controlled in Belgium than in Spain, may increase the importance of the ethnic recruitment strategies mentioned above. Two elements may play a role: for the employer, ethnic recruitment is cheaper, and it may serve to guarantee a selection of committed workers, minimising the risk of complaints to unions or inspections. For the ethnic community, it may increase the groups' chances to protect their section of the competitive informal labour market. In this way, Senegambian migrants in Belgium may find it more difficult to access informal work in construction or agriculture, given that the dominant ethnicities in these sectors protect their 'territory' by recruiting inside the community. In Spain, with a more booming economy and less control, there may be more open recruitment networks. This is a highly speculative hypothesis, not backed up in any of the literature available, and needs further investigation.

5.3 Reciprocity strategies

The analysis of labour market trajectories above raises many questions: how can recent migrants survive with the minimal incomes they receive? How do they overcome the frequent periods of unemployment? How can they still send money back in these circumstances? In order to find answers to these questions and to understand the labour market behaviour better, we need to include other crucial dimensions of the migrant experience: housing, solidarity mechanisms within the community, relationships with the host society.

Given the precarious nature of many employment situations, and given the limited income levels in the labour market, people may have to develop strategies in other spheres of integration from time to time. They need ways in order to smooth consumption and to protect themselves against loss of income or unexpected expenditures. Extra income could in theory be provided by redistribution mechanisms, but this option is almost excluded in the case of undocumented migrants; only asylum seekers can receive financial and material support during the time of their application, and very few respondents are in that situation. In Belgium, two men in different stages of the asylum received material support (housing, food) in the first stage of the application, and a subsistence income in the second phase. The third possible source of income and support is reciprocity, which will be explored in terms of the dimensions of accommodation, food, and organisation of life in general.

Housing

Most immigrants travelling had a point of reference in Belgium or Spain: a close family member, a distant relative, a childhood friend, an acquaintance, the brother of a former neighbour, someone from the same village of origin, or just a vague phone number. The first accommodation upon arrival is then obvious, based on the relationship or general solidarity: they stay for free in a spare room, a spare bed, or on the sofa, for some days, weeks, or months. However, the new migrant is bound to feel a burden or a parasite, and many express their embarrassment about this dependency. Most try to find a job as quickly as possible and start to contribute to food, rent and expenses, becoming an equal participant; others move out because of personal conflicts or long commuting distances. Normally three to eight people put money together to buy food, and they take turns in cooking and cleaning; this turns the evening meals into social gatherings, with friends and other people visiting (Stoller 2002). In the continuous flow of new arrivals, some addresses develop as more hospitable or reliable, and become real residences of passage, as the old hotel in Breixia, Italia, that is known as Little Senegal. Here, even the unconnected migrants can find a place to stay. A respondent explained how it worked (on a smaller scale) for houses in Antwerp; there were several in the same area functioning in the same way. The quote also illustrates how in this stage, the shared house is the basis of the network providing food, support and friendship.

> After staying with my brother and my cousin, it was a group house, a landing place, for people who just arrive and leave after; if you count, maybe you will see that more than 100 people passed there. It was a very popular house, everyone knew it, but the police never entered. We never had problems. Even now all of us we like to return and meet for meals, every Wednesday (Aliu, in Antwerp since 2001, regular status, unemployed).

Sometimes religious confederations can provide housing as well, the Murid brotherhood manages a system of houses throughout Europe.

Within this system of sharing apartments and co-residing, people move around a lot; visiting my original contact eight times over four years, I never found him in the same apartment.[7] This makes Adam (2001) say undocumented migrants live 'like nomads', ready to move quickly at every moment, which proves to be very stressful. Chavez proposes that by creatively forming and reforming coresident groups, undocumented migrants strategically and effectively use social organisation as a way of coping with changing conditions (Benson 1990; Chavez 1990). The reasons vary from changes of jobs and arrival of new friends and relatives, fear for police to problems with landlords, orders to leave the country but most often the community life itself is pointed at: gossip, problems over money, conflicts between housemates, the 'owner' forcing others to share rooms with more people.

> It is very difficult to live together with people, that is the problem; me I moved seven times... not for work, just for living together. When you are many in a house, the problems become, and then I go, because I am not a problematic person. If you are not the owner, you cannot do anything, so you go. Everybody has his way, you know, to cook, to organise, to clean, and people don't understand each other. People leave early for work, others just arrive, and there is noise in the house. And at the end of the month, when the bills arrive, the problems start. (Babacar, in Barcelona since 2000, regular status, transport)

Finding new accommodation is not easy for an undocumented migrant: regular signed contracts with proper names and bank accounts are out of the question. They have to mobilise networks to find a landlord who is ready to rent within these conditions; this often involves vacancies announced within a group of acquaintances. However, recruitment through networks does not necessarily mean noble intentions; in many cases, the quality of apartments is very bad, and conditions are often poor. The Spanish Secretary for Migration recently published a report on housing in Spain. According to this report, 47 per cent of the migrant population gain access to housing through sub-leasing and 19 per cent live in less than ten square meters. In addition, more than 12,000 use the so-called system of *camas calientes*, a practice which consists of the use and payment of a bed only for a limited number of hours (www.migrar.be).

The combination of characteristics that undocumented migrants look for in accommodation easily lead to a concentration in specific neighbourhoods[8]. The presence of more settled migrant communities who can support the undocumented ones, next to relatively cheap private renting or sub-renting housing possibilities, often takes them to low quality housing in deprived areas (Engbersen et al. 1999) and transition zones (Martínez Veiga 1997). In cases of danger of exploitation, undocumented migrants are vulnerable because of their judicial inferiority and incapacity to negotiate. But if a house is declared unfit for human habitation by the authorities (as some NGOs in Antwerp strive for) the inhabitants have no choice but to look for another slum dwelling as the few transit dwellings from the municipality are not meant to be for undocumented people (Frederix 2005).

In sum, housing is one of the most elementary needs for immigrants upon arrival and throughout their stay and reciprocity within the Senegambian community is definitely the main sphere of integration. Shared housing forms the link between spatial organisation and social structure (Martínez Veiga 1997). This corresponds with Chavez' statement that coresidential strategies are the undocumented immigrants' first level of defence against the economic and political constraints on their lives (1990). Burgers and Engbersen (1999) expect a weak housing position for migrants who do not belong to large settled, socially integrated communities (as the Moroccans in the Netherlands), as they have no choice but to rely on the market; however, in this Senegambian sample the solidarity seems to stretch quite far in most cases. This allows migrants to cope with limited incomes, to minimise disruption and to alleviate personal loneliness and social isolation.

Restricting activities

Life in the community is also a way to save money, to avoid spending. In an early phase, migrants limit their own life because all investments are made back home: many people share a room, no internet, never go for a coffee, no car, no trips, cutting costs on food, just go to work as much as they can and sleep.

> When everyone comes home between 8 and 9pm they are tired after a long day of work, someone needs to cook for the evening and for all of them to take something for lunch the next day; they need to wash and iron, call home and send money. Work, lack of work, extra hours of work, red eyes from the paint X uses, night work, and being tired are the most important topics of conversation and determine the exhausted atmosphere in house. (fieldnotes Barcelona)

Investing in education or training are mostly out of the question; partly because it rarely forms part of the migration project in the early stage of illegality; partly because of financial and administrative difficulties.[9] The odd person paying membership fees for an athletics club or buying a book is laughed at for being distracted from the main aim: earning money and going back. A labour union social worker tells us: 'it is impossible for people to think about learning the language or take trainings, it does not make sense: what they are interested in is work and papers, papers, papers'.

In this phase of the migration project, or even when planning to migrate, many people delay marriage or the formation of a family due to the precarious and temporal employment:

> I am not married yet, not here not there not anywhere. I am scared to marry, because of those reasons. I don't think about marriage because I think about other things. Marrying today would mean more responsibilities, and raise more issues... (Bubacar, in Barcelona since 2002, undocumented, agriculture)

People who were married before leaving and left a wife and/or children behind in Senegal have to put the family life on a hold. In more harmonious couples and families, the fact of being separated for years in a row is hard to bear and leads to fundamental loneliness. But in other cases, the migrant may have to solve the problems arising from this situation of long-distance relationship. The women tend to live under supervision of their family in law, taking care of the house, the children and possibly the elderly. Social control can be tight, particularly in the case of young women; divorce becomes more common as couples grow apart over time and distance, or as the fatherhood of children is debated (Barou 2001). Conflicts between wives and families often arise over the distribution of remittances of the migrant, who may have a difficult time trying to solve family arguments at long distance. At the same time they often feel they are not meeting the family expectations, because it is difficult to explain them the reasons, and the hard economic circumstances add to the insecurity and lack of safety.

Survival in group

The support of a large network is of crucial importance in facing many of the standard challenges at every stage of the migration process: from taking a shower and get help on the first day of arriving, to find emergency housing, to borrow their papers, and to share worries. Theoretically speaking, a wide network with a diversity of resources would be ideal; however, their network tends to be very homogeneous and very Senegambian. Both in the field of housing and work, social support is not of a kind to allow significant steps forward; it rather helps to overcome yet another problem.

It would be wrong, however, to interpret these networks only in the light of unconditional African solidarity. Sometimes there are clearly limits to the solidarity, particularly when it comes to substantial or long-term financial or social help. This is linked to the nature of the relationships: what brings them together is often need rather than shared interests or backgrounds. In addition, relationships suffer under the insecure nature of their labour market conditions, as Aliu explains:

> I know a lot of people, but nothing lasts. You meet because of circumstances, often you don't share similar background, one just needs a place to live, and after some months this leads to tensions and conflicts. Even with people that do become real friends, if you come back in one year, one has found a job somewhere else and has moved there, another went to Italy or Germany to find better luck... you loose contact and you forget each other.
> (Aliu, 30, in Barcelona since 2001, legal and in agriculture)

In many cases, financial support among respondents is confined to small and incidental help. Sometimes help is even refused indirectly, as in cases where the contact number from close friends or relatives seems to have been strategically changed.

> I had one Senegalese friend in Brussels, I started calling him and leaving him messages, but he never picked it up or replied,

and after one week the number was not valid any more. I was left without knowing anyone here. (Ousman, in Antwerp since 2004, undocumented, unemployed)

The increasing size of the community in Barcelona opens the possibility for a turn towards in-group competition instead of ethnic help, as in the case of Polish migrants in Brussels (2005). I did not find indication of this, but the flipside of community life entails also distrust, disloyalty and deceit. When Ousman arrives, his host tells him another friend would introduce him to selling cds and DVDs. What follows:

But this guy saw me as a competitor, he was not there to help me at all, he just left me in a dangerous point while he was further down the street. I displayed my stuff on a piece of cloth and tried to sell. I did not even know what a police officer looked like. When the first one came close to me, I offered him a dvd. They took my entire luggage and told me not to start again at any price. (Ousman, in Antwerp since 2004, undocumented, unemployed)

Engbersen (1999) distinguishes between three patterns of incorporation at the ethnic community level: 'communal sharing', 'bounded solidarity' and 'market patterns'. The first pattern of incorporation refers to substantial help given to an exclusive group of close relatives, covering a wide range of fields and often for long periods of time. This can be found mostly in the case of organised migration within a transnational community, for example, among Turkish residents in Rotterdam who bring over family members. The second pattern entails 'bounded solidarity', where aid is given to a less exclusive and larger circle of compatriots, but the support provided is limited and restricted. The African groups in the Amsterdam Bijlmermeer are his example. Finally, the market relations are forms of redistribution, which are paid in one form or another. I do not think that the Senegambian community can be given a particular place in this classification: the different models can be found, as relationships change over time and within the group.

Occasional support

The interviews show some evidence of the existence of occasional material and financial resources of private origin, expressing support from family and friends through borrowing or savings. As seen in the section on accommodation, absolute support is most evident between close relatives in early stages of the migration; in other cases, help is more limited or conditional; in still other cases, one might talk about exploitation or market behaviour. Next to the individual solidarity, there are also organised forms of reciprocity: these take the form of informal organisations based on Islamic brotherhoods, region of origin or ethnicity, which collect money on a monthly basis. This money can be used to support members who have family problems back at home (e.g. a fire has destroyed the family house, or a child is seriously ill), those who need to travel or, in the worst-case scenario, when their bodies have to be repatriated to the home country. But given that the community itself tends to be at the bottom end of society, the help is rather weak, uncertain and limited in time, and never sure or consistent enough to provide for life in difficult times. Rather surprisingly, two people mention receiving money from family members in Senegal, a real turn-around of the expectations and roles of migrant and family, illustrating that middle-class families also have migrants. Help from local Spanish or Belgian friends is never mentioned at this stage, nor did I find many signs of reliance on the solidarity of civil society through charity organisations giving food or shelter to undocumented migrants.

However, in Belgium a peculiar form of reciprocity arises when migrants have successive relationships with Belgian partners. Cases of real love happen of course, but some respondents are quite explicit about the advantages of such relationships: the Belgian partner may give you food and a hot shower, maybe a place to live for some weeks and, if you are lucky, also Dutch classes, presents, pocket money or even a holiday. An extreme example is a man who has an older married woman paying his phone, the rent, clothes and food; and in the meantime looks for other relationships.

> I try to sell sometimes but it is very hard, as I don't know anyone around, and I do not really want to enter business again, the papers [from another migrant] are not taking me anywhere. So it is very hard, I know women sometimes, they pay your restaurant and you can stay with them for a while, or they give you a little bit of money... 'on fait le gigolo' and I find it repulsive, but what can I do? (Ousman, in Antwerp since 2004, undocumented, unemployed)

We might consider this strategy of having multiple partners for extra resources as a mild form of prostitution. In her discussion of male prostitution, Van Bergen describes forms that lie outside pure market relations, and border more on reciprocity. In these cases there is no formal payment and 'the interest of the prostitute is income, housing and maintenance, while the client desires intimacy, sex and company' (Van Bergen 2003:245). Often feelings of friendship, attraction or even love may lay at the beginning, but the material and financial power of the 'client' always play a significant role, as made particularly clear in the case of big age differences between both partners. This is a gender-sensitive topic, but a very similar strategy has been described for Congolese women by Soenen (2003).

> So for many years I was selling and living with girls. I did not think about marriage because I did not want to stay here. I was sure I would go back to my country, so I did not care too much about the papers. But I was very young, only seventeen, and I was not thinking very well. I went selling, I met a woman, she took me to her village and told me to stay inside the house because the police would check me in the street and send me back to my country. I believed her, but she only wanted me to stay with her all the time. Afterwards other girlfriends came and told me not to go selling because they would be ashamed to tell their friends, or maybe somebody would recognise me in a bar. They don't understand and they think about their own benefit. (Idrissa, in Antwerp since 1993, regular status, unemployed)

In the case of a successful marriage or relationship, this dependency continues:

> If you don't have papers, you don't have the right to look for work. If you try to find a job, they will ask your papers. So I have to stay like this and it is my wife who carries all the charges till now. That is hard, you know. That is something very hard, someone who takes charge of you. It is not good, you know. I think it is not normal. I am a 34-year-old man and someone has to take care of me. It is not a nice thing. (Mustafa, in Antwerp since 2002, undocumented, unemployed)

The option of giving up

The next question then is: if people earn so little money, while living in bad conditions, why do they not give up their dream and go back to their country of origin? Why do they stay? This is question is sometimes raised by family members when a migrant complains about his situation without papers: 'if it is really so bad, why you are still there?'. Some respondents have in this phase considered going back to Senegal or Gambia, but they were unable to pay back the money family has invested in the trip, or they were not allowed to do so by moral pressure of their family (Dahou & Foucher 2004; Geets et al. 2006; Nwolisa

Okanga 1995). From the beginning, the migration project was a family strategy, that would at least result in visible economic prosperity of the wider family stayed behind, and, if possible, in a triumphant return of the migrant, with a project that allows to provide a better future for his whole family. In many cases, the limited remittances that migrants send home at this stage already represent an economic contribution that would be missed painfully:

> Also, I called my mother that I wanted to come back and that she should try to send me money, because I wanted to go back. She shouted at me, saying I was crazy... 'So many people are trying to go to Europe and you who are there you don't want to stay? Impossible, I tell you to stay there. A little bit of money is a lot of money here, you can make all the difference for us, you stay'. (Ndeye, in Antwerp since 1996, regularised, unemployed)

But second, if one would return without realising the shared expectation, so many others apparently succeeded, he must be an 'imbecile or a loser' as one respondent put it, and the whole family will share in the shame. After all the efforts they made, it would be difficult to accept that the money and time spent to come to Europe were useless; going back would be a public display of failure (Burgers & Engbersen 1999). Migrants therefore try to hide the ordeals and the suffering that they had to face throughout their life as a migrant, almost taking it as a 'rite of passage' typical for their generation.

> I cannot go back, that would be the ultimate shame, facing everybody, my wife, my children, my family, my friends, my colleagues. They don't know what I live here, not at all. My son is six and has his own computer and electric car, paid with the money I sent when in Italy. He is so proud of me, and he knows I am in Belgium, and he tells everybody he is 'Belgican'. How can I go back and disappoint him? (Ousman, in Antwerp since 2004, undocumented, unemployed)

> Also I was ashamed to tell this at home. In fact I would have liked to go back, but even though that would not have been a financial problem, I was too ashamed. They would see other people who live in Europe and succeed, so I would have been a failure, not working hard enough, not being man enough, so I stayed and did what it took. (Youssou, in Antwerp since 2000, undocumented, working in horticulture)

As an illustration, Segui was repatriated to Dakar after trying to make it to Europe for nine years without succeeding, and without money. When he called home, his mother was so ashamed about the gossip and humiliated by comments from family members, that she preferred him not to come home. This pushed him to leave again.

Instead of giving up, many undocumented migrants move around to look for better opportunities: between neighbourhoods, cities, and countries. Normally, people follow the advice of relatives or friends and go to stay with other members of the migrant community. Some of them even found themselves in countries as diverse as Portugal, Ireland, France, Italy, United Kingdom, and Poland before being an undocumented migrant in Barcelona or Antwerp, and I know of four undocumented migrants who have moved countries after the interview. Schuster (2005) confirms in her study how geographic mobility is very common due to financial difficulties, ending up somewhere else than planned. This shows their determination to try their luck in Europe instead of returning to their home countries.

Survival realised, but ...

Using these strategies, financial needs remain limited in this phase of the migration trajectory, and they help to explain the employment pattern discussed above. In the initial period, financial needs for housing and food may be zero – everything earned can be sent in remittances. Afterwards, people calculated that in Spain, the very minimum an immigrant needs to survive is 200 euro a month (80 euro a month for meals, 50 euro a month for a shared bedroom, plus some transport and phone calls). In Belgium, people say 500 euro allows you to live a decent life as an undocumented migrant. This allows for periods of casual work, even short-term unemployment, or jobs that generate limited incomes. Their situation is precarious but temporary; any money made beyond this tight budget can be sent home to the family. As Leman puts it: 'they thus understand all too well that they are in employment because others do not want to work under such conditions. They are able to accept and tolerate this situation because their ideas are permanently set on their region of origin and because they do not feel as if they 'live' in the host country' (Leman 1997:33; see also Van der Leun & Kloosterman 1999).

Notwithstanding this African frame of reference in terms of living conditions and consumption patterns, after a few months they can already stow away their dream to become quickly very rich and return subsequently to their home country. They do indeed send money home, which is initially a source for a feeling of success, but this allows only for daily consumption needs of the extended family in

Senegal. Making the savings necessary for an investment project that would continue to generate sufficient revenues for the whole family is more difficult. In addition, after the satisfaction of having arrived in the mythical paradise, they start to discover a reality that is difficult, lonely, and complex. Most respondents have never lived away from family before, and being alone in a house or a room for the first time may be a upsetting experience. Many knew they would have no papers but did not assess the consequences in daily life; they have made it to Europe, yet they have to continue a very African way of life. They see that being a regular migrant has many advantages, in terms of protection in the labour market, the possibility to travel home, and the security of residence. Therefore, the immediate aim changes in a next phase: they start thinking about trying to obtain legal residence and work status, as discussed in the following chapter.

> When you arrive in Europe and you do some months, you start to see another problem: the life conditions. If you don't have papers, you cannot work. If you want papers, you need work. But if you want work, you need papers. The life conditions are difficult. With papers you can find more work, that is sure, and better work also. (Sadani, in Barcelona since 2003, undocumented, casual work)

5.4 Conclusion: Better off in Spain

For me as a researcher, it was extremely interesting to gradually understand the functioning of a world parallel to the official one, at times completely separate from it, yet intrinsically linked, as Jordan also notes (2002: 114):

> What is interesting is to discover how self-sufficient this shadow world of undocumented commercial exchanges is in London, and how little need its participants have for the official world of recorded, tied transactions, registered workers, recognised citizens and legal entitlements.

In relation to the hypotheses that were formulated earlier, some findings should be highlighted. First, in terms of labour market participation, the general pattern of employment for undocumented migrants is necessarily one of precariousness, with low salaries and high levels of exploitation; unskilled devalorised manual jobs constitute the bulk of work, and migrants have mostly unstable jobs. The structure of the labour market provides them with limited economic resources. Search strategies are limited to count on fellow countrymen, family members and friends, and word of mouth. Because most are stuck in these ethnic networks, they are pushed into the same sectors. At the start, they have a very low reservation wage, because they need to provide for themselves; with time, it gets better; a larger network and some knowledge of the language seem to guarantee more options. In the informal economy, no highly educated jobs exist, so illegality makes human capital and skills disappear. Van der Leun and Kloosterman (2006) call this a legal ceiling, preventing the matching of skills and income.

Some explicit differences have arisen from this analysis, resulting in two ideal-typical trajectories, one in Barcelona and one in Antwerp. Collective networks seem to push undocumented migrant workers into hawking in Belgium, and into agriculture in Barcelona; however, Barcelona seems to have other informal sectors open for them as well, such as industries, services, selling. The exact role of economic and political factors in this pattern is difficult to identify. In both cities, recent trends have made entry into the two most common economic activities (agriculture and hawking) more difficult for the latest cohorts of arrival (also found in: Engbersen 2001; Van der Leun & Kloosterman 2006).

Although they cannot afford to lose a job, because they have no safety net, they are often unemployed. They make big efforts to keep working: mobility between areas and jobs has been shown to be of crucial importance in the lives of these immigrants. However, they are stuck in the shadow economy where they are vulnerable to abuse by employers and cannot ameliorate their position. In Spain, longer-term contacts often indicate that the worker has a bigger aim that makes him accept the circumstances: obtaining papers. For regularisation purposes, they need a contract, no matter how abusive, or they do not want to be expelled. In both Barcelona and Antwerp there seems to be increasingly difficult labour markets for undocumented migrants, due to increasing control or mounting competition or both.

The available openings or limits for undocumented immigrants are to some extent a consequence of elements of the economy and resulting labour markets, different degrees of control and regulation and, different welfare states and immigration policies. If legal work permits are organised to meet the need for high-skilled workers in the post-industrial labour market, the clandestine migration seems to feed by the underground economy with its need for low-skilled flexible jobs (Bribosia & Rea 2002). The Senegambian migration illustrates this best for Barcelona, but other groups fulfil a similar function in Belgium (eg. Polish construction workers).

Second, a relatively generous policy of reciprocity solves problems in all other areas of migrant life. In the face of an exploitative labour market and a hostile state, free sharing of housing, food and emotional support is crucial to their very survival. It allows them to lower the budget necessary for their own needs, and enables them to fulfil partially the obligations towards the family at home. The role of the state, the third structural factor, has received relatively limited attention in this chapter. However, because the only escape from this limited life is acquisition of papers, the strategies linked to this new aim will be discussed in the next chapter.

6 Documentation strategies as an undocumented migrant

> Foreigners are accepted, loved, and are even in demand only if they're outstanding in their field [...]. As for their integration policy, it only applies to their national football team. (Diome 2006: 125)

After having entered a country illegally, or overstayed a tourist visa, there is no easy way to obtain a residence permit; a new and different set of strategies has to be developed by responding to opportunities and actively trying to create improvements in their legal status. The differentiation between survival and documentation strategies can be debated as for many people being able to stay or seeking residence permits is simultaneously a survival strategy for themselves and their family, as they provide the basic material needs by living here (Adam et al. 2001).

In his attempt to describe the diversity of lives of undocumented migrants in Brussels, Leman (1997) launches a basic distinction between 'migrant employment illegality' and 'migrant residence illegality'[1]. He states that the first group involves people who clearly know and accept that they are residing illegally in a host country and do not expect much from institutions. They try to solve problems using their own resources or contacts; their aim is not integrate but to earn a given sum of money and go back. The second group, on the other hand, intends to regularise their situation in the host country at some stage; they may entertain certain expectation of institutions and see the host country as their new home country. In the case of Senegalese migrants, I would certainly argue that this distinction is not so clear-cut or better, that people move from one category to the other over time. After realising that earning the hoped-for capital may take somewhat longer than planned, Senegambian undocumented immigrants want to regularise their stay: to be at ease from a legal point of view, to have access to better jobs, and to be able to visit home.

> Before you have papers, you can only think of surviving. Afterwards, with the papers, you can think about other things, other plans. You can think to find a proper job, to study something like the language; you can plan to go back home, to see my family, my wife. (Elhadj, in Barcelona since 1999, regular status, construction)

Sometimes migrants are unable to maintain a new status because they no longer meet the conditions linked to the residence permit, or because of legislative changes in the country of origin or destination; this shifting between legal categories is called 'status mobility' (Schuster 2005).

The central questions in this chapter are: how do people try to legalise themselves and how are these strategies related to or influenced by migration legislation and its implementation? This section will be divided in two parts: firstly, a discussion of the strategies people develop to be physically able to stay (to avoid repatriation), and secondly, the strategies in order to be administratively allowed to stay (to obtain a residence permit, to enable settlement).

6.1 Being able to stay

There are significant differences in trying to live as an undocumented migrant in Spain and Belgium, the rights attached to this status and the risks involved. This is not a coincidence: I follow De Genova (2002) in that being illegal is as much a relationship to a state and an economy as being a citizen, that it is not a random side product of a system but rather a core element linked to society's structure. The differences will be discussed therefore in relation to the wider economic and political framework developed above.

Rights in daily life

Senegambian migrants tend to be hosted by friends, family or unknown co-nationals during the first days and weeks; the lessons they pass on about daily life as an undocumented migrant are rather divergent in both cities. According to PICUM, the international platform defending the rights of undocumented migrants, Belgium and Spain score generally well in guaranteeing a set of basic social rights linked to the international convention on human rights, compared to other European countries.

In Belgium, the exclusion of undocumented immigrants is very strong in every domain of life in the society. The foreigner who is not authorised to stay or settle in the country is by definition excluded from mainstream systems of housing and education, from social, medical and legal aid, and therefore from a dignified human existence. Contrary to Spain (see below), there are no rights attached to a valid passport or other proof of identity. For example, undocumented migrants in Belgium cannot have a bank account,[2] because they do not have an official address, and a year ago, it became impossible to send money through Western Union (Vlaams Minderhedencentrum 2004;

Vuylsteke 2006). It has nowadays also become standard practise to ask for an address when buying a mobile phone. Until recently, undocumented workers could not be members of labour unions – two unions have opened their doors for them in 2006.

However, undocumented migrants do have a set of basic social rights, and information is generally not passed on to the authorities, which makes the situation far less extreme than in Sweden and Austria, for example. Children under the age of eighteen are subjected to mandatory schooling, even if they are undocumented. A procedure for Urgent Medical Care has been elaborated for undocumented migrants, according to the Royal Decree of 12 December 1996 (PICUM). This system is quite comprehensive and includes preventive as well as curative interventions. From respondents' accounts, it sounds a rather complicated process, which poses immigrants with serious barriers in using it, to define what exactly is urgent is not easy, and mostly the migrant has to run from one service to another before everything is arranged to start up the procedure. At the same time, figures from the Ministry of Social Integration show that both the number of beneficiaries of the procedure as well as the costs have strongly increased over the last five years (*De Standaard* 15 June 2006), showing that gradually the procedure is becoming known. Their non-citizenship and lack of social protection, makes them dependent on the efficiency of humanitarian logics and actions (Fassin 1997). Doctors still see numerous cases of neglect and bad working conditions including diabetes and hypertension, but also small injuries, back pains, dental problems, industrial accidents; the most common strategy is hoping it will go away but in fact learning to live with it (Frederix 2005).

In Barcelona, on the contrary, migrants go as fast as possible to inscribe in the local residents' registry (*padrón municipal*),[3] a system which allows undocumented migrants to register in a safe way with the commune based on possession of a passport and proof of housing/ address[4]. This step gives them the right to universal health care, and education of the children. What is more, with their valid passport[5] they are able to rely on administrative services such as opening a bank account, and to be a member of the library, etc. The preconditions of registration at the town hall, however, excludes a number of groups from access to health care (for example, those who were never registered in their countries of origin) and a number of special health care centres focuses on those groups (PICUM 2001).

Concealing undocumented status

A rather common strategy that crosses the survival/documentation divide is to borrow, rent, buy or falsify somebody else's documentation, or what Engbersen (2001) calls 'manipulation of identities', to conceal their illegality.

In Spain, this strategy is mostly related to work opportunities; in Belgium to a lesser degree. One party, the legal migrant, has presently no job contract in his name: he may be travelling to his home country for some months, trying his luck in another European country, or he may be involved in informal activities.[6] The other party is the undocumented migrant who borrows the residence and work permit (or a copy) to obtain an official job using another name.

> With papers it is easier to work, that is sure. The bosses they are scared, they don't take you if you don't have papers. But you know, the black people, there are white people who cannot recognise us, like me, my picture, I can take the papers of someone else and I say it is me, but it is not true, but they cannot recognise us. (Ibu, in Barcelona since 2004, regular status, unemployed)

This strategy can be risky in unanticipated ways. One respondent was working with the papers of a certain Samba, when he heard this person had been involved in drugs dealing in France; scared to be arrested for some else's crime, he told his employer his father was dying in Senegal, and that he have to leave and quit the job. In other cases, there may be debts or unpaid bills behind the new identity one embraces; the person may have no qualifications, and you cannot present your own skills. An undocumented person working as a garbage collector with somebody else's papers had a bad cut in his foot treated in hospital. The proof of this treatment may serve in a legalisation campaign, so he registered under his own name; as the resulting sick note did not correspond with the name on his work permit, he went cleaning streets with the fresh stitches. Finally, the one who lends out the papers may get in trouble as well. During a trip to Senegal, Laye had given his work permit to a close friend; years later and working on the Canary Islands, he wanted to receive an unemployment benefit, but the social worker told him a contract was registered under his name in Barcelona. Until he proved to be the legitimate owner of the identity, his account was blocked. Conflicts between the two parties involved can easily arise when talking about money, as illustrated in the fragment below:

> A friend had recently got his papers and travelled to Senegal, so he gave me his papers to try and find a job. It was a construction site (...). But when he came back, he had spent all his own money, had some financial trouble and wanted to take a loan. But in the bank they saw that there was more than 2,000 euro on the account, my money, so they did not understand and did

> not want to give him a loan. So we made a deal between us, I did not really want to but I could not refuse as I was working with his papers. He borrowed 1,500 from me and promised to pay me back after three weeks; if he had not found the money, he would sell his car to reimburse me. But after one month there is no news, I go to talk to him, we have an argument and he asks his papers back – I did, but I never saw my money again. Up to now, he owes me money; he only paid me back 700. And all my hopes were gone, because I had lost the papers as well. (Ousman, in Antwerp since 2004, undocumented, unemployed)

In case of a regularisation (see below) the short-term strategy of borrowing papers may prevent a long-term solution, as the contract does not give proof of your presence in the country; it may even be difficult to confess to the employer and ask him to give the 'real you' a reference or contract.

In Belgium, some people use this strategy to work in agriculture, but it is more common as a defence against identity checks and the possible consequence of repatriation. As an extreme example, there was a time when four Belgian respondents shared the same paper, everyone holding a photocopy, but they had to be careful never to go out together.

> Yes, I have been checked but I had papers. I had other papers from someone who had asylum. Yes, I walked with this. And him also, he had his papers, and me a photocopy. Yes, you know, in a photocopy everyone looks the same. A copy of a picture of a black man, even we ourselves cannot recognise the person. Because the control was not so strong, you know. Because the most important it is that they don't find you doing bad things. [...] Because sometimes the police, they understand that the papers are not yours, but they let it go. They don't say anything. You understand? Because one day, a police officer told me this: 'This is not your papers. But you, Senegalese people, you are not dangerous. You only do business that is your only problem. I let you go'. And he let me go like this. Just like that. (Sal, in Antwerp since 1998, regular status, temping)

Checks inside the territory[7]

In Belgium, possible checks by federal and local police are manifold, in addition to control of the external borders. Particularly prior to 2000, when few black people held residence permits, police were said to be very tough in randomly checking people's identity on the street, in neighbourhoods with high concentration of foreigners, or in bars at night (Bernard 2000; Leman 1997). Because of this, risk reduction or 'operating strategically in public space' (Burgers and Engbersen 1999) is very important in the every day life of undocumented migrants in Belgium. Undocumented respondents in the 1990s reported a very immobile life after migration, trying to stay at home whenever they can, particularly in the evening, avoiding bars, public places and crowds; despite this, most of them had confrontations with the police at some time.

> In the beginning, we were all illegal, nobody had papers, we would only leave the house in the evening, just to go out and sell, and buy new stuff. It was a very hard and difficult life. It was because of police checks, because often there was so many checks, you don't dare to wander around in the days, because before, now things have changed, but before, you go out here, you are African, you go out, they ask you automatically your papers. We would take small streets and back ways to get where we wanted. Yes. Because you walk with a big bag. You leave, before leaving first you do a lot of prayers. Yes, seriously, a lot even, in order not to meet anyone, if they see you most often you have to be careful because they look at your instinct, they look if you are scared or not. For instance, when you see them, you have your bag, you see them, you run, and they find you immediately. But if you see them, you pray, you start to pray and you continue to walk... you pretend like it is not you, but then as soon as you go out of sight, you start to run. Or you enter a bar to have a drink, not take out the merchandise but just have your coke. This is what we did. If you stay cool, maybe they will not do anything. (Sal, in Antwerp since 1998, regular status, temping)

More recently, after the regularisation in 2000, attention has shifted to more targeted spaces, but without difference of colour or race: social inspection in work places or after being reported as undocumented; special actions against penal offence or crimes (like dodging fares on public transport or rack-rentings); or by chance in case of traffic accidents. In case of an arrest, they can be fined but not prosecuted for an illegal stay but they can be deported, which represents the worst punishment for most of them. According to Adam et al. (2001) and more recent undocumented respondents, by behaving strategically the majority of them have never been confronted with the police. Respondents say they avoid contact with authorities by being calm, behaving well, attracting as little attention as possible, and keeping away from the known targeted places (Engbersen 2001). They will avoid living in a dwelling shared by too many inhabitants, particularly if this goes together with too much movement, noise or conflicts in the building; they fear this may be perceived by the neighbours as suspicious and may form a reason for being detected (Soenen 2003). But these days it is possible to have a tea or walk the streets without being asked to show documentation.

In Spain, on the other hand, control inside the country seems to be more relaxed, as in other Southern European countries (Geddes 2003). In Barcelona and in city centres there are more checks, so people move away to avoid them. A house that I used to frequent and where a couple of respondents lived was actually located on top of a local police station; agents and undocumented migrants would exchange friendly greetings in the mornings and evenings. Bubacar was once checked on the road; he showed his health care card and police let him go, as they considered it not to be illegal.

> Till today I don't have papers, I am illegal, I have no papers. But still, there is an amount of liberty for the moment in Spain, you can move, not cross borders but in different cities yes. I am not scared of the police, if you don't cause problems or you don't go there where there is prejudice. I don't enter in jobs that could bring me problems. Sometimes they do carry out random controls, but that did not happen to me yet. (Bubacar, in Barcelona since 2002, undocumented, agriculture)

Repatriation

The ultimate touchstone for the influence of alien policy on social reality is the ability to make undesirable aliens leave (Caestecker 2000). Enforcement can take place at the border, and within the country, but both types usually capture only a fraction of illegal immigrants. Despite governments and police forces declaring that controlling illegal migration is a top priority (for Belgium, see De Walsche 2005), there is a consensus in Europe that it would simply be impossible to repatriate the millions of undocumented migrants, due to the financial and logistic costs, and because of the civil protest this 'hunt' would provoke (Engbersen et al. 1999). The immigration and local police often combat only those illegal immigrants who cause inconvenience and display criminal behaviour, and the others are tolerated. The implementation of the rather strict policies leaves freedom of interpretation or arbitrariness for the authorities in charge of checks.

In 2006, the Spanish government repatriated 97,715 migrants, 5 per cent more than the year before (*El País* 9 January 2007). A closer look at the numbers shows that the majority of migrants, 67,440, had been intercepted and sent back on their way to Spanish territory or at the border control; another 18,892 had returned voluntarily. This suggests that Spain prefers to control illegal immigration at the border rather than undocumented migrants inside the country (only 11,383). When a migrant is caught without a residence or labour permit, he can be administratively expelled, through an order to leave the country; this is rarely translated into a physical expulsion, except for some people who were caught in criminal offences. The order to leave has no consequences, though in case of a regularisation campaign this may prevent them from introducing a file. A labour union representative told me the following story:

> So, honestly, this morning there was a case, a Senegalese boy who asked me, really, he is here, he does not find work, no papers, he told me: 'What do I have to do for them to send me back?' because he has nothing, he wants to go back to his country, really. 'What do I have to do, should I steal? I don't want but I want to go back to my country.' But we only expel administratively, not physically.

In the specific case of Senegambian migrants, the same story applies: until very recently they were not physically repatriated, not even upon arrival because there was no return agreement with most sub-Saharan African countries. After the summer of 2006 brought many thousands to the Canary Islands, Senegal accepted the repatriation of 4,870 Senegalese migrants (*El País* 8 November 2006). These are mainly immigrants who were sent back from detention centres in the main arrival spots (such as the Canary Islands); in general, they are not the result of checks in daily life. As a result, respondents in Spain do not mention high levels of fear of repatriation.

In Belgium, a migrant who does not have the required permission to enter or to stay, can be expelled at any time. Different checks inside the territory result in about 30,000 orders to leave the country per year; many of those migrants disappear without anyone knowing where they are (*De Standaard* 20 July 2006). Some 3,000 migrants return voluntarily each year with support from IOM; in 2006, only eleven of them were Senegambian (IOM 2006). Distancing from the territory is frequently the method used by the authorities: statistics from the Belgian Aliens Office show that there are some 12,000 expulsions per year (*De Standaard* 20 January 2007). Upon seizure, the local police unit contacts the Aliens Office which decides whether the migrant is allowed to stay, receives an order to leave the country, or is transferred to a retention centre, where they can be held for three months waiting for their expulsion (Vuylsteke 2006). An NGO key informant explains that criminal involvement is an important criterion for reference to a detention centre; other factors that play a role are the countries of origin and repatriation agreements (Demets 2003). Respondents are aware of the existence of a list of priorities for physical repatriation, as Engbersen also notices (1999) and avoid criminal activities. In Belgium, fifteen Senegalese and one Gambian were expelled in 2006; despite this being a relatively low number, this policy is rather effective in its scaring effect:

> Repatriation happens, and it leads to big big fear. Here in the house people speak of nothing but that. We only talk about two or three recent cases, we never relate it to the total number of people around, but this is enough to make all of us very scared. Every couple of months we know of somebody who is in prison or on his way to be expelled. Recently a woman was in that situation, she had only been here less than a year. They can be checked in a phone shop, in the bus, in a car in a traffic check, just in id checks. It leads to a lot of tension and fear. (François, in Antwerp since 2003, regular status, in training)

People cannot be physically repatriated if their nationality is not identified. Although most respondents do have a valid passport from their country of origin, they never carry them with them; in case of a check, they may give a false identity or address. Orders to leave the country have to my knowledge never lead any of my respondents to go back; they throw the paper away and continue life as before, although it is often a humiliating experience. An artist with a visa for France for concerts was working for a while in Belgium and experienced first hand the tough approach of the Belgian police.

> They took our fingerprints and they put us in prison, they put us handcuffs. In Senegal, handcuffs is something very bad, they don't put it for small checks and things like that, we don't know it, it is only for big criminals. So that hurt me because I didn't do anything, I only came [from France to Belgium] to play, I didn't steal, I didn't do anything bad, and they put me in prison, from the morning till three o'clock. They told me I have to go back to France, leave the territory, because I don't have a Belgian visa. But because it was written in Flemish I did not even understand what they wrote, I took the paper and threw it away and I continued my work. (Mbaye, in Antwerp since 1995, regular status, musician)

However, there are many techniques for the police to find out, by phone numbers or people asking for you; and in case you manage to pretend being from another country, the prospect of being repatriated to unknown territory is scary enough to say the truth. The Senegalese embassy often collaborates with the Belgian authorities to identify citizens.

Emotional consequences

Living in these conditions has emotional effects. Frederix cites a psychologist who says: 'Everyone living in illegality has a significant chance of psychological problems. People have no safety, no stable place, little meaning in their lives or perspectives for the future, living in fear and isolation... the symptoms are head aches, stomach problems, insomnia, psychic and physical exhaustion. This so-called syndrome of Ulysses[8] is typical for refugees and is similar to a depression without suicidal tendency' (Frederix 2005: 40). Burgers (1999) also shows that stress and depression are the main problems for undocumented migrants, and more so when they stay illegally for a long time. Looking at the adult population, Leman (1997) uses a threefold typology of medical afflictions of immigrants: imported pathologies, acquired diseases, and adaptive pathologies. The latter two are the most important because they relate respectively to life conditions in the host country (nutrition, housing, climate, employment) and socio-cultural adaptation (mainly psychological and social).

In the case of Senegambians in Spain, those who made the trip overland and by boat do report traumatising experiences. In later stages, it is mainly the dependency on employers, the hidden racism and exploitation, and the separation from family and friends, that creates frustration and depression.

> The trip only was a surprise, but once I arrived here, I had problems but it was not sooooo hard. People helped me. Life without papers is a bit difficult but I have forgotten. Because if you are always thinking, you think work, you think papers, you think your family, you think many things... *Oooooo*, you will become crazy. (Assane, in Barcelona since 2001, undocumented, textile industry)

For migrants residing in Belgium, rather than the traumatic trip, the continuing atmosphere of fear and hopelessness create mental problems. Some respondents confess that they drink too much, and some make an explicit link to their undocumented status:

> I am ashamed of myself. I feel very bad, and even when I am with other people I am away, gone, somewhere else. I cannot

> enjoy things, I don't dare to watch myself in the mirror, I am so sick of this life and cheating and begging. I don't respect myself anymore and I can see how people would become mad in this kind of situation. (Ousman, in Antwerp since 2004, undocumented, unemployed)

One person who had some indications of mental problems back in Senegal tells how the different problems in his life in Belgium have made him fall back into psychoses that he might not suffer when staying in Senegal.

> I felt that I was falling behind compared to my friends who stayed in Senegal, I was not making progress, not going anywhere. And it takes so much energy to adapt to the conditions here, things not going the way you want them to go, and not much you can do to change it. Life as an undocumented migrant is difficult and hard, and you have to carry it alone. All of this triggered my illness (Sal, in Antwerp since 1998, regular status, temping).

In this context, people find refuge and support in their religion and spirituality; many people pray to ask for safety or health, a considerable number puts its faith in amulets and other protective measures (Nimako 2000; Nwolisa Okanga 1995). Leman (1997) shows how major religions offer specific religious services to undocumented migrants, as an ethno-religious extension of social life of home country, where they live without being there, and it fills in the gap. Undocumented migrants look for country mates and the atmosphere of home; sermons can offer support in terms of easing their guilt, or by maintaining a sense of ethno-religious self-esteem. The idea that fate is in someone else's hands makes it easier to accept everything that happens in their undocumented situation.

> In Belgium, you cannot do anything without papers. The only solution is to pray a lot, faith helps to live these conditions. There is a lot of checks. (Bakeba, in Antwerp since 1993, regular status, unemployed)

Others react in a different way: even though in an illegal situation, undocumented immigrants have acted politically, often supported by civilian society. Solidarity movements created around church and public building sit-ins in both Spain and Belgium have raised the interest shown for the precarious situation of the undocumented immigrants in both the general public and political circles. This has resulted in support for regularisation campaigns and easing of some of the most unrealistic and iniquitous aspects of control, but of course not in radical changes in the direction of political decisions (Bernard 2000; Vuylsteke 2006).

6.2 Being allowed to stay

Not having a residence permit has many unattended implications in the bureaucratic welfare states of Western Europe, ranging from the impossibility to travel or visit home, to the lack of social protection and administrative rights, and the stress of continuous hiding and extreme vulnerability. In order to realise their original and ultimate goal of saving a considerable sum of money, many people adopt a new mid-term aim: they try to obtain papers, in order to start a 'normal' life and thereby increase their chances of success. In the next sections, some direct and indirect strategies for ameliorating one's residence status are discussed (Wets 2001): asylum and regularisation are direct strategies, in which the goal and the act correspond perfectly. Marriage and job offers are indirect documentation strategies, as the right to stay in the country is a consequence of the person's status in another dimension of life.

Table 6.1 *Number of years in illegality before being regularised in Antwerp and Barcelona*

	Antwerp		Barcelona	
	Regularised	Still waiting	Regularised	Still waiting*
2 years or less	4	5	11	5
Between 2 and 5 years	7	5	5	9
More than 5 years	7	1	0	0

* Nine of these people had introduced files for the regularisation campaign February-March 2005; five others were trying to fulfil the conditions. In Belgium, the people waiting had no immediate prospect.

As an introduction, Table 6.1 gives an indication of the number of years people spent as undocumented migrants before obtaining residence permits. A first difference is that no one in Spain had been undocumented for more than five years, while eight people in Belgium had. In the same line, a large group of undocumented migrants was regularised in Spain within two years of arrival; in Belgium, this number stood at only four. This is a very rough indicator for generally longer waiting times in Belgium than in Spain. Below, I will explore how this reflects the different migration policies in both countries.

Asylum applications

In the absence of lasting civil war or political repression in Senegal and the Gambia, most western governments decide not to consider political refugee status for residents of these countries. However, some respondents do mention relying on the asylum procedure, mostly for improper aims such as gaining access or winning time.

Many black Africans entering Spanish territory by boat or through the enclaves of Ceuta and Melilla upon arrival declare themselves refugees from one of the numerous countries at war. During the investigation of their case, they cannot be expelled and receive a temporary permit; if not given refugee status, they just join the many undocumented migrants and wait for a regularisation campaign.

> When I entered in Ceuta I did two months, they give me the papers of refugee, residence card. Because there you don't declare your normal data, you have to name a country that is in war or that is very bad economically, and Senegal does not know these things. If you say Senegal they will send you to Senegal, and at that time there was war in Guinea Bissau, so I said that, so they give me paper for refugee and they transfer me to Spain. After one year, they know about how people cheat, so they invite everyone to come with the real passport. (Babacar, in Barcelona since 2000, regular status, transport)

Senegambians arriving in Belgium in the 1980s and 1990s would commonly apply for asylum, arguing they fled their country because of the war in the southern province of Casamance, the political troubles of 1988 (between President Abdou Diouf and the opposition), or the incidents with Mauritania in 1989. Knowing that these reasons were never really accepted for a refugee status, their aim was to have some time of relative freedom as their presence would be tolerated in case of an identity check. With the then long delays in the procedure, including the inevitable appeal against a negative decision, they might be safe for some months or even years. As Adam et al. mention (2001), people feel they become undocumented only after the final rejection of their case, although they were technically undocumented before. Some might even try successive asylum applications under different names.

Some people take on a fake identity, make up a corresponding refugee story, and continue to defend their case as such. An example are the Senegalese pretending to be Mauritanian; often original from the border region, they may have family on the other side or have spent part of their lives there, which makes it easier for them to pretend consistently. The common argument (that can only be used by lowly educated people, as a higher-educated migrant mentioned) would be that they used to be slaves there and if they would go back now they would be killed.

> Europe is very sensitive to slavery, they cannot accept it at all, and it works very well. But you need some family members there to get some papers, et cetera. Only people from the north tend to do it. (Musa, in Antwerp since 2004, undocumented, import-export)

If successful, as the three respondents in Belgium (see Table 6.2) another kind of problem arises: all documents linked to the original identity, like diplomas but also wedding acts and recognition of children are unusable now.

Regularisation

From Table 6.2, we can see that regularisation is the main strategy for obtaining residence permits in Spain, with twelve people succeeding in regularising their stay through this channel. Another nine were participating in the latest regularisation campaign (February to May 2005) that took place while I was finishing my fieldwork in Barcelona; many of them were accepted and are now regular workers.

Table 6.2 *Successful documentation strategies in Spain and Belgium*

	Antwerp		Barcelona	
Regularisation	5	(2)*	12	(9)
Marriage	13	(1)	0	
Work permit / Contingente	1		3	
Refugee	3		0	

* Bracketed numbers refer to people who are in advanced stages of a procedure that is not yet finished.

For Belgium, marriage is the dominant solution, which was successful for thirteen respondents. Five respondents were regularised, all of them during the one-off campaign in 2000. The legislative background to this outspoken difference will be explored below.

Spain

As mentioned in chapter 2, the subsequent regularisation campaigns in Spain coincide with changes in the law (Gortázar 2000). In 1985, the first 'Foreigners Act' was introduced and with the objective of legalising the stock of undocumented foreigners generated by the previous regulatory vacuum, 38,000 immigrants obtained a residence permit.

In 1991, pressures came from the considerable growth of the stock of undocumented immigrants, but also from the EU Schengen requirement to introduce visas for Maghreb countries. Regularising many of the Moroccan immigrants in exchange seemed a fair deal, and there was a substantial consensus among political parties, NGOs, and public opinion regarding the need to find a feasible solution: 109,000 new work permits were issued. In 1996, changes were introduced in the regulation that defined the application of the 1985 Law. For those who had lost residential status and for relatives of legal workers this resulted in 21,000 working permits. In 2000 and 2001, the regularisation coincided with new legislation again, resolving the undocumented status of 164,000 and 235,000 migrants respectively. Information about this policy choice is communicated widely among Senegambian migrants:

> Now my papers have expired, I have no papers here. It is very difficult. I chose Spain because everybody says when you got there is easier to get papers then other countries where you have to marry somebody that has papers. Here, when they are giving papers, you are lucky. So people say just try, here in Spain is safer. They police is not very hard, so even if I don't have paper, they will not deport me. So here I can try to have paper that is why. (Fatou, woman, in Barcelona since 2003, undocumented, textile industry)

The first campaigns were marked by the absence of a specialised agency staffed by experienced personnel and supplied with the necessary resources; later ones drew on the active cooperation of third-sector organisations, trade unions, and immigrants' associations. The initial one-year work permits issued need renewal on a regular basis, with early preconditions about proven employment representing a big difficulty for workers in a precarious labour market and undoing the effect of the campaigns; later ones were more flexible. Residence and work permits in Spain are always temporary in the beginning; they need to be renewed. A migrant should have contributed half the time of the permit to social security in order to renew it; this means having a labour contract, unless one has the statute of self-employed.

As a direct effect of the change of government, the latest regularisation campaign ran from February to May 2005 and gave renewable one-year legal residency to any foreign national who could show that he had a job contract and lived in the country for more than six months. This shows the main rationale behind the process: illegal immigrants and their employers, particularly in the agricultural, domestic and construction sectors are harming the economy by not paying taxes and social security. In addition, it was a solution for security problems on the level of the cities where they concentrate, as well as a symbolic issue for the socialist image. However, the conditions for regularisation of status were criticised by street-level organisations, who claim that the conditions were impossible to meet. Particularly the link to a labour contract was hard to obtain, which leads Domingo (2000) to point to an almost ridiculous spiral for an earlier campaign: to find a job an immigrant needed papers, but to get those papers he needed a job contract. Next to stimulating all kinds of frauds and insecurity, it also leads to an important dependency on the employers, as discussed below. In the case of Senegambian migrants, some key informants point out that the hawkers experienced problems: by the nature of their work they do not build the personal relationships to employers who may give them a job offer or pre-contract for obtaining papers, and they were therefore excluded from the regularisation process. In addition, the people working with somebody else's papers, or those for whom registration in the city register was impossible or scary, did not meet the conditions, and would thus remain undocumented. It is estimated that 573,000 residence permits were handed out.

On the other hand, employers use the system to tie workers to them. For most immigrants it is key to find an employer that would be prepared to give them a contract; this is more likely in a context of personal ties, a relationship of appreciation and trust, and therefore more probable in relatively small enterprises. This influences people's job strategies: Bubacar gave up a better-paid job in a Gambian phone shop, for harder work in agriculture, hoping that this may lead to a contract. With some respondents mentioning that 'contracts' are for sale at high prices, there is no need to say this strategy may lead to bad situations of dependency:

> You know, many Spanish, they don't want black people to have nothing. They pay us three euro per hour, that is nothing, and they think we don't know that. They think we don't know nothing, but we do know, we know. But we have to follow our interest, you know, that is why; we have no papers, that is why we accept. But we know it is little money (Mbacké, in Barcelona since 2000, undocumented, agriculture).

One year after this regularisation, Spanish authorities reported that there are again about one million undocumented migrants living in Spain (*El Mundo* 6 May 2006). This includes people who did not meet the conditions as well as new arrivals. The Socialist Party explicitly excluded a new regularisation, probably inspired by difficult position vis-à-vis the European partners. The avalanche of migrants arriving at the

Canary Islands over the summer of 2006 drove Spain to ask for help from European partners, who were reluctant to assist after they were not consulted about the unilateral Spanish regularisation decision. Fears are that immigrants benefiting from the amnesty will then be able to move freely throughout Europe. However, the ambition of a common EU immigration policy has been undermined by other member states signalling their readiness to regularise the status of undocumented migrants (Italy, Germany, the Netherlands and France).

The job offer is officially a way to recruit a particular foreigner for a job that is not filled by local work force; a good example is a percussion musician hired by a Belgian band. However, it can be used to regularise migrants already present in the country illegally, as happened in this case. For the three migrants in Spain, this involved going back to pick up the visa in the Spanish consulate of his/her country of origin, which is quite risky in case it does not end well. Therefore, an inventive system of paid local stand-ins partly solves this problem, requiring the immigrant to return only when the visa is stamped and ready for collection. However, as a flexible response to urgent needs in the labour market the system fails, because there is too much administration and check to verify if no local or EU worker can do the job. The remarks about dependency and exploitation 'balancing' the promise of papers, apply here in the same way as described above for common regularisation. Some established migrants ask their employer to do a favour for a relative back home; in that case, a new migrant comes over with a work visa, but in fact, there is no job waiting for him. The new arrival can legally try to find another job and maybe renew his residence permit showing he worked enough time. Over time, more than 150,000 immigrants have been regularised this way.

Belgium
When the migration stop was declared in 1974, it was followed closely by political actions and, as a consequence, a first mass regularisation for the foreign workers in irregular situations[9] (Ouali 1997). Some 7,500 work permits were granted, mostly to Turkish and Moroccan people (Bernard 2000). A second regularisation, and the last one so far, took place in 2000, due to a combination of societal factors.

In September 1998, Semira Adamu, a rejected asylum seeker from Nigeria, died during the state police's sixth attempt to expel her forcibly. This caused a shock in the general Belgian population and media, led to the dismissal of the minister of interior affairs, and proved to be a turning point for both the general awareness and the mobilisation of a movement to defend the rights of undocumented migrants (Kagné 2001). The solidarity movements created around church and public building sit-ins in the winter of 1998 later diversified and extended,

mobilising artists, scientists, universities and schools, but the socialist and Christian-democrat government did not give in. The 13 June 1999 elections brought a new government with both Walloon and Flemish socialists, liberals and ecologists, the last ones most closely associated with the social groups pushing for immigrant's rights. A stricter asylum policy was accompanied by a second and far larger regularisation campaign in January 2000 (Martiniello 2003). This aimed at a rapid regularisation of people meeting a set of individualised and precisely defined conditions: showing to have truly been in Belgium from 1 October, and fulfilling one of the following:
- having been engaged in asylum procedure for an abnormally long period without having been informed of a decisions (four years in general, three for families with minor children), if not a danger for public order and no breaches of the law after entering the procedure;
- not having the objective possibility of returning to one's country due to external reasons, for example, war;
- suffering a serious illness, or;
- having lived for six years in Belgium, showing humanitarian circumstances and lasting social ties.

More than 36,000 applications were handed in, involving more than 50,000 people, with large representations of the Moroccan and Congolese communities (Martiniello 2003). Some 25,000 files have received a positive answer, 6,000 a negative answer, and 1,240 are still being treated. Walckiers (2003) summarises two major complaints: the procedure was not transparent enough for the migrants (communication did not reach everyone, lots of details unresolved, no central information point, interpretation of arguments was not made clear) and the procedure was too slow to deal with the applications, with bad psychological consequences. Some respondents who participated are still waiting for the outcome, be it because they bought part of the necessary proof. Not everyone was reached by this campaign: some precarious (but not illegal) statuses were excluded, others did not trust the government and institutions, did not meet the criteria, did not possess proves, or were simply not informed (Adam et al. 2001). In Antwerp, almost 5000 applications were made, often including several people, 32 per cent residing in the North area, and 19 per cent in Borgerhout; five Senegambian respondents also took part in this procedure.

Today, there is no perspective of a new regularisation campaign. The only other possibility consists in case by case regularisations based on article 9, paragraph 3 of the 15 December 1980 law. This stipulates that a demand to obtain a residence permit when one is in the territory cannot be filed, except in 'exceptional circumstances'. The law does not make this precise, but seriously ill people, victims of human trafficking or people who have been in the country very long have a very small chance to be regularised. The obscure conditions contributed together with the rigidity in other channels to the build up of an important backlog of files: many of my undocumented respondents have tried their luck, and some repeat the application again and again, knowing very well that they have no new elements for their file (Frederix 2005). In 2006 the individual applications of 10,207 people were accepted, most of them because of unreasonably long asylum procedures (*De Standaard* 22 January 2006).

Common features
In both countries, new rumours about regularisation come up every year, often without clear reason, but most of the time taken seriously by desperate people. In order to be prepared for this mythological quest for papers, undocumented people try to find all kinds of proof of presence from the beginning of their stay. This includes registering as an inhabitant in the municipality in Spain, going to hospital for urgent medical care, having library cards made, having letters sent to you at a specific address, all of which they hope may serve as the proof they have been present in the country for the required time in case of a regularisation.

Next to the majority of 'deserving' immigrants following the correct way to apply, corruption, abuse and money-making from all kinds of middle-men is rife;[10] sometimes lawyers take advantage of people to give them hope and earn considerable amounts of money in the meantime, independent of the outcome (Burgers & Engbersen 1999). In the regularisation campaign of spring 2005 in Spain, people needed a job contract and a registration in the municipality for six months; almost immediately, these documents were for sale (Solé et al. 1998). A Senegalese civil servant is well placed to give some information:

> The government creates people who will sell contracts, registration in the municipality, false papers, that is all. You have to pay to have a contract, and you pay with your labour or with money. In the beginning of February the price for a contract was 4,000 euro, that is on average the salary of eight months of work, and now it has gone down to 3,500 [euro]; and of course you pay your own social security contributions.

In Belgium in 1999, one of the conditions was proof of integration and five years of residence in the country. As people were prepared to pay 250 euro for a proof of being in Belgium during five years, it stimulated an industry of fake or copied papers. The quote below shows how to buy them, and at the same time illustrates how multiple sets of papers and identities discussed above can come about:

> In 1999 when I was in Belgium for some months with my student visa, the regularisation was announced. I had an undocumented cousin in France who wanted me to introduce papers for him. I went to buy the documents, wrote his name, put my picture on it, and introduced the file. Where I bought the proofs? People who wrote letters for somebody photocopied them afterwards, or maybe others did it for money, anyway many were photocopied many times to serve a lot of people, with only the name changed. Also doctors and embassies helped. My cousin was 34 years old, but he died shortly after in a car accident in France. His documents are still in Belgium, so I can use it if I want. I use it only when I want to work, as I cannot do that with my student visa, but otherwise I lend it to other people. (Musa, in Antwerp since 2004, undocumented, import-export)

The administration discovered the abuse and is now checking everybody using the same witnesses.

To avoid mass arrivals of undocumented people from other countries when a country launches a regularisation campaign, or an attraction effect for criminal organisations, they are usually announced suddenly and unexpectedly, and application is limited in time. In addition, the government may considerably re-enforce its border checks ahead of and during the campaign.[11] Despite these efforts, my sample shows examples of people trying their luck several times, sometimes in other countries, until they are successful. They either go somewhere or send money and papers to have someone else take care of it.

> I left Belgium to go to Italy in 1998 to get the papers there. I got them and it was not difficult to renew them every time. But now it has become more difficult to renew them. But mine are 'license of commerce', not a working one, so I can still renew them without contracts. Italy used to be more open and friendlier to foreigners, but things changed rapidly for the worse. (Paté, in Antwerp since 1996, undocumented, restaurant)

However, despite this 'regularisation-tourism', it is not clear whether and to what extent large-scale regularisation campaigns generate additional illegal migration. Critics believe that this policy encourages immigrants to make often-dangerous journeys to the EU in the hope that they too will eventually be allowed to remain; evidence about this phenomenon seems hard to find in the European literature. In general, the economic picture of home countries would make it absurd to think that migrants need something to 'call them', although the relative ease to obtain papers may influence the choice of country.

This description shows how regularisation operations in some countries of the European Union is more a 'policy of fait accompli' than related to a new policy of immigration (Kagné 2001), because neither country intends to make steps towards structural regularisations.

Marriage

In Spain, only one respondent mentioned the possibility of a marriage, and also the elements that keep him from making the step:

> I cannot participate in the regularisation, so maybe I should marry. I say this because sometimes you need to be egoistic, you know, to get what you want. But also I don't want to hurt anyone. For me it is not good to marry a woman that you don't love, and then after she gives you the papers you throw her on the street and she will suffer, and this for me is not good because I have sisters, and I don't want them to live that situation. Therefore, I say it sometimes, but I think a lot… but in the end for me the person is more important than the papers. (Matar, in Barcelona since 2000, undocumented, shopkeeper)

In contrast, a marriage with someone legally residing in the country is generally seen as the only way out in Belgium. This seems to indicate that actively searching a marriage with a local is not the first choice in order to obtain a residence permit, but a final option turned to when no other perspectives exist. It was successful for thirteen Senegambian respondents, and is even recognised as such by outsiders.

> I contacted a lawyer in Brussels, the best for migrant problems, just to make an appointment to explain my case for a regularisation. But hearing I was Senegalese, he said 'Senegalese? No chance whatsoever. Just find a girl and marry her'. (Ousman, in Antwerp since 2004, undocumented, unemployed)

Large settled communities like the Turkish and Moroccan, may provide marriage partners for undocumented members of the ethnic group (Burgers & Engbersen 1999; Staring 1998); in the absence of a pool of legal counterparts, Senegambians have to look at other nationalities, mostly Belgians. The standard strategy is to go out to particular bars, festivals, or squares known for multicultural music and encounters, a way to maximise their chances to find a girl, or a woman: in a considerable number of cases, middle-aged women are part of the market[12]. Finding someone for the night is reported as very easy, as also explained in chapter 5, but finding someone who is prepared to marry is more difficult and may require some strategic profiling:

> You will not stop the relationship because marriage will solve some of your problems. If she wants to go to cinema and clubs, you will go with her because you are not free to speak your mind; but once you get the papers you can show your real character and say what you think and then she can decide whether she still likes you. (Sheikh, in Antwerp since 2004, undocumented, import-export)

Whether these are sham marriages, marriages of convenience, or based on genuine affective feelings is always food for questions from the surroundings of the couple: family, friends and civil servants. In my sample and fieldwork, I have not encountered signs of real sham marriages, involving people who never had a relationship, but where one partner paid the other; key informants confirm this. Much more common is what one respondent calls 'comedy marriages' in which the foreign partner pushes a girlfriend into wedlock prematurely. Other cases are based on friendship, with the marriage as a gesture for the undocumented migrant. Still others, and the majority, start with mutual attraction, love and shared plans for the future; the girl may really want to help because she understands the situation and may want to build a life together.

The fight against marriages of convenience was considerably increased in the last ten years (Bernard 2000), with a number of documents required and an obligatory pre-marital interview by the authorities. Whether a marriage of convenience or not, this procedure tends to raise nerves:

> They do not look at the love and the depth of our feelings for each other; and the possible consequences if they would not allow us to marry, how sad we would be. Really I love her a lot and that is why I want to marry her, she is a really good girl and will be a good wife. But they prefer to watch the negative things and to look for problems, it is their job, I understand. So now we will have to wait for the decision in a couple of weeks. If they want to repatriate me maybe I will be fine home with my family; but what about my wife? We will both suffer a lot if I am going to be expelled. I know many Africans get divorced, but me not, it is not everybody who is going to leave his wife after he gets the papers. We live in Antwerp now, and we are very happy together. I never thought I would live in Belgium, but love can

change things. The heart has its reasons. (Youssou, in Antwerp since 2000, undocumented, working in horticulture)

Afterwards, some stay together as a married couple; others leave the girl relatively quickly after the papers have come. Still others struggle with cultural differences and unequal positions (Bendadi 2005):

> You know, it is not easy with two traditions; it is difficult to stay together. I always say nobody has ever seen an old mixed couple; really, it is always small problems because we don't understand each other, so we divorced. (Mbaye, in Antwerp since 1995, regular status, musician)

This strategy may interfere with established family life back in Senegal. On the one hand, a wife back home may understand the need for this step:

> I do not go out and try to pick up girls, because my status as elderly person prevents me from doing that. But my wife told me to marry if that is going to improve my situation, she helps and supports me, we have been together a long time and she would understand this kind of decision. (Khadim, in Antwerp since 2003, undocumented, hawking)

In other cases, it can intervene in a bad way, as summed up nicely and surprisingly openly by this respondent:

> Why so many marriages fail? You have to look at the interest of the people. The man's interest is always to have the papers, so some of them marry somebody they don't love so much and leave it after they get the papers. Also, sometimes they don't earn anything and depend on the wife, and it is not easy to be like that, to depend on your wife, or to have a husband who depends on you all the time. Also, sometimes people are not very honest and don't tell you they have a wife and/or children in Senegal. Or maybe their family will not accept a white wife, so they take you to their country, but they present you somebody else's family, so nobody finds out. Sometimes the family in Senegal will make you marry a cousin or a relative, so you have two wives, one in Belgium, one in Senegal. And some Belgian women accept, particularly as they are sometimes a bit older, maybe divorced already, so they accept this situation. (Musa, in Antwerp since 2004, undocumented, import-export)

Residence permit realised, but...

In general, respondents refer to the acquisition of papers as the single event with most impact in their lives as a migrants, because of work and because they are geographically mobile again, with the possibility to visit family and friends at home (Schuster 2005). Some authors mention that the dichotomies of legal versus illegal immigrant are diffuse (Engbersen & Van der Leun, 2001), particularly in Spain where the short permits obtained in legalisation campaigns may be difficult to renew (Mendoza 1998). In my sample, I did not encounter examples of workers passing from illegal to legal and vice versa on several occasions. Only in the case of migrants who obtained residence and work permits in one country and then moved to another European country, their status is changing and volatile. However, it should be reemphasised that the apparent trajectory towards documented status is unattainable for some migrants.

If they did obtain the residence permit, many dimensions of life change. Particularly in Belgium, people need an official address where they live alone; sharing houses has fiscal consequences. The costs for rent, food, electricity and gas are suddenly considerably higher than before, in the arrangements between undocumented migrants. In Spain, migrants necessarily have to look for jobs in the official sector, given that the renewal of their permit depends on proven employment. In both cases, migrants need to pay taxes and have the opportunity to bring wives and children over.

> Yes, life changes with the papers... more individual, less community. When you have papers, you need an address, and with that you start to live like the Belgian people do, but we do not like it. We keep eating together with friends and family till today, many people come here or we go to eat somewhere else. Also you need to take a real job, it is too difficult to work in business with papers, too risky. You will need a car to go to work, you need a house for your family... and you need more money, just like Belgian people. (Bakeba, in Antwerp since 1993, regular status, unemployed)

This even leads to Bakeba getting nostalgic and longing for the simple life without documentation:

> Life was a lot better when we had no papers, now I am filled with nostalgia for the hawking days. They are two different styles of life: to have a house or a room alone, to be officially registered somewhere, to manage your life, an official life, fixed

address, pay all the bills that continue to come every month, try to save for the taxes – now everything is about rules and following the rules, you cannot create any problem. Before, that was less important. The life of a businessman is outside the laws, outside administration. The business life is flexible, and the community life is so good for us... Once you have the papers you are channelled, you cannot take risks. (Bakeba, in Antwerp since 1993, regular status, unemployed)

Many people underestimate the rising costs of living a 'western' life, reflected not only in increasing levels of financial expenditure, but also in terms of goal displacement. The mid-term goal becomes a better economic position; the focus of attention shifts to the family in the host country. The strategies need to change again, and return to the home country is postponed once more.

6.3 Conclusion: Different ways of 'being undocumented'

A first surprising element emerging from this chapter is the difference between the Western European adherence to administrative procedures and rules, and the flexibility of papers and identities in African social life. The 'holy faith' in the paper reality in Europe, is in Africa completely unknown. This is expressed foremost through the use of false identity papers, as identity, age, nationality, even marriage are not necessarily unchangeable facts as we tend to see them.

> If I want to be someone else tomorrow, I can buy the documents today. (Modou, in Antwerp since 2004, regular status, temping)

This can take shapes that European administrations can hardly imagine: someone got in trouble with one false name he had been using in Belgium to get married; he divorced, cancelled the name, got a new identity in Senegal (next to the real one that still exists) and came back to remarry the same girl but with a different name. Fake names and identities of course raise issues that continue to conflict with administrative rules: how to obtain a family reunification if one has a different nationality? This game with identities then extends to spheres of work, health insurance, driver licences, travel permits.

Second, the differences between documentation strategies in Antwerp and Barcelona have been highlighted in this chapter, and they confirm the hypotheses formulated above. Spain offers an easier life for migrants without papers, and the perspective of a next regularisation campaign is always present; Belgium is stricter and offers less perspectives. As anecdotal evidence, the circumstances under which I was carrying out the fieldwork can illustrate this difference. In Antwerp, my fieldwork coincided with the announcement and first activities of the 'X-stra' action in which targeted neighbourhoods were controlled door to door, in order to record social or housing problems and provide help.[13] As this information was passed on to the public prosecutor, civil rights movements and undocumented migrants were clearly scared that this would lead to repatriation. My Spanish fieldwork, on the contrary, overlapped with the discussion about and the launch of the last regularisation, which gave hope for a new life to hundreds of thousands of migrants. In short: for undocumented migrants life in Spain is better than in Belgium. Contrary to reality, many immigrants attribute this to a perceived longer experience with immigration in Spain than in Belgium. However, some respondents point to a factor that may be closer to the reality of undocumented migration:

> In Spain you have seen it, almost every year they give papers to the people, and Italy as well, because they need workers, so they regularise because so that the migrants can work for them. But Belgium does not do that at all. (Mbaye, in Antwerp since 1995, regular status, musician)

The specificity of the Spanish economy and migration legislation in the last decades has created an immigration process in which phases of irregularity are almost standard for the large flows of newly arriving migrants. After making it into the country, they search and find work in the informal economy; degrees of internal control are low, repatriation practically non-existent, and they have a number of rights and access to services. In short, migrants' lives can be characterised as 'quiet lives in the margins of society'. Afterwards many of them have succeeded to regularise their stay within reasonable timeframes (Pajares 2004), with the six waves of mass regularisation campaigns over the last 22 years presenting the main documentation strategy. That is not to say that life in Spain is easy, it is to say that the feel of repression is far less. For the hundreds of thousands who find themselves in irregular situations, the existing migration policy has conditioned a social framework that systematically promotes marginalisation and exclusion (King & Rodríguez-Melguizo 1999). The pending promise of 'papers' binds them to jobs and employers, providing Spain with a vulnerable and therefore obedient labour force for the informal sector. As Calavita (1998: 538) puts it:

> 'To preview the argument I make here, Spain's immigration laws – which systematically marginalize third world immigrants

but do not stem their immigration – provide the Spanish economy with precisely the type of vulnerable workers required to impose post-Fordist discipline on at least a substantial segment of the workforce.'

In Belgium, the situation is clearly different, with far smaller inflows of undocumented immigrants and stricter implementation of the law through active internal state control. Many areas of life are rendered difficult by the lack of identification and the subsequent lack of rights and access to services. The risks of police control and deportation causes restricted mobility; exploitation and abuse can be even worse than in Spain; a dignified human existence in general is difficult. In addition, because of the very small chance of obtaining papers in the future, Senegambian migrants are driven in the direction of marriage as a documentation strategy. Life as an undocumented in Belgium is clearly more stressful on a daily basis because of the active opposition of the authorities; it can be characterised as a 'hidden existence'. As Chavez puts it for the US: 'their continued presence in the US is an act of defiance to the powers that conspire to limit their opportunities and to keep them outside the society' (Chavez 1990: 58).

In the next chapter, I will take a closer look on how migrants try to organise their lives as documented migrants, through integrating themselves on the formal labour market, make different housing choices, stabilise family life and invest in education. The driving force is the wish to ameliorate their position, which is why 'mobility' strategies is an adequate term.

7 Mobility strategies as a legal migrant

So, under the grey European sky, or in unexpected sunlight, I walk on, counting my steps, each one bringing me closer to my dream. But how many kilometres, how many work-filled days and sleepless nights still separate me from that so-called success that my people, on the other hand, took for granted when I told them I was leaving for France. I walk on, my steps weighted down by their dreams, my head filled with my own. I walk on and have no idea where I'll end up. (Diome 2006: 3)

The most important change over an individual's migration time line is to obtain a residence permit: most respondents say regularisation changed their lives in a positive sense. In addition, the people who arrive legally enter the analysis now and start their careers at this point. Both situations allow job searching strategies and procedures to enter the official and regular labour market. However, they are bound to meet new challenges:

Life with papers is not easier; you will find other barriers and difficulties, so it is the same. You push, but always you meet new barriers: first it was the papers, now it is the work. (Ibra, in Antwerp since 2002, regular status, temping)

This chapter deals with the strategies migrants develop when they have papers, in order to improve their situation and with the aim of getting closer to their original goal. This includes looking at work experiences as well as strategies in other dimensions of life in order to secure a form of social mobility.

7.1 Work experiences for documented migrants

After regularisation, or upon legal arrival with a work permit, migrants normally enter the formal labour market, or they are at least entitled to do so. This changes their possibilities: to start with, they can use mainstream and more effective channels to find work; jobs are also better paid and come with guaranteed civil and legal rights, which allows them to have a 'normal' life. However, they soon discover that papers are not the only threshold: from now on, they will be faced with new barriers such as language, diplomas, and education. As they lose the competitive advantage of being undocumented (and therefore cheap), they may find that finding a job becomes more challenging.

This is the point where I should introduce the limited number of women respondents in the sample, as they mainly enter as regular migrants through family reunion (Marfaing 2003b). The biggest group of Senegambian women spend some years at home, taking care of children, prior to entering the labour market (Bodin & Quiminal 1991; Tellegen 2000). In Belgium, women can work officially from the first day they have received a residence permit. In Barcelona, on the contrary, an administrative difficulty is that women coming through family reunification do not automatically have a work permit, only residence; they have to change their status with a job offer, very much in the same way as the men regularise themselves.[1] The economic and financial dependency on the husband as a result of not having the right to work, is in stark contrast with the wish for integration and emancipation of immigrant women.

With or without working permit, many women engage in some forms of extra cash earning; most common are braiding hair of friends, catering meals or snacks or selling Senegalese products at home. Outside the ethnic community, informal cleaning is the most common activity, often using connections in the children's schools or from friends. Once working officially, it looks like their main sector is cleaning,[2] care for elderly people and temping – at least in Barcelona, where enough women have reached this stage; the Belgian respondents have mostly not entered this stage yet. Both Pajares (2005) and Anguiano Téllez (2001) note that black women are moving on to commerce, hotels and services. One illustration is Aisatu who is currently working as a cultural mediator. After five years caring for her children, she started cleaning in order to get a work permit; then a succession of temporary jobs in the environmental service of the municipality, in a plastics enterprise, cleaning in a hotel, to finally becoming a cultural mediator in the municipality for two years now. However, the largest group of respondents consists of men, and their trajectories will be analysed below.

In Antwerp

This new documentation situation requires some more explanation on the changes in job hunting strategies and the experience of temping and unemployment, as well as a closer look at some deviant strategies or trajectories that imply following courses and training.

Job hunting strategies

Friends remain a very important source of information for jobs in the formal sector. Many migrants find jobs through networks: someone who is working knows about a vacancy in this enterprise, and tells his friends about it. One example is someone who was offered a job in a slaughterhouse, but did not have the car needed to go there; he therefore informed another friend who went and took it. An exceptional illustration of this process is one particular industrial cleaning company in Antwerp, an enterprise that also sponsors the shirts of the Senegalese football club. Because of a Senegalese manager higher up in the hierarchy, up to six respondents have been able to work there at some point of their career. As one explains:

> My brother was working in industrial cleaning where they needed somebody, so I went there and worked for 3.5 years, until June 2004. Many Senegalese were working there, no Belgians; only immigrants. But they like Senegalese; they always ask if we know somebody to take a place, because they know we do well.
> (Idrissa, in Antwerp since 1993, regular status, unemployed)

The kind of friends therefore make a difference: Senegalese or 'local' friends provide different ways of access as seen in the informal strategies. A local wife or girlfriend can make a considerable difference.

Temping agencies are the second main channel through which jobs are found in Antwerp; the official Flemish employment agency is another central source of information and support; written sources are rarely used (Geets et al. 2006). Many people register in all agencies and go around every week to ask for a job in order to show their motivation to work. Two factors seem to help facilitate the process: speaking the Dutch language is a condition, and in addition, a car seems to be a prerequisite. Jobs are often located in industrial zones that are difficult to reach by public transport, particularly for work in shifts or at irregular times – someone without a car therefore misses out on jobs.

> I was lucky; I found jobs in interim very easily. For some people it seems to be more difficult. It is very important that you are able to speak the language, and also to have a car. Because sometimes you need to work outside the city if you cannot find something here. I took a language course but no job training. They are just the normal requisites, like for Belgian people.
> (Ibra, in Antwerp since 2002, regular status, temping)

In Antwerp, the Dutch language is often mentioned as problematic when looking for jobs. Many picked up some words or studied a little bit before regularisation (Geets et al. 2006), but most of the respondents are ready to admit that they don't speak Dutch well, even after several years and some courses. Then why do they not speak it, while Spanish Senegalese very quickly speak the local language? Next to the fact that Dutch and Spanish stem from different linguistic groups, with Spanish closer to French, and Dutch being rated as more difficult, one respondent explains that you will always find people in Antwerp who speak English or French, resulting in a lack of practice. In addition, the city of Antwerp organises language classes, but has had long waiting lists in recent years. Therefore, when applying for a job, language is problematic, and people are told to go and look for a course prior to starting a job. However, from the side of the migrants there are some doubts:

> Yes, they always tell me, because, you know, in the temping agency where I was, the woman, the girl, she is very difficult, she always tells me that I have problems with my Dutch, and she is partly right. Because if I talked well, very well Dutch, maybe I would not have so many problems to enter the labour market. But the work that they give me, this requires no Dutch... because surely Dutch, we, we cannot understand it like they want it. And they can always get you on this, they get you easily. Many agencies do what they refuse to say: they privilege the Flemish, the Dutch, the Flemish I mean, they give them first. (Sal, in Antwerp since 1998, regular status, temping)

The first step: Unskilled temping

Upon receiving a work permit there is a clear tendency for people in Antwerp to leave the field of business and hawking and to look for regular jobs that give more secure employment and social security rights. For most this opening of other sectors comes as a relief. Others would have liked to use their commercial experience, skills and networks to achieve the formal status of businesspersons, market seller or otherwise, but key informants say that regularising hawking is impossible because it would require the permission of all bartenders. To be a stallholder on markets you need a special permit, which is easy to obtain if you are Belgian, but foreigners have to prove ten years in the country.

> It could be a job, if they organise it, for those who have this experience, they could continue to do it, paying taxes and everything, being self-employed. I think this could be a solution instead of chasing the people to forbid it, there should be a

licence, put taxes on it, the state would benefit and the hawkers also. I think it could be a solution. (Aliu, in Antwerp since 2001, regular status, unemployed)

As shown above, a disproportionate number of respondents in Antwerp work in one specific industrial cleaning company. In addition, some three Senegambian migrants work in horticulture, mainly tomatoes and chicory; as noted above, they are partly formally but largely informally employed. Another four do unskilled jobs in a variety of industrial sectors. This corresponds with the distribution found by Desmarez et al. (2004) where Africans in Belgium are concentrated in the temping sector, others in catering industry or agriculture and horticulture; they particularly notice the underrepresentation in construction. However, it is difficult to decide on sectors of employment, as a typical trajectory could be as follows:

Sometimes I still work in the cleaning, some weeks or days to replace someone else. With a drivers licence I could start again tomorrow. So after, I work with temping jobs. I found a job, washing dishes, in a company canteen. I did many things... let's see... I worked as a worker in factories, I washed dishes, some time picking apples or being handyman... it was not easy; there were long periods without work. (Bakeba, in Antwerp since 1993, regular status, unemployed)

When looking at levels of education or training prior to migration, there is little or no difference: the people who have some university education can be found in selling, industries, construction, and shops; the less-educated are found in the same sectors.

On the level of wages and earnings, it is clear that respondents are overwhelmingly in low paid positions; this comes as no surprise, given that they are in sectors that are not attractive to locals because of the nature of the job combined with low salaries (Pajares 2005). Even in cases where hourly wage may be acceptable, employment is almost by definition unstable and insecure, resulting in volatile monthly earnings. Though migrants have many more good months than bad months, it is the case for many that their annual earnings approach the poverty threshold. Salary rises are rare, even after increasing experience, promotion is almost impossible for people hired exclusively on temporary contracts.

Several respondents mention examples of racism in the work environment, both from employers and colleagues: they are the first to be blamed when something went wrong or if something was stolen, they are confronted with negative remarks. A person managing to achieve a higher position says this:

> For racism, you need to struggle two or three times more than a Belgian person, you need to prove a lot more, but it is possible to do it and to have something. For instance white people do not want me to have this job or this position where I can tell them something. When I am in the central building, the centre of our enterprise, sometimes the people at the reception tell me that for deliveries, it is the other side... They cannot imagine that I work with them. Or in the floor of the managers, there are people who explain me that I am mistaken, that the workers cannot enter, but me I enter the code and I go to do my work, simply. You have to forget and continue, otherwise it has no sense. Flanders did not know many Africans before, so there still is work to do for us. There are prejudices, as if all of us have lived next to lions and elephants, or as if we cannot drive a car. (Lamine, in Antwerp since 1999, regular status, fixed position).

Thinking ahead: Longer-term employment
After spending a while wandering around in the temping segment of the labour market, most respondents realise that it is better to have a profession, with a diploma, in order to find better work.

> It is the same in every country, if you have no profession you are left with the lowest and hardest and worst paid jobs, but in Belgium even more important than in Senegal (Doudou, in Antwerp since 2002, regular status, temping).

Some have the opportunity to get 'on the job training' and to receive certificates of experience in building or forklift driving; others can move on to become supervisors in their teams. Belgium offers systems of subsidised contracts, where the cost of further training is compensated for the employer by six months contributions to the salary. Others invest in extra qualifications: a driving licence is most often mentioned. Although it is almost a precondition for employment, the time and money needed to pass the exam are often too much for respondents. One respondent, temporarily working in a transport company as a truck driver, had a drivers' licence from Senegal and had it converted here, helped by his Belgian wife. Five people have secured themselves longer-term contracts (more than one year), often because they have obtained a relative degree of specialisation in their field. One has been working at the reception of a hotel for 25 years, almost immediately after the moment he got papers through marriage; two others are working, one as a welder and the other as a skilled insulation worker, a third has made it to supervisor in the industrial cleaning company mentioned above.

In addition, a couple of people have made strong investments in education and pursued a professional career. One respondent is a shop owner and two others have high-skilled jobs as the branch manager of an industrial cleaning company and as a marine engineer respectively. A fourth is training to be a plumber.[3] The commitment and determination needed for those trajectories are illustrated by the decision to take Dutch classes as an undocumented migrant, and to prioritise them after legal possibilities to work, often combining lower-level work with studies. It requires a continuing belief in the sense and usefulness of long-term investments in the final goal, and not getting tempted by the relative comfort of fixed contracts at lower levels. One has to overcome the administrative maze of recognition of diploma's or settlement as a self-employed foreigner. Their own efforts in training are no doubt the most important factor for their success, but a number of factors in the context need to be right as well. Two people had Belgian wives supporting them and helping them to find the way to and around institutions. Another one inserted himself in a subsidised scheme of employment and courses, that also provided him with the links to institutions and, in the end, an organisation that gave him a loan for his shop. Strategic choices for job qualifications that are in demand are crucial to be reasonably able to expect that the hardship and sacrifices will pay off later. Finally, most of these respondents were not held back by a family waiting for remittances. They could afford not to send money home for some time, which left space to invest in training hoping for returns later.

A former mathematics student, Aziz spent eight years living as a hawker; however, at the moment of getting papers he had to make a choice, motivated as follows:

> At that moment I said look, I will do something, I understood, I was a bit realistic because I understood if I want to work according to my level in French, it will not work, because here, to learn Dutch at university level, to have a good job, I see that even the Flemish sometimes have problems. So one has to be realistic, I have a wife, I have a child, one has to be realistic, you have to do something. (Aziz, in Antwerp since 1994, regular status, shopkeeper)

Seeing that continuing his studies was not an option, he decided to invest in other kinds of training. He went for a one-year programme of the municipality combining language, social orientation and cleaning jobs, afterwards using these connections with the institutions to find information about an organisation that gives loans. He wrote a project for a grocery shop and was accepted, launching the enterprise about two months after. Given the limited size of the community in Antwerp, he targets a wider audience (as many ethnic entrepreneurs do) (Lambrecht et al. 2002):

> If you have a small business, like me, there are some Senegalese who come here but not many, and there is many Nigerians who buy here as well, and the Belgians, but with the Senegalese only it is not going to work. It is an African shop, a bit diverse, Senegalese food but also with fofou and other things that we don't eat, but with the Senegalese only I will not see anyone during three days. Also water and cigarettes for the Belgians, there is something for everyone really. (Aziz, in Antwerp since 1994, regular status, shopkeeper)

Unemployment

Temping goes hand in hand with shorter or longer periods of unemployment between jobs. Out of the seven respondents in temping jobs, three were unemployed at the time of the interview. In one case, a divorce interrupted a training job, and the person was unemployed for some months while reorganising his life and finding a job. Another stopped working in a recycling shop because the heavy physical work was difficult to combine with his age; he is unemployed because it is difficult to find a job when over fifty. Another one seems not too motivated to find something and makes a living from hawking. Respondents who had experienced this phase previously mention how difficult it is:

> I was then temping for a couple of months, but it was very difficult. One week they take you for three days, then you wait, then you work again maybe for six or seven days, then you wait again, and every time is another job, and other people, and you never know beforehand, and is not sure and not stable. (Bayfal, in Antwerp since 1998, regular status, temping)

In a chapter on the economic impact of migration, a recent OECD report about Belgium states that 'the foreign-born population is on average contributing far less to economic activity. Although employment rates have been increasing, foreigners have a low rate of labour force participation, higher unemployment rates, lower educational attainment and may face discrimination' (OECD 2005: 124). For the specific population I am discussing here, insufficient education and command of language as well as discrimination are the main reasons.

If one has worked long enough before, he is entitled to unemployment benefits; if not, most can rely on the subsistence income. This leads to the launch of another reason for unemployment, which is one of comfort: combining benefits or welfare with some hawking is considered sufficient income for some respondents.

> Many people who come here to Belgium do not really want to work. If they have papers, they are happy to receive the social benefits and go selling a bit on the side. Many of them do not want to work, it is too hard, or they feel they are too highly educated to do the kind of work available. Because the jobs are always about physical strength, they take us because of our bodies, but nothing else. It is difficult to find a job where you can use your mind. If you have the papers and you can have the OCMW, people are very happy and don't look for a job anymore. They have to take some course and go to school, that is not asked too much and it is not as heavy as going to work every day. In the evenings and the weekends, they go selling and earn a bit on the side. They can even send something to their families with that. (Musa, in Antwerp since 2004, undocumented, import-export)

On the other hand, some respondents clearly make efforts to get out of periods of unemployment or dependency on subsistence income. They may have been on subsistence income for a while because of mental problems, divorce, or because they did not work enough yet to receive unemployment benefits. These people can work for a year in municipal services or hospitals, carrying out cleaning or other low-skilled jobs with a coach and extra guidance, in order to integrate again into the normal labour market.

> In 2003 I entered unemployment, they tell me that they now look for special [subsidised] statutes that are less expensive, or people with a driver's licence. I don't like unemployment, it is not my thing, me I like to work. The unemployment money does not make you progress, and afterwards it is even harder to start working again. (Bakeba, in Antwerp since 1993, regular status, unemployed)

In Barcelona

As in Antwerp, people with work permits can rely on temping agencies in order to find jobs, in addition to the networks they used before.

> It is more easy to find a job, with the papers, before it was always contacts, people I know, but when I have the papers, there is offices where you can go and ask for work, no matter where, and they don't hesitate to take you because you are legal, you know, and then it pays better as well. (Thierno, in Barcelona since 1999, regularised, construction)

However, the trajectories in terms of sectors of employment are slightly different, which will be discussed below.

Escaping agriculture

After being regularised, Bakeba continued working in agriculture; he mentions being hired in a larger field and a bigger company, where he was taught to drive the machines. This suggests people with papers are eligible for slightly more specialised jobs. Then a new world opens for him:

> Afterwards, they tell me when you have papers, you can go to a temping agency to find a job. I went there, they ask me the papers, to fill in some forms, et cetera. The next day they called me, I went there, they say: 'The job is in a village 23 kilometres away, work starts at 6 am, you need a car. If you don't have a car, no problem, we can find you something else, only that it will take some more time". But me I wanted this work, so I said yes, I have a car, certainly, but I left it at home. They asked me many questions, they tell me not to come late at work. I say it is a Renault Megane, I have a licence from Senegal. I went to the company, I see that there is no problem; I will go to live there because I don't have a car. The first weeks I slept in the station, afterwards I got to know someone with whom I can live. That work, I liked it a lot, I had never had such a job, I went inside, everyone was wearing overalls, like uniforms, and then gloves, with lights and air conditioning, it was something else, you know, I had never worked in a factory. (Thierno, in Barcelona since 1999, regularised, construction)

We have seen earlier that agriculture is definitely the initial port of entry for many undocumented Africans; and that early migrants sometimes had long-term employments in agriculture. Looking at formal employment at the time of the interview, only four respondents continue to work in the fields. This is confirmed by numbers: in 2003 18.5 per cent of Senegalese migrants were working in agriculture, in 2005 only 14.4 per cent – a substantial decline, without counting the undocumented workers (Pajares 2005). Key informants in the Barcelona province also point out how the number of people working in agriculture declines every year, because the area for cultivation diminishes. A second important motivation seems to lie in the conditions of agricultural work that may be worse than in any other sector (Solé 1998): hard physical conditions in heat and rain,[4] with chemicals and pesticides, stooping for hours or lifting heavy weights, make respondents seek to escape from agricultural work. But also the insecure nature of the jobs, with high degrees of seasonality and casualisation and almost no full-year employment, force people to seek an income in other economic sectors, in order to secure an income through all or most of the year. This sensitises them to openings in other sectors, as well as making them aware that wages are higher elsewhere. A third reason lies in the changing attitudes of the immigrants. Parts of this group have become more stable and settled and start looking for a better job, enabled by better knowledge of information channels and networks (Kaplan 1998). Hoggart and Mendoza (1999) accurately describe the resulting status of agriculture in the immigrant labour market: 'Once in Spain, however, most African workers find that agriculture is a short-stay introduction to Spanish labour markets or, occasionally, a returned-to, short-term refuge from failure to secure a job in another sector'. Or in the words of Amadou:

> Before, all of us in the field, but now many in the factories. Because the field is very hard, and people have to leave it, and the immigrants working in the fields during twenty or 25 or 30 years, you see them [shows an arched back]. The people of the factories, this does not happen to them, the work never makes you rich but it is different from the field. It is not so hard, that's why the majority of the migrants change. Not all of them can change, but the ones who can. When they have papers, of course... Before, they have to sustain, there is no other way. (Amadou, in Barcelona since 1983, regular status, plastic industry)

This is of course is bad news for the agricultural sector, already under heavy pressure of global competition, and may point to problems for its longer-term future. The sector is characterised by an old age structure, and unwillingness of children to take over; the maintenance of competitiveness through a low-wage, anti-investment strategy (in which the low-paid migrant workers fit) will probably not bring long-term benefits for Spanish agriculture (Hoggart & Mendoza 1999). If migrants soon follow the labour preferences of the locals, they will not save the sector either.

The first step: Unskilled temping
Via temping agencies, friends or previous employers, some respondents succeed in shifting from agriculture into other economic sectors, moving into the manufacturing, construction and services sector. Most of the time they work on short-time contracts, changing sectors, moving around, working in shifts, often paid partly informally, as Thierno demonstrates resuming three years of formal work experience:

> I worked in Badalona, in a workshop, where they cut cardboard. I did nine months, but always contracts of three months, eleven hours per day. I left it, because I had to wake up very early to get there, so I arrived late sometimes. Afterwards I found a job in Mataro, in a company that makes glass, lamps, vases, plates in the shape of fruits, ashtrays, et cetera. I did four months, less paid than before, but I did only eight hours, sometimes in the morning, then the night, or after midnight. And I moved here to be close to work. Then three months in a supermarket, to replace someone who was ill. Another work was with a carpenter, without a contract, just in his home, he paid well. But in the end he exploits us, in the beginning he paid well, he wanted us to stay, but afterwards, sometimes we have to wait until the fifteenth of the month before he pays you. I worked in the glass company in Ocata, I started doing all kinds of different shifts with the fork lift, till I got a fixed contract for the night shift. [...]. Then a while in construction, but there is lot of abuse there. Therefore, I left the company and went to Fuertaventura on the Canary Islands, where I worked for construction; and afterwards maintenance in hotels. (Thierno, in Barcelona since 1999, regular status, construction)

This quote reveals why a detailed analysis of temping periods is almost impossible: respondents can make lists of subsequent locations and employers, but they are likely to forget some, and asking for labour conditions and incomes in all different periods is impossible. In her study of different migrant groups, Anguiano Téllez (2001) confirms that African migrants are found mostly in agriculture and construction, because of their demographic characteristics, limited networks and lack of experience. Nonetheless, there seems to be a limited mobility towards commerce, services and hotels (Colectivo IOE 2000; Pajares 2005; Tellegen 2000). However, when asking for a line or preferences throughout these periods, a common answer is:

> What I like more? But here, you cannot do a job that you like, that you choose. You will do the work that exists, you have no di-

ploma or nothing, so, you go where they ask you. What I like most is where I earn most... (Demba, in Barcelona since 2000, regular status, hawking)

Some respondents have come to temping after relatively long periods of employment with a single company before: two were working more than ten years in the textile sector, others in agriculture. However, as these sectors are in crisis, they push out workers, and it is difficult to find new work in same sector; respondents therefore shift to temping in hotel and gardening sectors.

When entering the formal labour market, proficiency in the local language becomes a selection criterion (Mendoza 1997), a rather problematic issue in Antwerp. In Barcelona, most people learn Spanish informally in a very short time, with friends and colleagues, in bars or on the street. As it is relatively close to French, it does not seem to create a significant challenge, and even after a couple of months people get by; some people even studied Spanish back in Senegal. Catalan is not often mentioned: on the work floor, the international migrants often work with former internal Spanish migrants who do not speak Catalan either, but it does facilitate access to higher-skilled jobs in administration as well as more contacts in society (Pérez 1995). There is however an impressive offer for language courses for adults in the city (Kaplan 1998), which some people use.

Just like Thierno, the most common profile of Senegambian migrants in Barcelona is one of rather low-skilled workers; temping agencies may ask for a written CV or a driver's licence; both can be problematic and limits employment possibilities. As a result, most do only unskilled work, and changes come down to shifting between low-skilled jobs, not making much progress, 'a regular pattern of unskilled worker job mobility' (Mendoza 1997). However, with better knowledge of the language, skills and experience, it seems like some are able to increase the time of employment moving from weeks to months to half years of temporary contracts. Nevertheless, in some cases, job changes are motivated by the search for better wages, particularly for those who are specialised, as we will see below.

More than education, an element which seems crucial for African employment is their inclination to accepting challenging conditions for themselves and their families (Trinidad García 2003). This includes long commuting times, staying at work for the week or working at night, no social benefits, temporary contracts, job instability, and dangerous working conditions. They are often prepared to move residence in search for work, a big comparative advantage.

In addition, respondents in this study reported on a wide array of mechanisms of exploitation and earnings abuse from employers, often based on the belief that migrants do not know their rights or are not in a position to complain somewhere. Also at the level of workplace safety and conditions, there are many abuses and accidents (Jounin 2004). The sectors of agriculture, transport and construction lead to most complaints (Pajares 2005); sectors like temping seem to be better organised, explaining why less complaints were registered in Antwerp. Pajares also shows that migrants revendicate and complain a lot less than their presence in the labour force would justify, often because they depend on the employer to get regularisation or a work permit. Abuse is clearly less than in the informal market; in addition, workers feel more confident to leave jobs because they do not get fair treatment or pay. Common wages at this stage are about 1,000 euro when working the whole month; many people try to work extra hours or weekends in order to get some extra income.

> I work for the train company, with the people who put the rails; it is a very hard work and the money is not worth the effort. They pay 965 euro, this is exploitation; that is why I did not continue. Sometimes you are in other regions, like the south, and the transport is not paid, and if you need to start on Monday morning, you have to travel on Sunday to be in time. I could work there my whole life, but I did not want, there is easier work to gain the same. (Bachirou, in Barcelona since 2000, regular status, temping)

Longer-term employment
Some people have managed to find longer-term employments, often because of specific professional skills they may have had before arriving. Salif for instance, a trained welder, was hired in Spain and was offered the opportunity to study and to get a Spanish diploma; he has been with the same company more than ten years. Pape is a shopkeeper in an African tourist shop; his knowledge of English and French, next to some computer skills, convinced the owners to hire him, and he has been in the same place for three and a half years. A rare exception is Omar, who arrived back in the 1980s and has worked more than five years in a plastics company, doing unskilled work during night shifts.

Sometimes, respondents have developed an active strategy of investing in training, inspired by knowledge of the importance attached to having a profession or specialisation in western labour markets; they were not among the higher educated in their country of origin, contrary to what Mendoza (1998) found. As in Antwerp, this requires a good insight into the functioning of the labour market, or help of a local friend to make one see the importance of training; a certain degree of freedom from the demands of the family back home in order to postpone immediate salaries for the sake of better and more regular employment later. One person trained as a steeplejack, another invested time after work in obtaining a drivers licence for large trucks and is currently an international trucker. None of these strategies guarantees a path of roses: the trucker was fired because he protested against exploitation, and is temping again for the moment. But this group shows a fragmented picture of job mobility for skilled workers, where job turnover is not necessarily the result of the end of a contract, but may arise from the search for better personal prospects in terms of stability or better wages (Pajares 2005).

One respondent with a university background started temping in commercial jobs upon arrival; when he became a member of the labour union, he was asked to be part of the team promoting social elections amongst migrant workers. He is a labour advisor in the labour union nowadays. Probably because of the importance of Senegambian migration in the province of Barcelona, as well as the progressive policies of the city, there is a rather large group of Senegambian people working in the public sector administration, as cultural mediators in hospitals and municipal services, in international development, labour union, etc. The equivalent in Belgium would probably be Turkish and Moroccans in social services.

Finally, four respondents have entered the status of self-employed shopkeeper; they tend to be among the people that had the longest residence in Spain, suggesting that a considerable sum of savings is necessary for the investment, which is often acquired in collaboration with others. A common characteristic is that being a shopkeeper requires man and wife working as a couple, with one being in the shop and the other doing purchasing, financial administration and tax forms.

In terms of gathering the money necessary for investment, there are several ways, one more creative than the other: Samba worked legally in agriculture for some years, than started to do some temping and finally met an Englishman who changed his life...

> He had a phone shop, well, in fact, he had four, but he wanted to leave the business. I worked with him free during one year, in order to take it over – I did not have enough money to buy it. In the evenings and weekends, I would do other small jobs, like in agriculture, to survive. (Samba, in Barcelona since 1997, regular status, communication centre owner)

He was able to run the business with some commercial experience in Gambia, and with support from a friend doing similar business; at present, he has two people working for him for the internet and phone services, as well as transfers of money abroad. Seck came to Spain in 1982 and worked for many years in agriculture, prior to moving on to temping in industries, and finally establishing himself in 1997 as a shopkeeper. It started with going to Andorra, buying cigarettes and suitcases on request, and selling them to customers. He limited the investment costs of the real shop by locating it inside a local butchery, with which he shared the space, rent and customers. He had just a calculator, a bag with spare coins and a table to present a limited array of products: beauty products, rice and tropical fruits. He and his four friends continued to work in industries and took turns for presence in the shop. Afterwards he and one companion invested in an appropriate location for his widening range of products. Serigne also had a standard trajectory, working in agriculture before papers, afterwards working in bars and temping until he grew tired of temping. He started to think about an arts and crafts shop, combined with a communication centre, and obtained a loan from the bank; a Catalan friend from the NGO-sector in which he was an active member served as guarantor.

In terms of the target audience, Serigne clearly aims at a Spanish and tourist public with his arts shop, an African street party to launch the opening, and a diversity of products coming from Senegal and also Mexico and India. When it turned out that this conflicted with the Africans customers of the communication centre who ring home, and stay in the shop hanging around to chat, the communication centre was moved to a different location. As an NGO activist, he combines talks and conferences with promotion for his shop.

> My strategy for the shop: there is a lot of competition, it is impossible to beat the Chinese in prices for clothes, so I try to be just a little bit different or bring new things, things that are more creative or special and unique. I also try to give a lot of explanations about African culture and try to function as a multicultural meeting place, with a gallery downstairs. That space also I can use it for Senegalese hairdresser, also percussion band. And I am going to talk in schools and for organisations, and always ask money for these things. (Serigne, in Barcelona since 1999, regular status, shop owner)

However, the grocery shops, hairdressers and the communication centres are clear examples of services explicitly aimed mainly at members of the diaspora, showing that the very existence of a significant community creates jobs as the segmented labour market theories suggest. This is shown by the special tariffs for calls to Senegal, Gambia, Mali and Mauritania, or by the offer of fruit and vegetables, different grains and cereals, herbs, skin and haircare products from 'home'. These things become more important as one is further away from home for longer periods of time (Martínez Veiga 2000). Some restaurants and bars in the city centre offer local dishes trying to be authentic for their own customers, but accessible enough to attract strangers as well.

Senegambian migrants in Barcelona also face periods of unemployment; the employment rate for Senegalese is estimated at about 64 per cent (Kaplan 1998). However, unemployment benefits are limited in time and directly linked to the number of months worked before, and in the near absence of a subsistence income, there is less time to stay without job; an additional pressure comes from the need to show employment in order to renew the temporary permissions. Some people were interviewed at exactly one of these in-between periods: one respondent just quit after his colleague died in an industrial accident, after working four years in the same construction company. His job implied often being away for the whole week, doing rather dangerous work. Another respondent, Boubacar, has had papers since 1982, but has been suffering from personal and family problems and faces long periods of unemployment in between casual jobs. However, long-term unemployment is seldomly mentioned. Contrary to Belgium, the current employment rates of migrant in Spain are even higher than those of the native-born population (OECD 2006).

7.2 Some remarks about the formal labour market

Undocumented migrants had rather divergent careers in Antwerp and Barcelona; after being regularised, their tracks seem to converge in the lower-skilled segments of the temporary labour market. They often try to obtain a higher income and more security by specialisation or additional training.

Informal activities on the side

All respondents, faithful to their common business heritage, continue to keep an eye open for an opportunity to buy or sell. People who used to hawk sometimes continue to sell in periods where they cannot find a job, others because they like it; sometimes to earn a little extra to make ends meet or because the profit is high given their established web of clients. In addition, everyone travelling to or from Senegal or Paris brings over some goods to sell with a small profit margin; others look for opportunities to be intermediaries in the transactions of others buying cars, filling containers or looking for false papers.

The sheer size of the local immigrant community provides for informal provision of internal services, particularly for parties and social events inside the community. Numerous respondents earn an occasional extra euro by acting as a hairdresser, photographer, cook, DJ, religious leader or tailor; some women sell home-cooked traditional dishes or have a small informal shop with Senegalese spices, sweets and cloth at home. Ibrahima is sewing African clothes after work and in the weekends, on command; living from this is difficult if not impossible:

> I also have a sewing machine, very old. And as I was not working much in the beginning, the people know that I sew. I have done this for many years. I would like to live from it, but here, the African people who sew, they don't have money. Because the African migrants they don't pay, they say at the end of the month, when the husband has his salary. So here I am, one owes me 30 euro, another twenty, but I cannot pay my house. I only do it in the end of the week, and when I am tired, I leave it.
> (Ibrahima, in Barcelona since 1994, regular status, horticulture)

This quote illustrates that postponing payments is frequent and informal contract enforcement is difficult, so that often considerable time is spent collecting late payments (Soenen 2003). In addition, the prices circulating internally are considerably lower than when providing for outsiders: for braiding, a hairdresser for European women earns up to 250 euro a head; in the community, prices vary with the level of friendship and can range from 15 to 30 euro or even up to 50 euro.

Many documented migrants also participate in informal activities in the host country environment, not only inside the ethnic niche, showing how there is no sharp demarcation between the formal and informal economies. The moonlighting may start as a necessity, when looking for a way to bridge periods in between seasonal work. On a modest level, possibilities arise in small extra activities such as guarding somebody's house during holidays, a low-level marihuana business, picking cones in public forests (an extreme example of precariousness). Working extra hours without contract is a common practice in agriculture, transport and construction, as shown below:

> Sometimes I would work in tomato fields, because they give you a contract for four or six hours a day, at the official rate of seven euro; but you do many more at 5.25 [euro] per hour. I also tried chicory for two days, but it was far too dirty and I did not like it, I quit. But sometimes I go to collect pears in the weekends or during my holidays, the boss pays me 7.50 [euro] per hour and he is

very good with me. It is without contract. (Malang, in Belgium since 1996, regular status, industry)

For Modou, his side activity has actually become his main source of income. Officially unemployed, and on the subsistence income, he has a contract for a limited number of hours in a cloth recycling enterprise, just enough to be able to keep the benefit – but in reality he is working more than fulltime at peak times when containers need to be filled. This combination offers him a salary of about 1,600 euro per month or more, which he invests in import-export. It is a risky enterprise for everyone, but most of all for people in the procedure of asylum, as it is forbidden. They often follow courses during their waiting period or engage in voluntary work to kill the time. Working partly undeclared creates other problems in the longer run, like not building unemployment or pension rights, but also other problems:

> Thierno calls me, he has moved to the Canary Islands. The job he had in Barcelona with the forklift was partly in black; as a result, he did not earn enough officially to be able to take a mortgage for a house. His company did not want to confirm that he works many hours in black and has a higher income, let alone increase his contract. He left this job, a dead-end street, because he is thinking about bringing his family over. (fieldnotes Barcelona)

The role of education

Armed with papers, migrants could in theory benefit more from their previous education or experience. For people with specific skills, problems of transferral pose themselves: an archivist in Senegal is dealing with paper, while in Antwerp many software skills are required; a car mechanic in Gambia solves problems that an average Spanish garage owner cannot even imagine. The same applies to a bookbinder, a soap maker and a sofa builder. For highly educated people, the recognition of diplomas is very difficult and can be expensive. Applying what one studied earlier is difficult, for a variety of reasons: the level of Dutch or Spanish necessary to pursue a professional career in nursery care, mathematics or as a physical trainer is too high; during the years of surviving as an undocumented migrant, a person may have lost his knowledge. The necessary networks may be lacking, as in the case of a sociologist/journalist who finds it difficult to access something more intellectual after all those years. This results in a wide diversity of jobs, mostly not corresponding to their educational level, leading a trained bookkeeper to say:

> A link between the level of studies in our country and the chances here? There is no link. You can have a PhD in Africa, but here, you should not dream, you get nowhere close. That is on the academic level; but also in the more technical field, for instance a car mechanic. He can do it informally, but it is sure that for a job they will ask him to do training in the VDAB. It is true that there is not always correspondence between the experiences. But in general it is difficult to find a link, mostly you are forced to do something else. (Aliu, in Antwerp since 2001, regular status, unemployed)

Another option would be to actively direct their careers and invest in training to increase their employment chances. In the beginning, most interviewees showed no interest in pursuing an education programme, as they feel it was contrary to the quest for immediate money that made them migrate. They see studying as a loss of time, particularly because they do not see their future here. Bakeba formulates it this way:

> I did not come to discover everything, understand everything, and to learn a language, only to earn enough money to invest afterwards in my country. (Bakeba, in Antwerp since 1993, regular status, unemployed)

Others do not believe it will actually result in better jobs:

> Training? Yes, there is training that one can do in Belgium... a small training in bricklaying, or something else for three months... but I don't see many results. Me personally I did not do it. Why do a ten-month training and then be a dishwasher in a restaurant? It is better to start working immediately. I did this and it worked well. Really, I am fine now, really well. (Fallou, in Belgium since 2001, undocumented, temping)

A number of respondents did chose to invest in training, courses and language learning, and although it is not an easy formula for quick success, they are generally better off in the long run. Many respondents have made the same analysis and started some form of education, but did not finish. This is due to a variation of reasons, mostly linked to the necessary means of time and energy, and the hard trade off between short- and long-term benefits (Geets et al. 2006). Some do not have the money to pay for training, although in many cases the fees are very limited. The difference between Spain and Belgium is that migrants in Belgium can often rely on unemployment benefits or subsistence income when taking a course, while Spanish migrants have no economic support. However, in either case, they need savings or part-time jobs to keep life going for the time of the course. With changing temping jobs and a variety of shift hours it tends to be complicated to show up for every class; many just let go. For others, the family pressure to send money holds them back: when entering the formal labour market they want to find a job as soon as possible, because the family back home has been waiting sometimes for years. They consider it not the right time to learn the language thoroughly or to invest in training. The only way out is to try and provide family members at home with a productive activity at home, like a car to run a taxi company, which can free the migrant from sending remittances for a while.

> I don't know, I think it is a problem of option, you have to choose. Some of us have the time to tighten their belts, not to engage immediately in hard work, but to follow rather a training, like me. Me I see, sometimes, there is problems [in Senegal], they call me, to inform me about problems, and me I cannot do anything for the moment, that hurts me a lot, but it is a choice, so I have to take it with the consequences. That is my case. But the family only knows the problems that they themselves have, not the problems that you encounter here. I think it is to the benefit of everyone: me, my family, Belgium, everyone, but it is hard. (François, in Antwerp since 2003, regular status, in training)

Being self-employed

The higher incidence of self-employed respondents in Barcelona than in Antwerp (four versus one) is a reflection of a number of factors, some of which are internal to the characteristics of the migration flow. Barcelona harbours a far bigger Senegambian community, which was also one of the first African groups to settle, which leaves them the space to start up their niche shops. In addition, based on the traditional business background, a more diversified set of opportunities also exist, such as bars, restaurants, African art shops, call centres and butchers. In Antwerp, a Senegalese nightclub, bar and grocery shop have closed over time. However, numerous Nigerian and Ghanaian communication centres, hairdressers, bars, video shops and grocery shops exist, suggesting that the absence of Senegalese entrepreneurs on the scene is due to their late regularisation. In addition, the community may not be large or settled enough to create a large employment market (Epstein 2000).

Another element is linked to the administrative and legal context of the host country, as suggested by the 'mixed embeddedness' notion developed by Kloosterman (1999). In Belgium, a basic requirement is of finishing secondary education (till age eighteen) or, alternatively, a management course taken in Belgium. Obtaining the necessary information and following the complex institutional procedure is often very complicated (Lambrecht, Verhoeven & Martens 2002; OCIV 2002; Wauters & Lambrecht 2006). Afterwards, the very strict implementation of different laws and checks from different inspection services are a constant source of worry as are the many different taxes one has to pay (Tellegen 2000). It is a written Antwerp policy to control systematically shops in areas with high concentrations of small migrant entrepreneurs, to limit the excesses of fierce competition (Planningscel Antwerpen 2004). Often problems arise with bookkeeping and contracts with banks, because of lack of information and not being familiar with the western system. The administrative demands for self-employed status are lower in Spain, resulting in people with a modest educational background opening shops; although the employment of self-employed workers could be facilitated (Dijkstra 2000), respondents complain less about checks, taxes and rules than in Belgium. It is estimated that about 3 per cent of the Senegambian population in Catalonia is registered as self-employed (Tellegen 2000). However, they are often involved in the lower end of the opportunity structure and have low profits because of the increasing competition.

The role of redistribution

Functioning in the labour market implies contributions to the social security system, and therefore implies mechanisms of social protection. Once the migrant has a residence permit and work permit, he or she is eligible for the services of most support institutions. This often includes the possibility to follow subsidised language courses, professional training, help when setting up a business, right to loans, etc. In addition, Belgium has the right to a subsistence income, for nationals and foreigners. In addition, working conditions are better protected in Belgium than in Spain, and salaries tend to be higher.

> I still prefer Belgium because once you have papers and a job life is more stable and of a higher standard, Spain is more like Africa. Here in Belgium, social protection is better, things are better organised, clearer, quicker, education is better, et cetera. (Tapha, in Antwerp since 2003, undocumented, unemployed)

In Belgium, quite a few respondents have gone through a stage of benefits dependency prior to securing a better income; a couple of respondents seem to abuse the temporary safety net for longer periods, settling for the subsistence income while combining this with moonlighting and/or hawking (as indeed some Belgians do). In Spain, unemployment benefits are linked to the number of months worked, and are limited in time.

> Belgium has a lot of facilities, like OCMW and social housing and things like that. This is very good, but it has two sides: some immigrants, like Belgians, take advantage of it and do not work anymore, because they can rely on the state. They want to take things easy, they don't really want to learn a language, it is difficult, I admit, but they don't want to work, because there is help. It may be an easy life, but they do not see that it leads to marginalisation, that is not where you will find respect, and that also their children are likely to do not so good in school... . (Lamine, in Antwerp since 1999, regular status, harbour)

Since 2004, Belgium has an obligatory integration trajectory, building on elements that existed earlier, based on voluntary participation: a combination of social orientation courses, language and work preparation. This came too late for most respondents, but the people on subsistence income also have to follow a similar trajectory. Those people claim it is useful and crucial in making the contacts.

> Me I receive OCMW, but honestly, I would have preferred not to receive it, but I am forced, because now I am doing the course. So I am in a hurry to find a job and go working. Me too I want to contribute, like everybody else, to pay taxes and everything. Only that with the taxes, now they pay me. It is a matter of conscience, my conscience tells me that I receive money form the OCMW, from the state, and what I want to do first, that is first, to know all the laws and to respect them, and to carry them inside myself. But the OCMW, they pay you exactly for the condition of need, and to allow people to organise themselves to get out. You see. Because what we receive, it does not allow you to have something extra, it is the three B's : bread, bed and [xxx]. Pfff. You will not die form hunger, but you cannot go to a bar often. Restaurant, cinema, that is excluded. [...]. But it is however good that is exists. Really, I really say thank you, thank you. And I am grateful. (François, in Antwerp since 2003, regular status, in training)

7.3 Other mobility strategies

Having a residence and work permit can open many doors; at the same time, an unattended consequence is that living costs increase, thereby taking migrants further away from their original goal of accumulating capital in order to go back home. In the next section, we will see how people both use the new opportunities and try to overcome the new difficulties. As we saw before, changing jobs and sectors is the first strategy; studying or become self-employed may be options for others; here I will look only at behaviour outside the pure labour market.

Continuing migration

Belgium or Spain may not be final destinations or places of fixed residence. I discussed above the seasonal migratory system in Spanish agriculture, and the mobility of hawkers following the tourist season. Sometimes inspired by adventure, the motivations to leave are most often the search for better work, a better life; particularly if things are not going well: 'they adapt to the economic and political conditions of the country of origin, juggle with chances for work and legislation' (Marfaing 2003b).

> I would like, in about a year, if things continue like this, I will change countries. I would like to go to a better place, like England or the US or Australia, things like that. It is better. I have an Australian friend, and she told me it is better, she explained me and I understood that it is better. It is not easy to enter, but if you try, if you are lucky, you go, otherwise, you try another country. What else can we do? We try till the day something works out. There are people in Senegal who would like to have my life here, and me I would like the position of someone in the UK. That is life, you know? I think that France and the UK are more developed than Spain; the Africans working there have better chances than the people here. (Pape, in Barcelona since 2000, regular status, shopkeeper)

Sometimes the mobility is not so much a well-planned project as a case of pure desperation, or based on vague rumours. Because of the risks involved, they tend to be single males (Mendoza 1997). One respondent was living and working in Germany for some years as a night receptionist. When he broke up with his girlfriend, he left his job and went back to France, just to continue travelling to England and finally finding himself in Spain.

> I remember it well, it was the World Cup of 1996. I stayed three or four months and I took my luggage direction UK, for more adventure. I loved the country, the ways of the people, I did two or three years there, I thought I would stay there (...) but in 1999 I went back to France for some months of holiday; I also went to visit Denmark, but that was just to visit friends and I did not like it enough to stay. And then I came to Spain... why... well, I saw a programme about Barcelona and decided to come to see it. Also they say that life is less expensive in Spain, you earn less but you spend less as well. I wanted to try my luck. (Bachirou, in Barcelona since 2000, regular status, temping)

This brings us back to the fraud with papers; the ones who move to other countries are often the ones who can now rent out their papers to others. They themselves, in turn, need a network of fellow countrymen to be able to travel with a fake visa, and arriving in the new destination country they change legal status again: they will need to work illegally, as the work permit is not transferable (Schuster 2005).

> I prefer to stay here, even if I have the residence permit in Portugal, but as there is no more work in Portugal, I prefer to come here. The last two years, or three, it has become more difficult. If the Portuguese themselves leave their country to find work elsewhere, and you are not even Portuguese, what are you expecting there? So in 2001 I left to come here, and other friends have left for Germany, and the UK, everywhere. (Bakeba, in Antwerp since 1993, regular status, unemployed)

The top dream countries tend to be the UK or the US, mostly because they heard the labour market is more flexible there, and because of the perceived greater toleration for black people. Fall notices that the Senegalese population in the US has a slightly older profile, probably because it tends to be a second step in the migration project, after years of investment in education and financial accumulation (Fall 2002).

The continuing mobility shows a variety of migratory movements: single and unidirectional, but also continuous, circular or return, transit and shuttle migration, sometimes seasonal migration, as Schuster found in her study in Italy (2005). This nuances the idea of transnationalism as moving between only two nation-states, origin and settlement and invites to move away from bipolar approaches. Some of these people can be called 'sojourners', moving from one country to another; between locals and cosmopolitans, some of them feel at home nowhere and everywhere (Sinatti 2006).

Bringing another family member to Europe

The leitmotiv in the story of Senegambian migration is the responsibility towards the extended family back home, a heavy burden for an individual; when he sees a possibility, he may try to get some help to support the family (Kaplan 1998). That would allow a degree of division of jobs, with someone concentrating on regular incomes while the other can invest in education or a shop. Several respondents thus invest in the travelling costs of a family member, or were themselves brought over by a predecessor. This chain migration often this results in families spread all over Europe: sisters, uncles, cousins and aunts in Italy, France, Spain and the US.

> Now that my brother is also here, he can help me with the house and the food, if I do not work two weeks or three weeks, if my money is finished, my brother can help the family, there is no problem. (Ablaye, in Barcelona since 1998, regular status, temping)

Even a migrant who would not consider bringing over someone else, because of the hardship and misery awaiting an undocumented new arrival, is likely to experience pressure from young male family members in the home country:

> I never wanted my brother to join me; life is too hard here, I don't want anyone I love to have to suffer like this. I rather wanted to invest in something that created work in Senegal for my brother, and that would allow him to make a living for himself and all our family. But after so many years of pushing I have now given up resistance and I am ready to pay the ticket: if they believe that my brother can do more for them here, can work harder and achieve more than me, we will see. (Thierno, in Barcelona since 1999, regularised, construction)

Housing investment

Chavez illustrated how types of living arrangements may be necessary, or desirable, over the course of an individual's life, as a resource which assists them in their struggle to live and work (Chavez 1990). The crowded conditions at the early start may be tolerated for a while, especially by recent arrivals; however, adjustments to this situation must be viewed as part of a process of migration and settlement (Burgers & Engbersen 1999). Often people will try to move to less crowded apartments, where everyone may have his own room (Kaplan 1998).

> It is difficult to find a room, because they judge on your origin. Because often I bought the newspaper, I select twenty or 30 phone numbers, and I swear, ten or twelve say 'I am sorry sir, but the owner does not want foreigners'. Just like this; it is frustrating. Or you call, they hear you are a stranger, they say 'oh, sorry, the room is already taken'. But this kind of things happen every day for us, we are used to it. But, notwithstanding, it still hurts every day. (François, in Antwerp since 2003, regular status, in training)

A very limited number of people have found the way to social housing; they tend to be well-informed people, sometimes working at the municipality, who have easier access and better understanding of procedures. Several key people mention in Spain that housing policies in social terms are almost non-existent, which causes significant problems for migrants; in Belgium the opportunities are greater, but waiting lists are very long. The husband of Penda waited two years, and then when she was pregnant they were given priority.

What is happening in Spain over the last years, and slowly also in Belgium, is a next step: Senegambian migrants move from renting to buying houses to fit their new strategies and expectations. The longer they stay, the more migrants feel that rents are very high, while their incomes remain relatively low. They may carry the social responsibility for family members who are also migrating (Benson 1990), or they start to see that they may be able to reduce housing costs by renting out rooms to undocumented migrants, completing the circle starting with their own experiences upon arrival. Rising housing prices and the idea of sharing the costs motivates many migrants to overcome the high mortgages (migrants often present higher risks for banks, and have less guarantees) and the costly administrative procedures (finding someone to act as guarantor, or borrow even the advance).

> It is a bit difficult to buy here; before, I was watching, I go to watch and I always leave it, it was not good. But the prices are always rising, so I decided for this. I have two cousins and a nephew, they have no papers, and we can live together, when they work they can help me with the rent to pay the bank, because now they always have to move and they could not live with me. (Niasse, in Barcelona since 2000, regular status, construction)

A final reason is that Spanish migrants thinking about family reunification may find it extremely difficult to rent something on their name in a racist environment, in order to meet the conditions they may prefer to buy (Terrones Ribas 2005).

I bought a house here to bring my wife over. Because look, I have no money to go to Africa this year, the money I send it to my mother, my children, my wife, when they have problems I send them everything. I cannot keep a penny. So I said I have to buy a house to bring my wife; if I cannot go, she can come here.
(Niasse, in Barcelona since 2000, regular status, construction)

In many cases, there is rhetoric that the investment in a house is not contradictory to the idea of return; on the contrary, it is considered a saving strategy. When they are ready to go back, they can sell the apartment and use the profit to realise plans back home. As Martínez Veiga mentions (1997), this comes down to subsistence ownership quite regularly: after paying the mortgage, there is no money left to spend anything on maintenance despite the generally low housing quality.

Acquiring nationality

Long-term migrants may consider taking the nationality of their host country or new home country: in Belgium this is possible as early as after three years of legal residency (Lambert 2002), in Spain after ten years[5]. The reasons to apply for a new nationality or to refuse it can be practical or emotional: the older generation may remember colonialism more vividly and want to stay loyal to their independent state and African identity. Others may take the new nationality as a way to express their integration or gratitude towards the new home; or just to be able to travel more easily, to have rights to a pension, or to go back to Senegal for longer periods. Paradoxically enough, obtaining the new nationality can be seen as a condition to go back to country of origin (Adam et al. 2001): they are certain to keep a link in case of failure, or they are guaranteed an easy travelling back and forth in the framework of business or visiting family in two continents.

While Western and Northern European countries used to adopt rather liberal policies based on the idea of naturalisation as a means of integration, Southern European countries tended to have nationality legislation aimed at protecting the relationships with their ex-migrant communities abroad (Moreno Fuentes). However, in the face of large immigration, they generally adopted highly restrictive attitudes towards naturalisation, with the exception of citizens from former colonies. Bauböck (2006) notices that since about 2000, more and more states introduce formal examinations of language skills and knowledge of society, as seen in Denmark, France, the Netherlands and the UK. Belgium is still an exception, but is considering lengthening the required residence period.

7.4 A better life realised, but...

Most people see this phase as the right time to start or resume family life. Bringing a partner over can be very difficult due to the requirements governments impose (salary slips, housing arrangements), and some do it without the necessary documents[6]. But when they succeed, yet another challenge starts. The cost of maintaining a household in terms of food and housing costs is considerably higher again than the sharing of accommodation typical for previous stages of bachelor life. If family members come over when the migrant has not been able to organise decent conditions, it can lead to worsening financial or administrative insecurity, or even marginalisation (Diop 1996). In addition, the wives and children bring with them a whole new set of issues[7] and expectations, often related to the possible conflict between traditional and modern interpretations of family roles, leading to problems with hierarchy and frustration (Barou 1987). The children, belonging to the second generation, will grow up between two cultures (Andall 2002). These prospects sometimes inspire men to say they will never bring their wife to Europe (Marfaing 2003b). In Spain, this process started earlier than in Belgium, due to the earlier regularisations; in Belgium, people have started bringing their wives over only after the 2000 regularisation.

When an undocumented migrant obtains legal status and starts a new life, his living expenses increase considerably with every step he takes: a car, a family, another apartment. Consumption patterns and lifestyle changes over time, although they hardly match the local habits. The minimum of 200 to 500 euro no longer suffices, and has risen to 800 or 1,000 euro.[8] With salaries that are normally situated in the lower echelons of the distribution, these migrant families have to finance the same basic needs as local households, but carry in addition the responsibility for an extended family in the home country (Barou 2001).

For the ones who intended to build a life in a new country, they may at this stage have succeeded in their plan, and be satisfied. However, many still stick to a vague or specific myth of return inherent in the original migration plan, mostly formulated with a careful 'inshalah' (Kaplan 1998): 'if God wants'.

> People always want to go back, we always feel like the real life is back in Senegal, and what we are doing here is just 'between brackets', while we are preparing and planning everything we will do there. We are always hoping, but nobody returns. Maybe it is just a fantasy that allows us to continue the life we have here. Me too I am always making plans to go back, but I know nobody did and my wife does not want to... and among older

> immigrants we tend to joke about it (Malick, in Antwerp since 1989, regular status, industrial cleaning).

Although they may have secured a better life, most migrants have to keep postponing return to the home country, adapting their initial project always in the same direction: to stay just a couple of years longer. There is a logical explanation: the low wages and marginal economic status discussed above, combined with the continuing immediate needs in the home country, curtail the migrants' potential to accumulate resources for productive activities which could generate wealth and employment (Marfaing 2003b).

> So, with maybe 1,200 or 1,400 euro per month, you will never have the money that you had planned to go back to your country; that dream will not come true. But still, it is my dream and it is what we are working for, although playing on the lottery may prove more effective to reach my aim. (Malang, in Belgium since 1996, regular status, industry)

Being unable to fulfil their initial plans within short periods, most delay their return home until after the children's education is finished, after retirement, and often only to be buried.[9] With time, the choice between old and new home country becomes more painful, when the children have established their lives in Europe and one sometimes feels a stranger in Africa (Mateo Dieste 2002). The nostalgia for the Senegambian rhythm of life, atmosphere, and weather has to be traded against better educational provisions for the children, or better health care institutions when elderly. Although the dream of going back home seems important to cope with their situation (Kaplan 2001), most longer-term immigrants favour the idea of a 'commuting life', alternating longer periods of work in Europe with family time and some business in the country of origin. Although migrants have always kept in touch with home, Castles (2002) suggests that increasing numbers of immigrants orient their lives to two or more societies. The impact of this trend to transnationality on nation-state sovereignty and autonomy, as well as the process of migrant belonging, multiple identities, and multi-layered citizenship remains an open question.

Profile of migrants in Barcelona and Antwerp

As an unanticipated outcome, I found considerable differences in the Senegambian community level in both cities. In the theoretical chapter, I took community and networks as a constant dimension, assuming it would not differ between the two research settings, but that premise is now modified. It shows that the diversity and pluralism of black African migration should be taken into account (Kuagbenou 1997; Soenen 2003).

While Senegambian migrants in Barcelona represent a large variety of geographical origins and ethnicities, it looks like Antwerp only knows a specific type of migrant. Through a process of self-selection,[10] people from rural origin and non-Wolof ethnicities are channelled towards Barcelona, while the urban-based Wolof are overrepresented in Antwerp.[11]

> It is true that Belgium has more city-people than Spain or Italy. Comparing the level of life in Belgium and Italy or Spain, you need to think carefully. There in the South, people tend to live in community, they always live the African life without reservations, they eat together rice every evening, and the level of their expenses is far lower than here. Many people in a room, no internet, never go for a coffee, just go to work as much as you can and go to sleep. They do not invest anything in their lives in Europe; they just survive and send almost everything back home. Immigrants in Belgium are well dressed, have good shoes, they eat well and healthy. They want to live in the Belgian way, go out for a meal, go to the cinema sometimes... I would never like to go south because I cannot live like on the countryside. (Malick, in Antwerp since 1989, regularised, industrial cleaning)

As Malick describes, the lifestyle in the community is different in both cities (Kuagbenou 1997): Belgium is supposed to be more developed and individual, while Spain is considered a bit closer to the African rhythm and atmosphere. This is reflected in the relationship with home, and the remittances sent back. Spanish migrants are generally more driven by the desire to save as much as possible, and economise on any extra dimension of life. The traditions of tontines, reciprocity, and investment savings are rife in Spain, as more people come directly from the countryside where they have seen and lived these habits, while people in Dakar and large cities tend to be more individualistic. Due to a generally stronger feeling of community, the rural migrants in Spain more often marry in their home country, sometimes because their family opposes a white wife, and concentrate on solidarity with the home country. The city migrants generally find it easier to prioritise their own lives in Belgium, and cut down on remittances.[12] In addition, due to the different labour markets in combination with different consumption patterns, the rural migrants in Spain are able to collect more money than those in Belgium. The remittances are also worth more in the countryside, where daily expenses as well as land prices are low compared to the capital.

7.5 Conclusion: Better off in Antwerp

Overviewing the results, the main theories are confirmed: Senegambian migrants are employed in declining industrial sectors like textiles, in family-based as well as industrial agriculture, in the service sector, and they occupy flexible jobs in the temping sector. African nationals are restricted to limited occupational and sector niches within European labour markets, which are not based on immigrant skills, but on the availability of unwanted, unskilled work (Chavez 1990). By selection through language and education, and the reliance on collective networks for job information, they are concentrated in specific sectors and sometimes even enterprises. Despite the suggestion of some long-term mobility in terms of sectors, most change in work still occurs within the lower-paid unskilled occupational niches, and often because of labour market conditions rather than as the result of worker choice. Very similar to their undocumented situation, documented migrants have to accept socio-professional downgrading.

In a nutshell, it seems that Belgium is more attractive for documented migrants: life is more stable and of a higher standard, and social protection is better. However, the Spanish labour market seems to offer more possibilities in the low-skilled temporary segments (much as it does for its citizens, thus reflecting life in general). Some respondents previously living in Spain, Italy or Portugal expressed their wish to have a more comfortable life, and therefore moving to Belgium or other Western European countries; the opposite was never mentioned.

It is important to stress that these immigrants have already achieved the most significant step in their personal mobility process by making it to Spain. Most respondents point out that migration on the personal level may be a complex, unjust, difficult and lonely process that was not what they dreamed[13] (Kaplan 2001); the family back home benefits and that is worth doing it for. De Jong et al. (2002: 860) also found that 'if migrants feel they can better meet family needs by working abroad, and if these responsibilities are paramount in decision making, then they may move even if specific types of satisfactions do not improve'. As long as large international inequalities continue to exist, transcontinental migration will remain the option for upward mobility.

8 Conclusions

> If you think it's better to try and get by at home, why don't you come back? Come and prove yourself that your ideas can work. This place where you want to keep me, yes, this place, does it still mean anything to you? (Diome 2006: 159)

To conclude the interview, I asked respondents to look back on their migration project and evaluate it. Many expressed mixed feelings about their success, saying they have been able to help their family economically, but at the expense of their own quality of life. The continuing adaptation to a new home country, the confrontation with loneliness and racism, and their generally lower position in European society weighs heavily on the satisfaction of improving living conditions at home; some explicitly refer to the word 'sacrifice'. Increasingly against their better judgment, most stick to the final aim: collecting enough money to be able to return home and guarantee the extended family a decent standard of living. While this plan is pushed forward until another set of conditions is met, and the ties to the homeland become more vague and imagined, they advise younger family members to stay at home and build their future there. As seen in the quote form Salie's brother above, this suggestion is seldom accepted with gratitude, with family members blaming the migrant for not caring about them any more – a painful accusation for the ones who often make great efforts to be able to send the monthly remittances.

Parallel to my respondents, it is time to conclude this research project and evaluate the balance of success and weaknesses. The main research question raised in the introduction was about how newly arrived uninvited labour migrants find a place in European urban labour markets: I wanted to explore the employment patterns of recent immigrants in a context of socio-economic change. The economic context is shaped by a post-industrial labour market that needs low-skilled, low-paid flexible work in a variety of sectors, and a state that tries to regulate migration. These elements interact with the strategies migrants develop to earn enough money to guarantee a higher and more stable income for themselves and their families back home. The outcomes of this complex interaction depend on many factors: different groups and individuals seem to vary with respect to their ability to take advantage of the opportunities a society offers; over time migrants may change their preferences or their assets in relation to certain jobs; in addition, opportunities differ by country.

The most typical trajectories, the deviant cases, and the detailed conclusions have been discussed before, and will not be repeated here. In Spain, I can state that the overwhelming majority of my respondents started working in agriculture. Though being a key element for understanding Senegambian formal and informal employment patterns, when compared to the 1990s, the share of agriculture seems to decline in decades from the 1960s. After the 1990s, we see more different sectors and jobs, but more precarious and temporary, more difficult with time; respondents also pointed at more control against moonlighting. In Antwerp, the move is generally from hawking to temping, without so much difference over generations, only that hawking has become less profitable. In general terms, the analysis has shown that the majority of respondents change jobs within the lowest segments of the labour market, thereby confirming dual and segmented labour market theories. For the illegal migrants the picture is a rather extreme one, where strategies are directed at survival and at obtaining papers, leaving them in a very vulnerable situation. Those who have acquired the conditions of legal workers have a wider range of opportunities, some of which may lead to some stability and capital accumulation – a possibility not covered by the two theories mentioned above. In short, in a segmented labour market in which some individual characteristics play a role, next to discrimination and macro-economic trends, immigrants are both the exploited solution and creative and productive actors.

In addition, I argued that in order to study this topic, special attention should be paid to a number of issues often overlooked in the literature. This approach was subdivided into a set of questions, which the first part of this conclusion will try to answer, discussing the empirical findings in a more overarching way, evaluating how useful these points of attention have been. The second part will take the discussion forward into policy implications and suggest further research.

8.1 General research conclusions

This research was, in the first place, a plea for a more dynamic approach to the migrant experience, taking into account various forms of mobility. The dimension focused on was time, and asked about the importance of dynamics over the life course, and the possible existence of certain phases or typical trajectories. Second was the necessary focus on mobility in a set of areas such as geography, legal status and employment. Third was the added value of international comparison between two cities, with the aim of highlighting the structural political and economic forces influencing migrants' strategies. Finally, was the method of qualitative life-course analysis an appropriate tool to capture these dynamics?

Life-course dynamics

First, respondents tend to show a trajectory that takes them from an intended temporary stay to becoming a permanent settler, matching the original starting point of Piore (1979). However, in this research the underlying dynamics and changing priorities were documented through qualitative life-course interviews, allowing for a far more detailed analysis. The key is a process of continual adaptation to changing and limited circumstances, trying to get by in shifting economic situations. This sketch resulted in some new insights, changes, and nuances.

To start with, three major stages of the migration experience were distinguished, based primarily on the main concern driving their strategies in that stage: as an undocumented migrant, the focus is on economic survival of the individual and, where possible, the family back home. In a second phase, they invest in documentation strategies, trying to regularise their stay in order to have a better chance of achieving their goal. Thirdly, once they have become a regular migrant, most of them try to accomplish some form of progress, in the form of upward mobility. This changing set of priorities also reflects different levels of security as well as economic standards of living: over time, most migrants do manage to realise a more stable life, where questions about their very survival are replaced with questions about a decent standard of living. This evolution also implies different emotional stages, not in the least linked to the maintenance, reunion, or formation of families. This chronological way of presenting the process may suggest that there is a necessary trend of climbing up the ladder, but there is no evidence whatsoever to suggest that there is a one-way trajectory leading to longer-term positions for everyone; some people get stuck in stages where they stay throughout many years, or even go backwards.

A specific point in which this research has contributed to the existing knowledge is by stressing the documentation strategies, which are central in the process of integration in all dimensions of life, including in the key dimension of the labour market. The necessity to regularise their stay constitutes a crucial element in the daily lives of undocumented migrants, if not an obsession, yet little attention has been paid to these strategies in scientific literature. Another insight derived from the interviews is how the labour market trajectories should be placed in the wider context of life as an immigrant, including family back home as well as in the host country, the importance of legal status, consumption as well as education. In all these dimensions migrants report changing needs and objectives over time, as well as the changing strategies to meet these aims.

My second aim was to stress the importance of mobility in an individual's life course in terms of legal categories, jobs, houses, cities and countries. The empirical material has shown that a more 'open interpretation' of many categories is necessary. First, studies about employment should always take into account the informal sector, as main or as additional source of income. A much wider interpretation of concepts of market and work, including all forms of part-time, temping and occasional employment has shown its relevance in this study. Second, the strict division between undocumented and regular migrant status is often blurred, partly because of documentation strategies of migrants, partly because of formal toleration practices by the authorities. Third, migration should not be seen as a simple movement between two places: both in the past and in the plans for the future many more locations play a role, other possible destinations, as well as the home country. The transnational dimension of the migration experience is without doubt a key one.

International comparison

A basic point of departure in this book was to contrast the ways in which structural forces influence migrant trajectories: how are economics and politics central to the way in which migrants organise their lives? Despite the undeniable influences of globalisation, substantial differences in terms of labour markets and immigration policies influence the lives of migrants in Antwerp and Barcelona. This understanding of the background of external possibilities and constraints in different countries forms an important modification of Piore's scheme. The integration of immigrants in the urban labour market is a complex process, marked by the interaction between multiple processes operating within the same space. My evidence suggests that different processes are at stake, mainly political and economic, in which characteristics of the receiving country play a major role: the political regime, the salience of migration politics, the public opinion about migrants, as well as the perceived need for migration, economic growth, size and role of the informal economy, and the type of welfare state. The migrants develop strategies that interact with these elements, which can lead to a variety of conditions of social inclusion or exclusion in the daily urban life.

The main differences can be summarised as follows: having no documents in Belgium is far more risky than in Spain, and regularising their stay is more complicated as well, often leaving only marriage as a way out. Spain seems to presents a larger variety of sectors for informal employment, with agriculture often representing the entrance door, but offers possibilities in manufacturing industry and construction as well. In Antwerp, Senegambian migrants are generally left with no option but to work as hawkers. The combination of a relatively peaceful life in the margins with easier access to work in Barcelona, compared to a hidden life and difficult access to work in Antwerp, inspires me to say that the experience of being undocumented is shaped by the state. However, also documented migrant's rights are constructed and created in a context of interests and priorities of the local political and economic setting. When having papers, working options also seem to be more limited in Antwerp, but social protection schemes provide more support than in Spain. This confirms what Sassen found for labour migration over a longer period of time (Sassen 1999: 134):

> the evidence for the last two centuries shows that labor migrations are patterned in terms of geography and duration. It is not an irreversible flow that only keeps growing. It is highly modulated (...). Labor migrations took place within systemic settings and there appear to have been multiple mechanisms contributing to their size, geography and duration. From a macro societal perspective, these can be seen as a type of equilibrating mechanisms. It could be argued that precisely because labor migrations never became mass invasions, they are parts of a system, and are conditioned by the latter's characteristics.

Third, the choice for a semi-longitudinal approach, by reconstructing trajectories, has shown its relevance in suggesting how the agency of individual actors is influenced by structural factors in different dimensions of life. Using the rich material of the interviews and observation, I was able to create a rare insight in the lives of these migrants, showing the interaction between different fields of life. A purely economic and individual approach falls short of understanding the wider social, emotional, and ideological context. In addition, it cannot grasp the complexity, precariousness, and volatility typical of contemporary migratory experiences. The method reveals the strategies they develop; although choices are limited as a result of the restrictive migration regimes and economic adverse conditions, it shows that agency remains important. The qualitative life-course methodology has also allowed for the depiction of general trends and similarities but also adds the local nuances and differences, due to the thick embeddedness of local socio-economic and institutional dynamics; this complexity is often lost in more general theories. However, a research question focussing specifically on one set of transitions, one dimension of mobility would have to develop a more specialised method. The most limiting factor is basically the memory of respondents, who generally do not remember the exact date of starting jobs, moving houses or countries.

8.2 Policy implications

Most experts foresee larger and more diverse international migrant flows over the next few decades, because of structural elements in the economies and societies of both countries of origin and destination. In the short run, market liberalisation is likely to create labour-market dislocations that intensify migration pressures: the demand for new workers in Europe's ageing and flexible labour markets will continue, and the surplus labour from developing countries is likely to increase. Migrants are able to earn wages that they otherwise could not obtain, and their families, communities and governments assume that remittances will continue to pour in. Increasingly, European countries start to accept the reality of immigration as a natural part of global economic integration, although they find it difficult to explain this to their wider public.

Away from a total migration ban or completely open borders, the challenge is to manage labour migration in a manner that is just, stable and transparent, and that releases the beneficial potential rather than detailing the related problems (Black 1996). Some conditions and starting points are outlined before.

Undocumented migration and informal employment

Illegal immigration has become a growing problem for the EU, leading to social injustice and exclusion. In the case of undocumented migrants, a series of valid and convincing arguments can be developed to defend their basic social rights in Europe. From a purely humanitarian point of view, for example, a minimum degree of emergency medical help and labour market protection should be guaranteed. Politically, there is a cost to completely excluding a considerable percentage of the actual population: it can lead to a dual society, with dangers that can affect everyone. Unsafe housing conditions for undocumented migrants can result in fires as seen in Paris in the summer of 2005, carrying risks for neighbours and passers-by. Inadequate health policies may result in the spread of diseases that Europe had previously combated successfully. Concentrations of people without any prospect for the future and nothing to lose can result in crime. For the benefit of the wider population, access to adequate shelter, nutrition, clothing, health care, and education for minors might be considered. Third, the legal obligation for states to respect human rights is already a fact; although they often fall short in the implementation of the existing ones for undocumented migrants. A migration policy might build here on international documents such as the UN Convention on the Protection of the Rights of All Migrant Workers and Members of Their Families (2003) and the ILO's formulation of a social justice that also includes irregular employees.

What is more, undocumented migration tends to be linked to illegal forms of employment. The acceptance of exploitation on the labour market can de facto result in the gradual dismantling of general workers' rights. It must be recognised that labour markets are using unskilled cheap labour and that this labour is cheap in part because the workers are foreign, and in part from illegality. The accumulation of seasonal and temporary jobs, with limited social rights, is installing an intolerable form of segregation that benefits some sectors and employers. This shows the risk that globalisation, instead of increasing income everywhere in the word, could import conditions and practices only seen in developing countries into the core of our society. Only that the growth of new downgraded and informal sectors of the labour market staffed by socially marginal migrants is not an imported phenomenon but rather 'part and parcel of advanced capitalist strategies of deregulation, for the enhancement of 'flexibility' in terms of a networked economy and society, and a fragmented labour market' (Schierup, Hansen & Castles 2006: 299). The implication may be that legal immigration of the unskilled is again desirable, along with affordable social protection for these workers.

Directions for new policies

Policy trends in Europe take a number of divergent directions. On the one hand, the pleas for more restriction and more control continue, as showed in the proposed crackdown on bosses that employ undocumented migrants in the underground economy. However, with the continuing demand and supply of cheap labour, it might be that more people will enter illegally at the back door if the front door is closed. On the other hand, there seems to be a consensus that some forms of migration should be encouraged. This contradiction can be found in discourses: it is unclear how governments afraid of a migration-adverse public opinion will be able to explain the advantages of selective immigration, to defend or justify the increasing need for foreign workers. At the same time, the EU is moving forward in that direction.

A first, relatively new tendency is the collaboration with countries of origin in order to tackle the growing problem of illegal immigration. The summer of 2006 has shown how collaboration between Spain (and the EU as a whole) and countries of origin was necessary, but also how migration has emerged as a topic on the foreign policy agenda. In this framework, a number of summits have been held between EU and African ministers, with shared declarations about joint monitoring of sea and border routes, repatriation, as well as the tackling of poverty, one of the root causes of immigration. A network of information centres is planned, which will be matching the supply of legal migrant labour for low-skill sectors such as agriculture, public works and tourism, to demand in EU states; probably in a system of quota. At the same time, it will seek to increase jobs in Africa by promoting investment in labour-intensive sectors there. The first experimental job centre was supposed to open in Mali in February 2007.

A second line of thought seems to be the launch of temporary migration schemes, as in the rotation of guest workers. It is argued that they are a good match between the needs of some labour markets, the migration pressure, the fear of brain drain, and the potential of return migration. From a theoretical point of view, if the system is transparent, predictable, and rights-based, it could be a realistic and cost-effective policy option (Baldwin-Edwards 2004; Ghosh 2000). However, in practice, a set of conditions would have to be implemented in order for the temporary migration to be successful: this would include penalties in case of overstaying the permissible period, deferred payments, and limiting the right for family reunion. However, if foreign workers do not wish to return home, there is an almost inevitability to the creation of a population of undocumented immigrants.

Thirdly, there is also an increasing understanding across Europe about the inseparability of immigration from integration. There can be no doubt that successful immigration policies rely heavily on the successful integration of immigrants, not least because of the 'dual crisis of the welfare state and the nation' (Schierup, Hansen & Castles 2006). Public opinion may only accept increasing numbers of migrants if they feel the social protection and the perceived identity of the nation is secured. On the other side, one wonders what will become of these first Senegambian generations when they lose their physical power, or when they are replaced by other, cheaper workers. The new countries of immigration could find many answers in the experiences of older destination countries with post-war migration, whose first generation is already at the stage of retirement, homes for elderly people, and increased health care needs. In addition, lessons should be learned from the situation of many children from migrant origin, second and third generations, who often find themselves with educational and professional disadvantages when they enter the labour market. An early investment of means (money and energy) in integration policies that benefit not only the current immigrants but also the generations to come would be highly recommended.

In the quote at the beginning of this chapter, the brother left behind in Senegal asks the migrant sister if she still cares about their home country, and he asks for proof of that commitment. In the same way, potential migrants and the governments of developing countries will ask the West about their dedication to diminishing the inequalities in the world, root causes of migration. In the comprehensive and collaborative approach needed for success in managing migration, their needs and suggestions should be taken into consideration, which would mean not only considerable amounts of aid but more equitable systems of trade and development (Martin 1994). If host countries think they can pay just lip service to these principles, while trying to realise their own agenda, people will continue to come, more creative, determined, and desperate than western legal and policing systems can imagine or deal with.

Further research

This study has focused on immigrants' socio-economic trajectories in two cities characterised by different labour markets, migration politics and welfare regimes. It has, in the first place, revealed the importance of a dynamic approach, taking into account various forms of mobility. This work constitutes one step in this direction, but it leaves many questions unanswered. Future research could look in more detail at specific forms of mobility, such as the systems behind the continuously changing employment patterns, and the factors influencing it. The impact of casual, temporary and part-time work on the lives of migrants as well as native workers should be studied more closely. In addition, more insight is needed in the diversity of structural factors influencing the migrants' strategies. Some elements have been brought to light here in the presentation of empirical results, but there is no doubt that comparisons between other cities, countries, labour markets, ethnic groups and welfare regimes would show a larger diversity of mechanisms. Thirdly, the agency perspective is crucial, as an insight in their own pre-existing aims and the way they change over time is essential to understand their priorities and strategies. More work could be done on the psychological process that lies behind this. As mentioned above, the growing importance of the presence of women and a second generation should be taken into account when looking at the further trajectories.

A bit further away from the main research question developed here, some other lines of research might be suggested. In order to explain the disadvantageous situation for most migrants in the labour market, more work on discrimination and anti-discrimination measures by policymakers and other social partners should be encouraged. This might help to put to use the considerable amount of neglected but available immigrant resources. The question of the continuing role of the country of origin could also be looked at more closely, a framework in which the ideas of co-development could be developed further.

The final aim, in my regard, should be a world in which nobody needs to migrate in order to secure his life or that of his family, but where everybody would have the opportunity to travel in order to study, work, or just discover. Western societies have kept this privilege for themselves, but every world citizen has the right to claim it.

Appendix A Topic list for questionnaire

Personal data
- Year of birth
- Gender
- Origin (country, city, village)
- Ethnicity
- Family status

Migration experience
- Year of leaving home
- Year of arrival in Europe
- Means of travelling
- Trajectory in Africa & Europe
- Trips back home
- Where living now
- Mobility plans

Legal status
- Phases without papers
- Phases with papers
- Documentation strategy
- Administrative status now
- Education/training
- Education and training back home
- Education and training in Europe
- Language proficiency

Job career
- Trajectory (sector, contract and level)
- Labour conditions
- Reasons to change jobs
- Search strategies
- Actual job
- Difficulties?

Social networks
- Family in Europe
- Family in Senegal
- Friends in Europe
- Associations

Evaluation of migration project

Appendix B List of key informants

Barcelona

Name	Organisation	Sector
Natalia Gonzalez	Caritas Barcelona, Migration Unit	NGO
Babacar Mbaye	Municipal Service for Reception of Immigrants, Sabadell	municipality
Quim Pons	Migrastudium, before in San Pau, Mataró	NGO
Ousmane Mballo	UGT (General Workers' Union), Migration Unit AMIC	labour union
Miguel Pajares	CCOO (Workers Committees) Ceres Center for Labour Union Studies and Research	labour union
Ousseynou Niang	president ACRS (Catalan Association of Senegalese Residents)	self-organisation
Chelo	SAIER Bolsa de trabajo (Support Service for Foreign Migrants and Refugees, Labour market Guidance)	municipality
Idrissa Djiba	CCOO (Workers Committees) CITE (Information Centre for Foreign Workers)	labour union
Papa Sow	Doctor in Geography	academic, self-organisation
Aliou Diao	Catalan Fund for Development cooperation	regional authority, self-organisation
Adriana Kaplan	Centre for Demographic Studies, Universitat Autonoma de Barcelona	academic
Saoka Luzolo	Generalitat de Catalunya (Catalan authority), Migration secretariat, Area of of Citizenship and Participation	regional authority
Abdu Mawa	ACRS (Catalan Association of Senegalese Residents), responsible for social area	self-organisation
Bombo Ndir	Granollers municipality, labour insertion	municipality, self-organisation
Merced Janer	Municipality of Barcelona, Migration Department	municipality
Marta	Oficina d'Informació a l'Estranger Mataró (Office for Information to the foreigner)	municipality
Isabel	Sair Mataró	NGO
Mohamed	UGT Granollers (General Workers' Union)	labour union

Antwerp

Name	Organisation	Sector
Omar Ba	VZW Sunugaal	self-organisation
Wilfried Pfeffer	Migration Observatory, Centre for Equal Opportunities and Fight against Racism	federal government
Evans Eguavoen	De Acht, Antwerp Minority Centre	NGO
Baba Ba	Senegalese sociologist and migrant	academic
Nele Verbruggen	PICUM (Platform for International Cooperation on Undocumented Migrants)	NGO
Karen Poisson	Social worker at the OCMW	municipality
Katrijn Pauwels	OCIV (Discussion Centre for Integration of Refugees), Return migration	NGO
Abdoul Ba	Doctor in Geography	academic
Anissa Akhanaf	City of Antwerp, Integration Services	municipality
Yves Bocklandt	Social Service BZN (Confederation without Name)	NGO
Chris Van Kapellen	City of Antwerp, Information Centre for Enterpreneurs	municipality

Appendix C   Letter

The letter below and the introductory text preceding it are reproduced from www.wikipedia.org.

> Yaguine Koita (aged 14) and Fodé Tounkara (aged 15) were stowaways who froze to death on a Sabena Airlines Airbus A330 (Flight 520) flying from Conakry, Guinea, to Brussels, Belgium, on 28 July 1999. Their bodies were discovered on 2 August in the airplane's rear right-hand wheel bay at Brussels International Airport, after having made at least three return trips between Conakry and Brussels. The boys were carrying plastic bags with birth certificates, school report cards, photographs, and a letter. This letter, written in imperfect French, was widely published in the world media.

Excellencies, Messrs. Members and officials of Europe,

We have the honourable pleasure and the great confidence in you to write this letter to speak to you about the objective of our journey and the suffering of us, the children and young people of Africa.

But first of all, we present to you life's most delicious, charming and respected greetings. To this effect, be our support and our assistance. You are for us, in Africa, those to whom it is necessary to request relief. We implore you, for the love of your continent, for the feeling that you have towards your people and especially for the affinity and love that you have for your children whom you love for a lifetime. Furthermore, for the love and meekness of our creator God the omnipotent one who gave you all the good experiences, wealth and ability to well construct and well organise your continent to become the most beautiful one and most admirable among the others.

Messrs. Members and officials of Europe, we call out for your solidarity and your kindness for the relief of Africa. Do help us, we suffer enormously in Africa, we have problems and some shortcomings regarding the rights of the child.

In terms of problems, we have war, disease, malnutrition, etc. As for the rights of the child in Africa, and especially in Guinea, we have too many schools but a great lack of education and training. Only in the private schools can one have a good education and good training, but it takes a great sum of money. Now, our parents are poor and it is necessary for them to feed us. Furthermore, we have no sports schools where we could practice soccer, basketball or tennis.

This is the reason, we, African children and youth, ask you to create a big efficient organisation for Africa to allow us to progress. Therefore, if you see that we have sacrificed ourselves and risked our lives, this is because we suffer too in Africa and that we need you to fight against poverty and to put an end to the war in Africa. Nevertheless, we want to learn, and we ask you to help us in Africa learn to be like you.

Finally, we appeal to you to excuse us very, very much for daring to write you this letter to you, the great personages to whom we owe much respect. And do not forget it is to you whom we must lament about the weakness of our abilities in Africa.

Written by two Guinean children,
Yaguine Koita and Fodé Tounkara

Notes

Chapter 1

1 This does not mean that strategies would be the only stimulus and sole determinant to action. They are constructs people use to make sense of their world; they can be reviewed and amended in the light of events, and they can differ in different spheres of life.
2 For many centuries, host of migrants have been agricultural workers, who lived and worked in the countryside; in this study, however, I will focus on migration to metropolitan areas.

Chapter 2

1 Even more recently, the term 'new migration' has been used for the movement of Eastern Europeans from the enlarged Europe to the 'old' Europe.
2 Art. 2(1), International Convention on the Protection of the Rights of All Migrant Workers and Members of Their Families, 1990.
3 It is my opinion that the term 'migrant' should be reserved for the person who moved, not for children born in the host country. In Belgium, this is solved with the reference 'allochtonous population', with 'second generation'; elsewhere with 'ethnic minority'.
4 The term *'sans-papiers'*, launched in the academic world by Bourdieu, is not a legal category, but a concept picked up by the French media during the first collective occupation in 1996, in the Saint-Bernard church.
5 Convention relating to the Status of Refugees, Art. 1A(2), 1951 as modified by the 1967 Protocol.
6 If he is low-skilled, of course; high-skilled migration is often seen as good.
7 In a somewhat related framework, Portes (1995) refers to the concept of 'embeddedness' to explain the process of insertion of immigrants into various social contexts. On the one hand, the structural embeddedness of the process of immigrant settlement consists of the limits and possibilities offered by the policies and characteristics of the society at large; the assistance and constraints offered by co-ethnic community can, on the other hand, be defined as instances of relational embeddedness.
8 Awad's exhaustive list of policies (2004) affecting labour migrants goes from migration control laws, welfare systems in receiving countries, education and labour market policies, to macro-economic trade, monetary and fiscal policies. Here, only a fraction of the most relevant factors will be discussed.
9 According to estimates from Europol and the International Centre for Migration Policy Development in Vienna, some 400,000 to 500,000 people annually enter Europe illegally, adding to an undocumented population of several millions.
10 The wider 'uban area' of Antwerp has 944,900 inhabitants (OECD 2005).
11 The biggest minority actually consisted of substantial numbers of Dutch citizens, who in recent times have come to the city, partly for tax-related or housing-related reasons, due to its vicinity. In addition, there is the the presence of the long-established Jewish minority.

12 Population Data for January 2006, Stad Antwerpen, Databank Sociale Planning.
13 In a previous political programme it included proposals for restrictions on migrants' right to property ownership, a revision of all naturalisations granted since 1974, the repatriation of non-European unemployed migrants, a separate education for Muslim children or even the withdrawal of the status given to Islam by the Belgian state (Govaert 1995). This lead to a conviction for racism in April 2004, but contrary enough changing names (now Vlaams Belang) might guarantee them even bigger public support.
14 In Wallonia the extreme right is divided in several small political groups, torn by numerous internal divisions, so their electoral significance is small.
15 The three Communities (French-, Flemish- and German-speaking) and three Regions (Walloon, Flemish and Brussels Capital) overlap but do not correspond, and each have specific legal powers, as well as the remaining federal institutions (the King, the federal Parliament and the national government).
16 Despite the colonial links to Rwanda, Burundi and the Democratic Republic of Congo, the African community in Belgium is not large. Due to endemic racism until the 1950s, an atypical history developed where strong limits were imposed on emigration from the colonies in Belgium: in 1945 only ten Congolese were found in Belgian population statistics (Jacquemin 2002). In the 1950s, students started coming to Belgian universities, but in the subsequent inflow of labour migrants, Congolese workers did not play any role. Today, after an increase in asylum applications due to continuing wars in the area, the community counts around 15,000 to 20,000 people but apart from footballers and musicians they can count on limited popular sympathy (Kagné 2001).
17 According to official numbers from the federal police, 11,000 files were opened in Zeebrugge in 2003; this includes people who were caught several times (De Walsche 2005). This has leaded the British government to offer financial and logistic help in developing detection systems.
18 Confusion between refugees and migrants, as well as the image of 'cheaters', may stem from this improper use of the asylum procedure by economic migrants (Meert et al. 2006).
19 A first peak occurred in 1993 with about 25,000 applications, and in 1999/2000 around 40,000, to a large extent linked to the Kosovo war (Lennert and Decroly 2002).
20 However, this trend has been recorded everywhere in Europe, where applications in 2005 have diminished with 34 per cent compared to 2003, according to figures of the High Commisioner for Refugees.
21 Congolese, Rwandese and Burundese citizens of the former Belgian colony of the Congo do not benefit from any special treatment.
22 As for Subsaharan Africans, the earliest presence must have been a limited number of university students from Guinea Equatorial (Spanish Colony) from the 1960s onwards. A few sub-Saharan Africans on their way to France or other northern European countries passed through the area and worked temporarily in industries and construction in the metropolitan area of Barcelona or in intensive agriculture in the peri-urban area. Few stayed, most of those because of the closure of the French border in 1974.
23 In June 2006, a Catalan referendum backed by the central government gave the region greater autonomy. The Catalans won nation status within Spain and the region's parliament gained extra powers in taxation and judicial matters.
24 Spanish judiciary has even commented on elements of the law going against basic rights of individuals.
25 In 2002, more than half a million people from Latin America entered with tourist visa, and only 86,000 returned (*El País*).

26 This schematic representation used for analytical purposes might suggest a necessarily upward social path for migrants, which would be misleading. It is not an automatic process; many people are stuck in one stage or another, drop out of the process, or fall back. In addition, this is not to say that this analytical distinction is that clear in everyday life; people may combine strategies from different analytical periods at a single moment in time.

27 Other authors (Adam et al. 2001; Burgers & Engbersen 1999; Engbersen 2001; Soenen 2003) use the distinction between 'survival' and 'residence' strategies in the context of undocumented migrants. As 'residence strategies' may be confused with housing strategies, I prefer the term 'documentation strategies'. The chronological approach and addition of the 'mobility' strategies is my responsibility. Brun also suggest a certain trajectory by using a categorisation of recently arrived undocumented migrants, settled undocumented migrants, foreigners who were recently regularised and those with permanent permit (Brun 2003).

Chapter 3

1 In Spain, I initially built on the network of a friend I knew in Senegal many years before; joining him for visits to friends and shops introduced me to many people. Actually, spending time with him in this environment, being confronted with the reality of migration formed the inspiration for this study, as explained in the introduction. After he moved to a different part of Spain, I kept in touch with earlier respondents and the process continued. A Senegalese key informant independently provided me with another set of contacts. In Belgium, the story starts with a far acquaintance knowing a Senegalese man; I explained my research over a cup of tea. Though hesitant in the beginning, he encouraged me at the end. He turned out to be a figure of reference for part of the community, and the younger man he appointed as my guide proved to be a great help. On my first day in Antwerp, I was introduced in a house where people come together weekly to share a meal: the ideal place for making my initial contacts. I was extremely lucky: today this house is uninhabited, the community dispersed over several locations and to a large extent out of touch.

2 Unless one has the means to organise an 'ethno survey' suggested by Massey and Capoferro (2004), which combines detailed life histories with data compiled at the household, community, national and international levels.

3 Recently statistical techniques are being used to improve the method, compensating for the fact that the sample was collected in a non-random way (Atkinson & Flint 2001). In respondent-driven sampling, for example, respondents recruit their peers, as in network-based samples, and researchers keep track of who recruited whom and their numbers of social contacts. A mathematical model of the recruitment process then weights the sample to compensate for non-random recruitment patterns (Heckathorn 1997).

4 Or others. In an example from my research, a jealous girlfriend alarmed by my calls to a respondent called me after the interview. She understood my explanation, but then shifted to asking for my help in resolving the question of whether he really loved her or just wanted to marry her for papers. He had talked about this issue in the interview, but I did not disclose the information.

5 I learned to ask 'If God hears your prayers, where would you like to live in the future?' instead of the more straightforward and secular Belgian approach, in order to avoid the inevitable polite lectures about how it is not man but God who determines the future.

6   Despite this setting, I never felt insecure or unsafe (Kenyon & Hawker 1999); respondents were without exceptions caring and courteous.

Chapter 4

1   In Senegal, a low-level separatist war was going on between 1982 and 2004 when a peace pact was signed. The rebellion was fuelled by complaints among Casamance's Diola population that they were being marginalised by the more numerous Wolof people of northern Senegal in the allocation of national development resources. In the Gambia, the elected government was toppled in a military coup in 1994; the country returned to constitutional rule two years later when its military leader ran as a civilian and won a presidential election. Despite attempts to unify Senegalese and the Gambian territories in a political union in 1982, political disputes are rather common: a conflict over ferry tariffs led to a border blockade in 2005.
2   External debt is another major constraint to development in Africa. At $313 billion in 1994, it was equivalent to 234 per cent of Africa's total export income and 83 per cent of its GDP, representing the highest debt burden for any world region (UN 1996a). As of 1994, average per capita spending for debt service was $43, compared with only $35 on education and health. With nearly two-thirds of its export earnings devoted to debt service, the region's capacity to mobilise resources for socio-economic development and employment is severely constrained (Adepoju 2004).
3   African destinations like Nigeria and Gabon became less of an option, due to their political instability and economic crisis after the 1970s, and their ad hoc repatriation actions of non-citizens to their countries of origin. Only Ivory Coast continued to attract a lot of people, until civil war hit the country in 1999.
4   I wish to refer again to the letter of Guinean teenagers Yaguine Koita and Fodé Tounkara, explaining how the lack of perspective made them risk their lives as stowaways in a plane (see annex C).
5   As professionals also look for economic and social mobility, the risks for brain drain are well-known (Ajibewa & Akinrinade 2003). It is very difficult to decide the final picture of the total cost-benefit analysis of migration for the country of origin, and also the discussion about the 'brain drain' is very complex. It includes elements as diverse as the 'return brain drain' of for instance Indian IT-specialists, unemployment of high-skilled people, new forms of colonialism, and the effect of remittances on the level of dependency, economic development or new entrepreneurship (Asiedu 2005; Diatta & Mbow 1999).
6   I was able to witness this throughout four visits to Senegal between 1992 and 2004.
7   What may play a role, according to me, is that the material and financial benefits of migration are quickly visible and widespread. The emotional price, on the contrary, in terms of loneliness and racism in the daily battle for subsistence are almost unimaginable for ambitious young men. Therefore, even if migrants tell true stories at home, which is not always the case, it seems unlikely that this will discourage other possible migrants to try their luck.
8   Artists, businesspersons, religious leaders and diplomats often travel for professional reasons with an entourage; part of this group sometimes decides to stay behind instead of travelling back. Sometimes a business develops: vacant places in these missions are on offer with the aim of migration. The Congolese singer Papa Wemba was sentenced in France for smuggling hundreds of people under cover of his musical activities over several years (*De Standaard* 16 November 2004).

NOTES

9 Within Catalonia, Senegambians are also concentrated in the province of Gerona where they are often employed in agriculture (Mendoza 1998). Because of the urban focus in this study, I leave this group on the side.
10 Other Southern European countries face the same challenge: in 2006, Italy saw 22,016 undocumented migrants arriving at the coasts of Sicily and Lampedusa, predominantly coming from Morocco, Egypt, Eritrea and Tunisia (*De Standaard* 6 January 2006).
11 It is estimated by the police labour union (Sindicato Unificado de Policía) that arrivals in boats represent only 5 per cent of the total inflow; the majority, 55 per cent, uses the airport of Barajas, Madrid, and 25 per cent more El Prat in Barcelona; another 15 per cent uses the roads. Since the announcement of visa requirements for Bolivians from 1 April 2007, the number of tourists from this country has increased considerably, from 5,000 in May to 14,100 in November. They amounted to between 800 and 1,200 arrivals daily in Madrid in December 2006; in addition, between 200 and 300 Brazilians and about a hundred Paraguayans enter daily (*El País* 4 January 2007).
12 Effective is not always synonymous for correct: many migrants complain about being dumped in desert areas bordering Algeria or the Western Sahara (*El País* 29 August 2006) or suffer abuse from policemen (Médecins Sans Frontières 2005).
13 The traffickers and their networks have also been targeted by police services, with more than 50 arrests in different West African countries.
14 Although the numbers diminished during the winter months, some 1,500 migrants already made it to the Canary Islands in the first eleven weeks of 2007 (*El País* 24 March 2007).
15 The most recent trend is that the African waters become transit routes for Asian migrants travelling by boat to the Canary Islands. In March 2007, two boats with each more than 300 migrants from India, Pakistan and Sri Lanka were intercepted by Frontex.
16 This is parallel to the East End concept of 'ducking and diving'.
17 This name comes from the fact that many Senegalese are called Modou, abbreviation of Mamadou, after the prophet Mohamed; the term used to refer to seasonal migrants from the agricultural peanut basin, in search of additional income by informal trade in big cities such as Dakar. In Senegal, it is now the generic name used for all international migrants even if they do salaried work; inside the European migrant community, it only refers to those who are involved in hawking.
18 Ecuadorian migrants also sell art from their country, Pakistanis sometimes sell flowers and, recently, Chinese have been entering the hawking business.
19 Statistics released by the European Commission show that customs services of the 25 EU countries took possession of more than 75 million counterfeit goods in 2005, which represents probably only 10 per cent of the total business; more than 25 per cent was intercepted in Belgium (*De Standaard* 15 November 2006). The World Intellectual Property Organization calculated that the global economy lost 77 billion euro to counterfeit business (*De Standaard* 31 January 2007).
20 Sadly enough, this intention and practice tends to change personal relationships: when somebody calls, it is probably to ask for more money, even close family members hardly ask how the person is feeling, never sympathise with hardship or problems. Some migrants complain that their family would no longer welcome them to live back at home because they run the risk of cutting their most effective survival strategy. It is hard to distinguish friendship or love from sheer interest when on a return visit: everyone wants something from you, and girls in Senegal now want to marry only migrants, under the motto of three Vs: *venant, villa et voiture* ('return migrant, villa and car').

21 The World Bank estimated that in 2005 almost 200 million migrants sent officially 232 billion dollar remittances home; an additional 80 billion was transferred through informal channels. developing countries received 167 billion, more than double the total amount of development aid. The World Bank estimates that 2.5 million people escaped poverty through remittances.
22 Most quotes are therefore from men; I will stress it when a woman is being quoted.
23 This goes contrary to the fact that West Africans (particularly Nigerians and Senegalese) have the highest rate of second degrees in Britain and France. Maybe people with higher education tend to go to countries where they hope to benefit immediately from their education.
24 In Koranic schools pupils learn to recite Arabic, not to speak or write the language in itself.

Chapter 5

1 It should be repeated that the informal labour market is by no means the territory of undocumented migrants alone; on the contrary, moonlighting is in the first place an activity of nationals and legal foreigners (European Foundation for the Improvement of Living and Working Conditions 2005). For local workers undeclared work is generally a strategy to generate extra income after hours or in an inactive period protected by social rights; it seldom provides the basic income. Some documented migrants may copy this behaviour or return to informal work during periods of unemployment.
2 Original name changed; the street name has become a common name to refer to this particular house and community of hawkers.
3 A square known for its concentration of African bars and restaurants, in an area with many African residents. At weekends, it functions also a meeting place for African communities from Paris, Germany and the Netherlands.
4 Spanish labour unions do receive complaints from undocumented workers, and do follow up their files as they do with other clients. However, many immigrants consider how the consequences of a complaint could be worse for themselves: they may lose their jobs.
5 A recent estimation pointed at about 75,000 undeclared workers in Belgium, resulting in a 'shortage' in social contributions of 6 per cent, 2 billion euro. In addition, considerable numbers of unemployed or registered employed also moonlight (*De Standaard* 3 October 2006).
6 In the first year, 10,000 new 'proper' jobs were created through this subsidised system.
7 This can easily lead to problems with correspondence (e.g. about asylum applications or regularisation) arriving in previous addresses.
8 In Antwerp, this process is further aggravated by the arrival of asylum seekers, who at the start of their application are 'allocated' to a municipality according to a dispersal plan. However, some municipalities sometimes prefer to pay for accommodation in big cities, rather than providing them with convenient accommodation on their own territory (*De Standaard* 11 April 2006).
9 In both countries, there is a right to education for children from parents without papers. An undocumented child gets a diploma, is insured, and can do an internship, but cannot be paid. Schools cannot report the children or the parents to the police or the Department for Foreigners.

NOTES   213

Chapter 6

1   He misses a third distinct category, consisting of the group of undocumented migrants who settle in and around existing ethnic communities. Examples are the undocumented Moroccans that form part of the established Moroccan community that Engbersen describes.
2   Again, the solution for this can be mainly found in community organisation, such as tontines. In this system of rotating credit, people contribute a fixed amount a month; the total is given each month to a certain person of the group, designated by luck or negotiation, taking turns until the whole group has received. Group pressure forces a certain discipline in saving, while the system allows people to make important investments (Lelart 1990; Soenen 2003).
3   There have been reports about public officials rejecting to register undocumented migrants without any justification, municipalities making the procedure unreasonably difficult, or property owners refusing to provide proof of address. A civil servant in Barcelona explains how the city prioritises registration as part of their reception policy:
    In Barcelona, we pushed a lot for *empadronamiento* to be an important tactic, like a condition for normalisation. There are cities that don't ask it so much, because they may stay only very short, question of fear for intervention from the police... some people have problems with this. In Barcelona, we support actively a policy of *empadronamiento*, it is the only instrument against marginalisation, to use schools, basic health services, social. It has been five years a strong pressure but we move on with this accumulated stock.
4   Since the Aliens Act that went into effect on 22 December 2003, police are now able to consult data of foreigners registered at municipalities through a special procedure. Undocumented migrants may feel it is no longer safe to register at the municipality, thinking that they run the risk of being apprehended by the police and possibly deported (although the procedure has not yet been used).
5   Migrants travel overland without documents, leaving the identity card at home, in order to hide their nationality and avoid immediate repatriation upon arrival. Once settled, the family back home sends the documents, with which they can get a valid passport in the Senegalese embassy.
6   One example was particularly absurd, as it concerned the work permit of a deceased elderly Senegalese man being used by a youngster.
7   As opposed to the control of external borders.
8   Ulysses was the leading character in the ancient Greek epic poem the *Odyssey*, describing the ten years it took him to get home after the Trojan War. He is thus a symbol of long travelling with terrible ordeals.
9   A considerable flow of spontaneous migration occurred parallel to official guest worker schemes, induced by intense recruitment campaigns, and normally solved by regularising them after arrival even though not part of a bilateral scheme.
10 *El País* reports on the arrest of four people including one police officer, for selling false documentation in exchange for money (up to 6,000 euro) or sexual services (28 July 2006).
11 Belgium used the Schengen agreements to limit access to the territory. These agreements authorise its members to remove the obligations of free movement of EU citizens, by re-imposing the checks at the borders, for short periods during special circumstances.
12 Without much scientific basis, one can see some reasons for this: older women have greater resources and can offer more security to a migrant; also, if single they are often lonely and less likely to find a national as a partner. In a couple of cases, these women got to know their African partner in the country of origin, an brought him

over after marriage. Without excluding the possibility of real love, we have to recognise the existence of sex tourism industry with the specific objective of picking up a young virile black man; from the black male's perspective, the possibility of this leading to a migration opportunity is attractive.
13 The results of the first four streets were as follows: in 342 families, together totalling 622 people, 43 per cent had Belgian nationality; 38 per cent were native Dutch speakers, 21 per cent had a European language as their mother tongue and 41 per cent spoke a language from outside Europe. Only 28 per cent had a job, 41 per cent lived off social security, 3 per cent from the OCMW and 18 per cent has no official income. Housing was inadequate in 49 per cent of cases, and 65 families resided in the city illegally (*De Standaard* 16 May 2006).

Chapter 7

1 A way around this is to wait five years until receiving the permanent permit, which automatically includes both.
2 Internal domestic work is not often done by black women: in that sector, there seems to be a preference for Christian migrant women who speak the language already, such as Latin Americans. In addition, African women often have their husband and children in Spain, making residential work difficult; the Dominican women on the contrary mostly come on their own.
3 In addition, two respondents are artists and have been so all their lives; they have tried different statuses, as employee or self-employed, but always made a living from their music (giving percussion classes, playing in bands, assisting other musicians, organise concerts, give workshops). They seem relatively happy although many comments can be made on provisions for artists. They build on previous experience and talent; as this is not a route for many others, their trajectories will not be analysed in detail here.
4 And this is only Catalonia; the many African workers in Almería face temperatures up to 50 degrees (Kaplan 2001).
5 For residents from most countries; for some Latin American countries, it is only three years.
6 There is also a cultural complication in the process of family reunion: the European lawmaker's nuclear conception of a 'family' does not coincide with the African structure of polygamy and extended families (Timera 1997). Polygamy is prohibited in Europe, thus there is every incentive to hide polygamous relationships. Informally this practice can continue in transnational space: the husband can live in Europe while all the wives are in Africa; he can bring only one to Europe, or they can take turns; and he might marry several in Europe, without registering the marriage officially. For the children, this may be solved with complicated partial reunification, with one or some children staying in Africa in order to keep the link with the rest of the family; they may join the migrants later, legally or illegally. In any case, the social protection of the women and children can be in danger (Barou 2001; Bryceson & Vuorela 2002; Salzbrunn 2002; Timera 2002).
7 This sadly includes practices of genital excision, dowry, and divorce by repudiation (Scales-Trent 1990). European criminal laws forbid clitoridectomy and infibulation, making mothers hesitant to have daughters excised in Europe. They may simply return to their home country for a short visit to have the excision performed there, where it is legal; however, on their return they can be punished.
8 A more or less representative spending pattern is as follows: Segui works as a specialised worker in construction, earning between 1,200 and 1,300 euro per month. He

NOTES

pays the bank 700 euro per month for the apartment, 200 euro for the car. Renting out two rooms, he makes 200 euro a month. That leaves him 500 to 600 euro a month for expenses remittances. If he would have his wife and child in Spain, the extra on the budget would soon melt down.

9   My research in Antwerp and Barcelona deals with, by definition, only people who have yet to return, making it impossible to estimate the number of those who did return.
10 This probably happens through a variety of mechanisms. A first element is the mode of transport during the migration trip, based on disposable income: the migrants who travel over land and sea tend to be poorer, of rural origin, end up in southern Europe. The ones who have the connections and money to obtain a visum and airplane ticket can travel to anywhere in Europe. Second, this trend is reinforced by chain-migration: most respondents chose their destination based on links to an established community from their region of origin. Through this filter of networks, Bubacar, from Mandinka and rural origin but travelling by plane to Germany, ended up in Spain because of recommendations inside his ethnic community.
11 This model is reproduced inside the Spanish case; the people living in the city centre correspond more with the Belgian image, while those in the satellite towns, to the community model.
12 This difference is also found by Romaniszyn in the Polish community, but more as a characteristic of individuals without the ethnic link as I found in my research (Romaniszyn 2000).
13 As illustrated by Musa: 'I don't want to stay in Spain. Life here is not worth living, people are not friendly, money is not enough to live a life. Migration is not worth the trouble. I thought I would find a better life, but on the contrary... . This is not a life. This does not make sense. What does it rhyme to? Work, sleep, eat. And sometimes problems. There is no future, no perspectives, no security.' (Musa, 32, in Barcelona since 2003, undocumented, textile factory).

References

Adam, I., N. Ben Mohammed, B. Kagné, M. Martiniello & A. Rea. (2001), *Itinéraires des Sans-Papiers en Belgique*. Brussels, Liège: Fondation Roi Baudouin.

Adepoju, A. (2004), 'Trends in International Migration in and from Africa', in Douglas S. Massey & J. Edward Taylor (eds.), *International Migration: Prospects and Policies in a Global Market*, 59-76. Oxford: Oxford University Press.

— (2005), 'Review of Research and Data on Human Trafficking in Sub-Saharan Africa', *International Migration* 43:75-98.

Adriaenssens, S. & D. Geldof (1997), 'La Polarisation Sociale et Spatiale d'Anvers', in Albert Martens & Monique Vervaeke (eds.), *La Polarisation Sociale des Villes Européennes*, 191-201. Paris: Anthropos.

Agrela, B. (2002), 'Spain as a Recent Country of Immigration: How Immigration Became a Symbolic, Political and Cultural Problem in the "New Spain" '. La Jolla: University of California-San Diego.

Ajibewa, A. & S. Akinrinade (2003), 'Globalisation, Migration and the New African Diasporas: Towards a Framework of Understanding', unpublished conference paper presented at International Workshop on Migration and Poverty in West Africa, 13-14 March 2003, University of Sussex.

Alexander, M. (2004), 'Comparing Local Policies toward Migrants: An Analytical Framework, a Typology and Preliminary Survey Results', in Rinus Penninx, Karen Kraal, Marco Martiniello & Steven Vertovec (eds.), *Citizenship in European Cities*, 57-84. Aldershot and Burlington: Ashgate.

Andall, J. (2002), 'Second-generation Attitude: African-Italians in Milan', *Journal of Ethnic and Migration Studies* 28:189-407.

Anderson, M., F. Bechofer & S. Kendrick. (1991), 'Individual and Household Strategies: Some Empirical evidence from the Social Change and Economic Life Initiative', unpublished paper.

Anguiano Téllez, M. E. (2001), 'Inmigración Laboral Extracomunitaria en España: Explorando Perfiles y Trayectorias Laborales', *Migraciones*:111-134.

Asiedu, A. B. (2005), 'Some Benefits of Return Visits to Ghana', *Population Space and Place* 11:1-11.

Atkinson, R. & J. Flint. (2001), 'Accessing Hidden and Hard-to-Reach Populations: Snowball Research Strategies', *Social Research* 33,1-4.

Awad, I. (2004), 'Concept and Practice of Labour Immigration Policies in European Mediterranean Countries', in *Fifth Mediterranean Social and Political Research Meeting*. Florence.

Ba, A. H. (1997), 'Diaspora Sahélienne et développement des pays d'origine ou "l'effet boomerang"', *Revue Espaces Marx*, Lille, no.10, Afrique Subsaharienne, 132-139.

Baldwin-Edwards, M. (2004), 'Immigrants and the Welfare State in Europe', in Douglas S. Massey & J. Edward Taylor (eds.), *International Migration: Prospects and Policies in a Global Market*, 318-334. Oxford: Oxford University Press.

Barou, J. (1987), 'In the Aftermath of Colonization: Black African Immigrants in France', in Buechler Hans Christian and Buechler Judith-Maria (eds.), *Migrants in Europe: The Role of Family, Labor and Politics*, 77-90. Westport: Greenwood Press.

Barou, J. (2001), 'La Famille à Distance. Nouvelles Stratégies Familiales chez les Immigrés d'Afrique Sahélienne', *Hommes & Migrations* 1232:16-25.
Barros, L., M. Lahlou, C. Escoffier, P. Pumares & P. Ruspini (2002), 'L'immigration Irrégulière subsaharienne à travers et vers le Maroc', in ILO (ed.), *Cahiers de Migrations Internationales*, 54 F. Geneva: ILO.
Barry, B. (1992), 'Commerce et Commerçants Sénégambiens dans la Longue Durée: Etude d'une Formation Economique Dépendante', in Leonhard Harding & Boubacar Barry (eds.), *Commerce et Commerçants en Afrique de l'Ouest*, 35-58. Paris: Harmattan.
Bauböck, R., E. Ersbøll, K. Groenendijk & W. Harald. (2006), 'Acquisition And Loss Of Nationality. Policies And Trends In 15 European States'. Results of the EU-project: The Acquisition of Nationality in EU Member States: Rules, Practices and Quantitative Developments (NATAC). Austrian Academy of Sciences. Vienna: Institute for European Integration Research.
Bava, S. (2000), 'Reconversions et Nouveaux Mondes Commerciaux des Mourides à Marseille', *Hommes & Migrations, numéro monographique "Marseille, carrefour d'Afrique"*, 1224:46-55.
Bava, S. (2002), 'Entre Marseille et Touba: le Mouride Migrant et la Société Locale', in Momar Coumba Diop (ed.), *La Société Sénégalaise entre le Local et le Global*, 579-594. Paris: Editions Karthala.
Beauregard, R. A. (2003), 'City of Superlatives', *City & Community* 2/3: 183-199.
Bell, N. (2003), 'Le Goût Amer de Nos Fruits et Légumes: L'Exploitation de Migrants Clandestins dans l'Agriculture en Europe', *Migrations Societé* 15/85:49-65.
— (2004), 'The Exploitation of Migrants in European Agriculture', in Michele LeVoy, Nele Verbruggen & Johan Wets (eds.), *Undocumented Migrant Workers in Europe*, 41-46. Leuven: Acco.
Bendadi, S. (2005), 'Trouw met Mij', *Mo** 21:51-54.
Benson. (1990), 'Households, Migration, and Community Context', *Urban Anthropology* 19:9-29.
Bernard, F. (2000), 'La Régularisation des Étrangers Illégaux en Belgique', in Philippe De Bruycker (ed.), *Regularisations of Illegal Immigrants in Europe*, 97-160. Brussels: Bruylant.
Bertoncello, B. (2000), 'Les Marins Africains de Marseille: Histoire d'un Ancrage', *Hommes & Migrations, numéro monographique 'Marseille, Carrefour d'Afrique'* 1224:22-35.
Bertoncello, B. & S. Bredeloup (2000 a), 'Commerce Africain, Réseaux Transnationaux et Société Locale', *Hommes & Migrations, numéro monographique 'Marseille, Carrefour d'Afrique'* 1224:5-21.
Beuving, J. J. (2006), Cotonou's klondike: A sociological analysis of entrepreneurship in the Euro-West African second-hand car trade. Amsterdam: University of Amsterdam.
Black, R. (1996), 'Immigration and Social Justice: Towards a Progressive European Immigration Policy?', *Transactions of the Institute of British Geographers* NS 21:64-75.
Black, R., M. Collyer, R. Skeldon & C. Waddington (2006), 'Routes to illegal residence: A case study of immigration detainees in the United Kingdom', *Geoforum* 37:552-564.
Black, R. & R. King (2004), 'Migration, return and development in West Africa', *Population, Space and Place* 10:75-83.
Blion, R. & S. Witeska (1998), 'Revenus, Epargne et Transferts d'Economies des Immigrés Maliens et Sénégalais en France', *Hommes & Migrations* 1214:38-46.
Blommaert, J. & M. Martiniello (1996), 'Ethnic Mobilization, Multiculturalism and the Political Process in Two Belgian Cities: Antwerp and Liege', *Innovation* 9:51-73.
Blommaert, J. & J. Verschueren (1991), 'The Pragmatics of Minority Politics in Belgium', *Language in Society* 20:503-531.
Bodin, C. & C. Quiminal (1991), 'Le Long Voyage des Femmes du Fleuve Sénégal', *Hommes & Migrations* 1141:23-26.

Body-Gendrot, S. & M. Martiniello (2000), 'The Dynamics of Social Integration and Social Exclusion at the Neighbourhood Level', in Sophie Body-Gendrot & Marco Martiniello (eds.), *Minorities in European Cities. Dynamics of Social Integration and Social Exclusion at the Neighbourhood Level*, 3-25. Basingstoke: Macmillan.

Borjas, G. J. & R. B. Freeman (1992), 'Immigration and the Work Force: Introduction and Summary', in George J. Borjas & Richard B. Freeman (eds.), *Immigration and the Work Force: Economic Consequences for the United States and Source Areas*, 1-15. Chicago and London: University of Chicago Press.

Boswell, C. (2003), European Migration Policies in Flux: Changing Patterns of Inclusion and Exclusion. Oxford: Blackwell.

Bouhdiba, S. (2006), 'Les Conséquences socio-légales de la migration clandestine de l'Afrique sub-saharienne vers l'Afrique du Nord', paper presented at the Seventh Mediterranean Social and Political Research Meeting, 22-26 March 2006, European University Institute, Florence.

Bousetta, H. (2000), 'Political Dynamics in the City: Three Case Studies', in Sophie Body-Gendrot & Marco Martiniello (eds.), *Minorities in European Cities. Dynamics of Social Integration and Social Exclusion at the Neighbourhood Level*, 129-144. Basingstoke: Macmillan.

Bovenkerk, F., R. Miles & V. Gilles. (1990), 'Racism, Migration and the State in Western Europe: A Case for Comparative Analysis', *International Sociology* 5:475-490.

Boyd, M. (1989), 'Family and Personal Networks in International Migration – Recent Developments and New Agendas', *International Migration Review* 23:638-670.

Bredeloup, S. (1993), 'Les Migrants du Fleuve Sénégal: A Quand la "Diams'pora"?', *Revue Européenne des Migrations Internationales* 9:67-92.

Brettell, C. B. & J. F. Hollifield (2000), 'Migration Theory: Talking across Disciplines', in Caroline B. Brettell & James F. Hollifield (eds.), *Migration Theory: Talking across Disciplines*, 1-26. New York and London: Routledge.

Bribosia, E. & A. Rea (2002), 'Le Débat sur les Nouvelles Migrations en Belgique à la Lumière des Politiques Migratoires Recentes', in Emmanuelle Bribosia & Andrea Rea (eds.), *Les Nouvelles Migrations. Un Enjeu Européen*, 233-260. Brussels: Editions Complexes.

Briggs, C. L. (1983), 'Questions for the Ethnographer: A Critical Examination of the Role of the Interview in Fieldwork', *Semiotica* 46:233-261.

Briggs, V., Jr. (1984), 'Methods of Analysis of Illegal Immigration into the United States', *International Migration Review, Special Issue: Irregular Migration: An International Perspective* 18:623-641.

Brun, F. (2003), 'Les Immigrés et L'Evolution du Marché du Travail en France', *Migrations Societé* 15.

Bryceson, D. & U. Vuorela (2002), 'Transnational Families in the Twenty-first Century', in Deborah Bryceson & Ulla Vuorela (eds.), *The Transnational Family: New European Frontiers and Global Networks*, 67-78. Oxford and New York: Berg.

Bryman, A. & R. G. Burgess (1994), *Analyzing Qualitative Data*. London and New York: Routledge.

Burgers, J. & G. Engbersen (1999), De Ongekende Stad 1. Illegale Vreemdelingen in Rotterdam. Amsterdam: Boom.

Burgess, R. G., C. J. Pole, K. Evans & C. Priestley (1994), 'Four studies from one or one study from four? Multi-site case study research', in Alan Bryman & Robert G. Burgess (eds.), *Analyzing Qualitative Data*, 129-145. London and New York: Routledge.

Byron, M. (1994), The Unfinished Cycle: Post War Caribbean Migration to Britain. Aldershot, Hants; Brookfield: Avebury.

Cachón, L. (1999), 'Immigrants in Spain: From Institutional Discrimination to Labour Market Segmentation', in John Wrench, Andrea Rea & Nouria Ouali (eds.), *Migrants, Ethnic Minorities and the Labour Market*, 174-194.

Caestecker, F. (2000), *Alien Policy in Belgium, 1840-1949*. New York and Oxford: Berghahn Books.

Caixa Catalunya (2006), 'Razones demográficas del crecimiento del PIB per capita en España y la UE-15', *Informe semestral I/Economía Española y Contexto Internacional*. Barcelona: Caixa Catalunya.

Calavita, K. (1998), 'Immigration, Law, and Marginalization in a Global Economy: Notes from Spain', *Law and Society Review* 32:529-566.

Camara, A. M. (2002), 'Dimensions Régionales de la Pauvreté au Sénégal', *Belgeo* 1:17-28.

Carlier, J.-Y. & A. Rea (2001), Les Etrangers en Belgique: Etrangers, Immigrés, Réfugiés, Sans-Papiers?, Dossier no. 54 du CRISP, Brussels.

Castles, S. (2002), 'Migration and Community Formation under Conditions of Globalization', *International Migration Review* XXXVI:1143-1168.

Castles, S. & S. M. Miller (1993), The Age of Migration: International Population Movements in the Modern World. London: MacMillan.

Chavez, L. R. (1990), 'Coresidence and Resistance: Strategies for Survival Among Undocumented Mexicans and Central Americans in The United States', *Urban Anthropology* 19:31-61.

— (1992), *Shadowed Lives. Undocumented Immigrants in American Society*. Fort Worth: Harcourt Brace Publishers.

Chiswick, B. R. (1984), 'Illegal Aliens in the United States Labor Market: Analysis of Occupational Attainment and Earnings', *International Migration Review; Special Issue Irregular Migration: An International Perspective* 18:714-732.

Chiswick, B. R. & T. J. Hatton (2002), *International Migration and the Integration of Labor Markets*, Bonn: Institute for the Study of Labor.

Clark, W. A. V. (1998), 'Mass Migration and Local Outcomes: Is International Migration to the United States Creating a New Urban Underclass?', *Urban Studies* 35:371-383.

Cohen, I. J. (1989), Structuration Theory: Anthony Giddens and the Constitution of Social Life. Hampshire and London: MacMillan.

Cohen, R. (1991), Contested Domains: Debates in International Labour Studies. London: Zed.

— (1996), 'Diasporas and the Nation-State: From Victims to Challengers', *International Affairs* 72:507-520.

Colectivo IOE (1998), 'Inmigración y Trabajo: Hacia un Modelo de Análisis. Aplicación al Sector de la Construcción', *Migraciones* 1998:35-70.

— (2000), Inmigración y Trabajo. Trabajadores Inmigrantes en la Hostelería, OFRIM Suplementos June.

Collinson, S. (1994), *Europe and International Migration*. London: Pinter for Royal Institute of International Affairs.

Collyer, M. (2006), States of insecurity: Consequences of Saharan transit migration, Oxford: University of Oxford, COMPAS.

Conteh-Morgan, E. (1997), 'Senegal: Political Unity in the Face of Economic Austerity', *Africa Contemporary Record 1994-1996*, 157-166.

Copans, J. (2000), 'Mourides des Champs, Mourides des Villes, Mourides du Téléphone Portable et de l'Internet', *Afrique Contemporaine* 194:24-33.

Cornelius, W. A. (1982), 'Interviewing Undocumented Immigrants: Methodological Reflections Based on Fieldwork in Mexico and the U.S', *International Migration Review, Special Issue: Theory and Methods in Migration and Ethnic Research* 16:378-411.

Couper, K. & U. Santamaria (1984), 'An Elusive Concept: The Changing Definition of Illegal Immigrant in the Practice of Immigration Control in the United Kingdom',

International Migration Review, Special Issue: Irregular Migration: An International Perspective 18:437-452.
Criado, M. J. (1997), 'Historias de Vida: El Valor del Recuerdo, El Poder de la Palabra', *Migraciones* 1997:73-120.
Cross, M. & R. Moore (2002), Globalization and the New City: Migrants, Minorities and Urban Transformations in Comparative Perspective. Hampshire: Palgrave.
Cross, M. & R. Waldinger (2002), 'Migrants and the Urban Labour Market in Europe and North America', in Malcolm Cross & Robert Moore (eds.), *Globalization and the New City: Migrants, Minorities and Urban Transformations in Comparative Perspective*, 16-31. Basingstoke: Palgrave Publishers.

Dahinden, J. (2005), 'Contesting transnationalism? Lessons from the study of Albanian migration networks from former Yugoslavia', *Global Networks-a Journal of Transnational Affairs* 5:191-208.
Dahou, T. & V. Foucher (2004), 'Le Sénégal, Entre Changement Politique et Révolution Passive', *Politique Africaine* 96:5-21.
Daum, C. (1993), 'Quand les Immigrés Construisent leur Pays', *Hommes & Migrations* 1165:13-17.
Davis, M. (2004), 'Planet of slums – Urban involution and the informal proletariat', *New Left Review* 5-34.
De Genova, N. P. (2002), 'Migrant "Illegality" and Deportability in Everyday Life', *Annual Review of Anthropology* 31:419-444.
De Jong, G. F., A. Chamratrithirong & Q.-G. Tran (2002), 'For Better, For Worse: Life Satisfaction Consequences of Migration', *International Migration Review* 36:838-863.
De Lourdes Villar, M. (1990), 'Rethinking Settlement Processes: The Experience of Mexican Undocumented Migrants in Chicago', *Urban Anthropology* 19:63-79.
De Walsche, A. (2005), 'Illegalen Tussen Wal en Schip', *Mo** 21:18-19.
Demets, F. (2003), 'Dossier Illegalen: De Engelandvaarders', *Humo* 2003:124-127.
Deslé, E. (1997), 'Brussel 1968-1995: De Politieke Constructie van een Migrantenprobleem', in Els Deslé (ed.), *Migrantenpolitiek in Brussel*, 7-24. Brussels: VUB Press.
Desmarez, P., P. Van der Hallen, N. Ouali, V. Degraef & K. Tratsaert (2004), Minorités Ethniques en Belgique: Migration et Marché du Travail. Analyse Démographique, Statistique et des Mesures Juridiques et d'Action en Faveur des Migrants sur le Marché du travail. Gent: Academia Press.
Dewilde, C. (2004), Vormen en trajecten van armoede in het Belgische en Britse welvaartsregime. Multidimensionele armoededynamieken bestudeerd vanuit de sociologie van de levensloop, Doctoraat in de Politieke en Sociale Wetenschappen. Antwerp: University of Antwerp.
Diao, A. (2004), 'Migraciones y Desarrollo Local', *MUGAK* 27-28:26-27.
Diatta, M. A. & N. Mbow (1999), 'Releasing the Development Potential of Return Migration: The Case of Senegal', *International Migration* 37:243-265.
Dijkstra, T. (2000), 'Fufu en Masjela in de Polder: Afrikaanse Ondernemers en Produkten in Nederland', in Ineke van Kessel & Nina Tellegen (eds.), *Afrikanen in Nederland*, 183-198. Amsterdam: Koninklijk Instituut voor de Tropen / Leiden: African Studies Centre.
Diome, F. (2006), *The Belly of the Atlantic*. London: Serpent's Tail.
Diop, A. M. (1990), 'L'Emigration Murid en Europe', *Hommes & Migrations* 1132:21-24.
— (1990), 'Le Mouvement Associatif Négro-Africain en France', *Hommes & Migrations* 1132:15-20.
— (1996), 'Conditions des Retraités Ouest-Africains en France', *Migrations Societé* 8:1996.

Diop, M. C. (2002), 'Regards Croisés sur le Sénégal', in Momar Coumba Diop (ed.), *La Société Sénégalaise entre le Local et le Global*, 9-25. Paris: Karthala.
Diouf, M. (2000), 'The Senegalese Murid Trade Diaspora and The Making of a Vernacular Cosmopolitism', *Public Culture* 12:69-702.
Domingo, A., A. Kaplan & C. Gómez Gil (2000), *Easy Scapegoats: Sans-Papiers Immigrants in Europe, Report on Spain*, Barcelona: Centre d'Estudis Demogràfics.

Ebin, V. (1990), 'Commerçants et Missionnaires: Une Confrérie Muselmane Sénégalaise à New York', *Hommes & Migrations* 1132:25-31.
Eggerickx, T., C. Kesteloot, M. Poulain & L. Dal (1999), De Allochtone Bevolking in België. Algemene Volks- en Woningtelling op 1 Maart 1991. Monografieën no. 3. Brussels: Nationaal Instituut voor de Statistiek.
Engbersen, G. (1995), 'The Unknown City', *Berkeley Journal of Sociology* 10:87-111.
— (2001), 'The Unanticipated Consequences of Panopticon Europe: Residence Strategies of Illegal Immigrants', in Virginie Guiraudon & Christian Joppke (eds.), *Controlling A New Migration World*, 222-246. London: Routledge.
Engbersen, G. & J. van der Leun (2001), 'The Social Construction of Illegality and Criminality', *European Journal on Criminal Policy and Research* 9:51-70.
Engbersen, G., J. van der Leun, R. Staring & J. Kehla (1999), *De Ongekende Stad 2. Inbedding en Uitsluiting van Illegale Vreemdelingen*. Amsterdam: Boom.
Ensign, J. (2003), 'Ethical issues in qualitative health research with homeless youths', *Journal of Advanced Nursing* 43:43-50.
Epstein, G. S. (2000), *Labor Market Interactions Between Legal and Illegal Immigrants*. Bonn: Institute for the Study of Labor.
Epstein, G. S. & I. N. Gang (2004), *The Influence of Others on Migration Plans*. Bonn: Institute for the Study of Labor.
Escrivá, A. (1997), 'Control, Composition and Character of New Migration to South-west Europe: the Case of Peruvian women in Barcelona', *New Community* 2:43-57.
Esping-Andersen, G. (1990), *The Three Worlds of of Welfare Capitalism*. Cambridge and Oxford: Polity Press in Association with Blackwell Publishers Ltd.
Espinosa, K. & D. S. Massey (1999), 'Undocumented Migration and the Quantity and Quality of Social Capital', in Pries I. Ludger (ed) *Migration and Transnational Social Spaces*, 106-132. Aldershot and Brookfield: Ashgate.
Estevão, M. (2002), 'Regional Labor Market Disparities in Belgium', Washington, D.C.: International Monetary Fund, European I Department.
European Foundation for the Improvement of Living and Working Conditions (2005), 'Industrial relations and undeclared work', *EIRO thematic feature*. Dublin: European Foundation for the Improvement of Living and Working Conditions.

Faist, T. (2000), 'Economic Activities of Migrants in Transnational Social Spaces', in Sophie Body-Gendrot & Marco Martiniello (eds.), *Minorities in European Cities. Dynamics of Social Integration and Social Exclusion at the Neighbourhood Level*, 11-25. Basingstoke: Macmillan.
Fall, A. S. (2003), Enjeux et Défis de la Migration Internationale de Travail Ouest-Africaine, Internation Migration Papers. Geneva: IOM.
Fall, P. D. (2002), 'Ethnic and Religious Ties in an African Emigration. Senegalese Immigrants in the United States', *Studia Africana* 13:81-90.
Fassin, D. (1997), 'La Santé en Souffrance', in Didier Fassin, Alain Morice & Catherine Quiminal (eds.), *Les Lois de l'Inhospitalité. Les Politiques de l'Immigration a l'Epreuve des Sans-Papiers*, 95-106. Paris: La Découverte.

Favell, A. & A. Geddes (1999), European Integration, Immigration and the Nation State: Insitutionalising Transnational Political Action? Florence: European University Institute.
Favell, A. & R. Hansen (2002), 'Markets against Politics: Migration, EU Enlargement and the Idea of Europe', *Journal of Ethnic and Migration Studies* 28:581-601.
Flick, U. (2002), An Introduction to Qualitative Research. London: Sage.
Frederix, S. (2005), 'De Onzichtbare Stad. Illegaal in Antwerpen', *Mo** 29:37-41.
Freeman, G. P. (1995), 'Modes of Immigration Politics in Liberal Democratic-States', *International Migration Review* 29:881-902.

Gambaracci, D. (2001), 'L'Occasion Manquée. La Filière Automobile entre Marseille et Algerie', in Michel Peraldi (ed.), *Cabas et Containers. Activités Marchandes Informelles et Réseaux Migrants Transfrontalières*, 199-236. Paris: Maisoneuve et Larose.
Garnier, C. (1990), 'Migration, Flux Monétaires et Economie Villageoise', *Hommes & Migrations* 1131:13-18.
Geddes, A. (2003), 'Migration and the Welfare State in Europe', in Sarah Spencer (ed.), *The Politics of Migration: Managing Opportunity, Conflict and Change*, 150-162. Oxford: Blackwell.
Geddes, A. (2003), *The Politics of Migration and Immigration in Europe*. London, Thousand Oaks and New Delhi: Sage.
Geets, J., F. Pauwels, J. Wets, M. Lamberts & C. Timmerman (2006), *Nieuwe Migranten en de Arbeidsmarkt*. Leuven and Antwerp: HIVA/Oases.
Ghosh, B. (2000), 'New International Regime for Orderly Movements of People: What will it Look Like?', in Bimal Ghosh (ed.), *Managing Migration: Time for a New International Regime?* 6-26. Oxford: Oxford University Press.
Giddens, A. (1993), *The Constitution of Society*. Oxford: Blackwell.
Giménez Romero, C. (1997), 'Migración y Desarrollo. Su Vinculación Positiva', *Ingenieria sin Fronteras. Revista de Cooperación* VI/9: 6-10.
Glaser, B. & A. L. Strauss (1967), The Discovery of Grounded Theory: Strategies for Qualitative Research. Chicago: Aldine De Gruyter.
Glick Schiller, N., L. Basch & C. Blanc-Szanton (1992), 'Transnationalism: A New Analytical Framework for Understanding Migration', *Annals of the New York Academy of Science* 1992:1-24.
Gogia, N. (2006), 'Unpacking corporeal mobilities: the global voyages of labour and leisure', *Environment and Planning A* 38:359-375.
Gonin, P. & V. Lassailly-Jacob (2002), 'Les Réfugiés de l'Environnement. Une Nouvelle Catégorie de Migrants Forcés', *Revue Européenne des Migrations Internationales* 18:139-160.
Gordon, I. & S. Sassen (1992), 'Restructuring the Urban Labour Markets', in Susan S. Fainstein, Ian Gordon & Michael Harloe (eds.), *Divided Cities – New York and London in the Contemporary World*, 105-127. Cambridge and Oxford: Blackwell Publishers.
Gortázar, C. J. (2000), 'The Regularisation of Illegal Immigrants in Spain', in Philippe De Bruycker (ed.), *Regularisations of Illegal Immigrants in Europe*, 291-342. Brussels: Bruylant.
— (2002), 'Spain: Two Immigration Acts at the End of the Millennium', *European Journal of Migration and Law* 4:1-21.
Govaert, S. (1995), 'Flander's Radical Nationalism: How and Why the Vlaams Blok Ascended', *New Community* 21.
Grillo, R. & B. Riccio (2003), 'Translocal Development: Italy-Senegal', *Population, Space and Place* 10:99-111.
Guest, G., A. Bunce & L. Johnson (2006), 'How Many Interviews Are Enough? An Experiment with Data Saturation and Variability', *Field Methods* 18:59-82.
Guèye, C. (2002), *Touba, la Capitale des Mourides*. Paris: Editions Karthala.

Guilmoto, C. Z. (1997), *Migrations et Institutions au Sénégal: Effects d'Echelle et Determinants*, Paris: Centre Français sur la Population et le Développement.

Harding, L. (1992), 'Les Grands Commerçants Africains en Afrique de l'Ouest: Le Cas du Sénégal et de la Côte d'Ivoire', in Leonhard Harding & Boubacar Barry (eds.), *Commerce et Commerçants en Afrique de l'Ouest*, 5-34. Paris: Harmattan.

Hareven, T. K. (2000), *Families, History and Social Change: Life Course and Cross Cultural Perspectives*. University of Delaware: Westview Press.

Harris, C. (1987), 'The Individual and Society: A Processual Approach', in Alan Bryman (ed.), *Rethinking the Life Cycle*, 17-29. London: Macmillan Press Ltd.

Harris, N. & D. Coleman (2003), 'Does Britain Need More Immigrants?', *World Economics* 4/2:57-102.

Heckathorn, D. D. (1997), 'Respondent-Driven Sampling: A New Approach to the Study of Hidden Populations', *Social Problems* 44:174-199.

Held, D., A. McGrew, D. Goldblatt & J. Perraton (1999), *Global Transformations. Politics, Economics and Culture*. Cambridge, Oxford: Polity Press and Blackwell Publishers.

Herman, E. (2006), 'Migration as a family business: The role of personal networks in the mobility phase of migration', *International Migration* 44:191-230.

Hoggart, K. & C. Mendoza (1999), 'African Immigrant Workers in Spanish Agriculture', *Sociologia Ruralis* 39:539-560.

Holkup, P. A., T. Tripp-Reimer, E. M. Salois & C. Weinert (2004), 'Community-based participatory research – An approach to intervention research with a native American community', *Advances in Nursing Science* 27:162-175.

Honsberg, B. (2004), 'Undocumented Migrants in the Construction Sector in Europe', in Michèle LeVoy, Nele Verbruggen & Johan Wets (eds.), *Undocumented Migrant Workers in Europe*, 41-46. Leuven: Acco.

International Organisation for Migration (2006), Return and Emigration of Asylum Seekers ex Belgium, Statistical Data, Brussels: IOM.

IOM (2005), *World Migration 2005*. Geneva: International Organization for Migration, United Nations.

Jacquemin, J.-P. (2002), 'L'Immigration Congolaise dans la Belgique Coloniale', *Migrations Societé* 14:65-72.

Jettinger (2005), *Senegal Country Study*, Oxford: COMPAS.

Johnston, R. J. (1993), 'The Rise and Decline of the Corporate Welfare State: A Comparative Analysis in Global Context', in Peter Taylor (ed.), *Political Geography of the Twentieth Century: A Global Analysis*, 115-170. London: Belhaven Press.

Jordan, B. & F. Düvell (2002), *Irregular migration: the dilemmas of transnational mobility*. Cheltenham/Northampton: Edward Elgar.

Jounin, N. (2004), 'L'Ethnicisation en Chantiers. Reconstructions des Statuts par l'Ethnique en Milieu du Travail', *Revue Européenne des Migrations Internationales* 20:103-126.

Jovchelovitch, S. & M. W. Bauer (2000), 'Narrative Interviewing', in Martin Bauer & George Gaskell (eds.), *Qualitative researching with text, image and sound: A practical handbook for social research*, 57-74. London: SAGE.

Kagné, B. (2001), *Easy Scapegoats: Undocumented Immigrants in Europe – Belgian Report*. Liége: Center for Studies on Ethnicity and Migrations (CEDEM).

— (2001), 'Sans-Papiers en Belgique. Eléments d'Analyse d'une Catégorie Sociale a Facettes Multiples', in Antoine Pickels (ed.), *A La Lumière des Sans-Papiers*, 41-59. Brussels: Revue de l'Université de Bruxelles.

Kane, A. (2002), 'Senegal's Village Diaspora and the People Left Ahead', in Deborah Bryceson & Ulla Vuorela (eds.), *The Transnational Family: New European Frontiers and Global Networks*, 245-264. Oxford and New York: Berg.
Kaplan, A. (1998), De Senegambia a Cataluña, proceso de aculturación e integración social. Barcelona: Fundación "la Caixa".
— (2001), 'Los Procesos Migratorios. Una Motivacion Económica: Senegambianos en Cataluña', in Museu Etnologic (ed.), *Barcelona, Mosaico de Culturas*, 37-52. Barcelona: Museu Etnologic.
Kenyon, E. & S. Hawker (1999), 'Once would be enough': Some Reflections on the Issue of Safety for Lone Researchers', *International Journal of Social Research Methodology* 2:313-327.
King, R. (2000), 'Southern Europe in the Changing Global Map of Migration', in Russell King, Gabriella Lazaridis & Charalambos Tsardanidis (eds.), *Eldorado or Fortress? Migration in Southern Europe*, 3-26. Basingstoke: Macmillan.
King, R., A. Fielding & R. Black (1997), 'The International Migration Turnaround in Southern Europe', in Russell King & Richard Black (eds.), *Southern Europe and the New Immigrations*, 1-25. Brighton and Portland: Sussex Academic Press.
King, R. & I. Rodríguez-Melguizo (1999), 'Recent Migration to Spain: The Case of Moroccans in Catalonia', in Floya Anthias & Gabriella Lazaridis (eds.), *Into the Margins – Migration and Exclusion in Southern Europe*, 55-81. Aldershot, Brookfield, Singapore, Sydney: Ashgate.
Kloosterman, R. (1996), 'Mixed Experiences: Post Industrial Transition and Ethnic Minorities on the Amsterdam Labour Market', *New Community* 22:637-654.
Kloosterman, R., J. van der Leun & J. Rath (1998), 'Across the Border: Immigrants' Economic Opportunities, Social Capital and Informal Business Activities', *Journal of Ethnic and Racial Studies* 24:249-268.
Kloosterman, R., J. van der Leun & J. Rath (1999), 'Mixed Embeddedness: (In)formal Economic Activities and Immigrant Business in the Netherlands', *International Journal of Urban and Regional Research* 23:252-266.
Knights, M. (1996), 'Bangladeshi Immigrants in Italy: From Geopolitics to Micropolitics', *Transactions of the Institute of British Geographers* NS 21:105-123.
Koser, K. (2000), 'Asylum policies, trafficking and vulnerability', *International Migration* 38:91-111.
— (2003), *New African Diasporas*. London: Routledge.
Koser, K. & H. Lutz (1998), 'The New Migration in Europe: Contexts, Constructions and Realities', in Khalid Koser & Helma Lutz (eds.), *The New Migration in Europe: Social Constructions and Social Realities*, 185-198. Hampshire and London: Macmillan Press Ltd.
Krissman, F. (2005), 'Sin Coyote Ni Patron: Why the "Migrant Network" Fails to Explain International Migration', *International Migration Review* 39/1:4-44.
Kuagbenou, V. K. (1997), 'L'Immigration Noire Africaine en France: Pour une Approche Ethnique', *Migrations Societé* 9:5-26.

Lacomba, J. (2000), 'Immigrés Sénégalais, Islam et Confréries à Valence (Espagne)', *Revue Européenne des Migrations Internationales* 16:85-103.
Lambert, M. (2002), Longing for Exile: Migration and the Making of a Translocal Community in Senegal. Portsmouth: Reed Elsevier.
Lambert, P.-Y. (2002), 'Nouveau Code de la Nationalité Avant-Gardiste', *Migrations Societé* 14:59-67.
Lambrecht, H., H. Verhoeven & A. Martens (2002), 'Allochtone Ondernemers of Ondernemende Allochtonen? Ondernemers!' in VIONA (ed.), *Werkt de Arbeidsmarkt?*

Beleidsgericht Arbeidsmarktonderzoek in Vlaanderen, 95-108. Antwerp: Standaard Uitgeverij.

Lelart, M. (1990). *La Tontine*. John Libbey Eurotext. Paris: AUPELF-UREF.

Leman, J. (1997), 'Undocumented Migrants in Brussels: Diversity and the Anthropology of Illegality', *New Community* 23:25-41.

Leman, J., B. Siewiera & A.-M. Van Broeck (1994), *Documentloze immigranten te Brussel*. Brussels: Cultuur en Migratie.

Lennert, M. & J.-M. Decroly (2002), 'La Belgique Prise d'Assault? Les Flux Migratoires Étrangers en Belgique', in Emmanuelle Bribosia & Andrea Rea (eds.). *Les Nouvelles Migrations. Un Enjeu Européen*, 261-272. Brussels: Editions Complexes.

Light, I. (2002), 'Immigrant place entrepreneurs in Los Angeles, 1970-99', *International Journal of Urban and Regional Research* 26:215-228.

Linton, A. (2002), 'Immigration and the Structure of Demand: Do Immigrants Alter the Labor Market Composition of U.S. Cities?', *International Migration Review* 36:58-80.

Magone, J. M. (2004), *Contemporary Spanish Politics*. London/New York: Routledge.

Marfaing, L. (2003a), 'Investir au Sénégal: Les Sénégalais résidant en Allemagne entre le Retour Virtuel et le Va-et-vient', *Migrations Societé* 15:83-98.

— (2003b), *Les Sénégalais en Allemagne. Quotidien et Stratégies de Retour*. Paris: Editions Karthala.

Martín Pérez, A. (2006), 'Doing Qualitative Migration Research as a Native Citizen of the Host Country: Reflections on a Research in Spain', in *Forum Qualitative Sozialforschung/Forum: Qualitative Social Research*. www.qualitative-research.net/fqs-texte/3-06/06-3-1-e.htm.

Martin, P. L. (1994), 'Reducing Emigration Pressure: What Role Can Foreign Aid Play?', in W.R. Böhning & M.-L. Schloeter-Paredes (eds.), *Aid in Place of Migration*, 241-156. Geneva: International Labour Office.

Martínez Veiga, U. (1997), 'El Lugar Estable y Móvil de los Inmigrantes, las Paradojas de su Vivienda en las Ciudades', in Manuel Delgado (ed.), *Ciutat i Immigració*, 127-147. Barcelona: Centre de Cultura Contemporània.

— (1999), 'Immigrants in the Spanish Labour Market', in Martin Baldwin-Edwards & Joaquín Arango (eds.), *Immigrants and the Informal Economy in Southern Europe*, 105-128. London, Portland: Frank Cass.

— (2000), 'Evolución y Clasificación del Trabajo Doméstico Inmigrante', *OFRIM Suplementos* June:77-96.

Martiniello, M. (1997), 'Construction Européene et Politique D'Immigration', in Marie-Thérese Coenen & Rosine Lewin (eds.), *La Belgique et Ses Immigrés. Les Politiques Manquées.*, 121-143. Paris and Brussels: De Boeck Université.

— (2003), 'Belgium's Immigration Policy', *International Migration Review* 37:225-232.

Massey, D. S. (1999), 'International Migration at the Dawn of the Twenty-First Century: The Role of the State', *Population and Development Review* 25:303-322.

Massey, D. S., J. Arango, G. Hugo, A. Kouaouci, A. Pellegrino & J. E. Taylor (1998), *Worlds in Motion: Understanding International Migration at the End of the Millenium*. Oxford: Clarendon Press.

Massey, D. S. & C. Capoferro (2004), 'Measuring Undocumented Migration', *International Migration Review* 38:1075-1102.

Massey, D. S. & J. E. Taylor (2004). *International Migration: Prospects and Policies in a Global Market*. Oxford: Oxford University Press.

Mateo Dieste, J. L. (2002), 'L'Immigration et les Paradoxes de la Mémoire Coloniale en Espagne', *Migrations Societé* 14:83-95.

Mauthner, N. S. & A. Doucet (2003), 'Reflexive Accounts and Accounts of Reflexivity in Qualitative Data Analysis', *Sociology* 37:413-431.

May, J., J. Wills, K. Datta, Y. Evans, J. Herbert & C. McIlwaine (2007), 'Keeping London Working: Global Cities, The British State, and London's New Migrant Division of Labour', *Transactions of the Institute of British Geographers* 32:151-167.

Mayer, K. U. & N. B. Tuma (1987), *Applications of Event History Analysis in Life Course Research*. Berlin: Max-Planck-Institut fur Bildungsforschung.

Mazzucato, V. (2005), *Ghanaian migrants' double engagement: A transnational view of development and integration policies*. Geneva: Global Commission on International Migration, Global Migration Perspectives no. 48.

Médecins Sans Frontières (2005), Violence et immigration. Rapport sur l'immigration d'origine subsaharienne en situation irrégulière au Maroc. MSF-Espagne.

Meert, H., K. Stuyck, J. Blommaert & K. Peleman (2006), ' "Oh, ik ga schrik hebben". Attituden tegenover asielzoekers', in Marie-Claire Foblets, Jogchum Vrielink & Jaak Billiet (eds.), *Multiculturalisme ontleed. Een Staalkaart Van Onderzoek Aan De K.U.Leuven*, 115-134. Leuven: Universitaire Pers Leuven.

Mendoza, C. (1997), 'Foreign Labour Immigration in High-Unemployment Spain: The Role of African-Born Workers in the Girona Labour Market', in Russell King & Richard Black (eds.), *Southern Europe and the New Immigrations*, 1-25. Brighton and Portland: Sussex Academic Press.

— (1998), New Labour Inflows in Southern Europe: African Employment in Iberian Labour Markets, unpublished PhD: King's College London.

Mikkelsen, B. (1995), *Methods for Development Work and Research: A Guide for Practitioners*. New Delhi, Thousand Oaks, and London: Sage Publications.

Miller, R. L. (2000), *Researching Life Stories and Family Histories*. Thousand Oaks, London and New Delhi: Sage Publications.

Morén Alegret, R. (2002), 'Gobierno Local e Inmigración Extranjera. Aproximación a los Casos de Barcelona y Lisboa durante los Años 90', *Migraciones* 2002:25-81.

Moreno Fuentes, F. J. (2000), 'Immigration Policies in Spain: Between External Constraints and Domestic Demand for Unskilled Labour'.,unpublished paper presented at ECOR workshop, Copenhagen, April 2000.

— (2001), 'Migration and Spanish Nationality Legislation', in P. Weil & R. Hansen (eds.), *Towards a European Nationality. Citizenship, Immigration and Nationality Law in the EU*, 118-142. London: Palgrave.

— (2004), 'Evolution of Spanish Immigration Policies, and their Impact on North-African Migration to Spain', *Working Paper 2004/211*. Madrid: Juan March Institute.

Moreno, L. (2006), 'Le modèle de protection sociale des pays d'Europe du Sud: Permanence ou changement?', *Working Paper 06-07*. Madrid: Unidad de Políticas Comparadas (CSIC).

Ndiaye, I. C. (1996), 'Dynamisme et Isolement des Toucouleurs (Peuls) de France', *Migrations Societé* 8:77-83.

Ndiaye, M. (1996), *Le Goorgi, Type Moyen de la Société Sénégalaise Urbaine Post-indépendance*. Tome 1 de: "L'Ethique Ceddo et la Société d'Accaparement. Ou les Conduites Culturelles des Sénégalais d'Aujourd'hui". Dakar: Presses Universitaires de Dakar.

Nimako, K. (2000), 'De Ghanese Gemeenschap: Van Migranten tot Etnische Minderheid?', in Ineke van Kessel & Nina Tellegen (eds.), *Afrikanen in Nederland*, 11-41. Amsterdam: Koninklijk Instituut voor de Tropen/Leiden: African Studies Centre.

Nwolisa Okanga, E. O. (1995), 'Les Nigérians sans Documents', in Johan Leman (ed.), *Sans Documents: Les immigrés de l'ombre. Latino-américains, polonais et nigérians clandestins*, 76-92. Brussel: De Boeck Université.

OCIV (2002), Refugee Contribution to Europe. A feasibility study on the establishment of a Fund for Refugee Employment and Education (FREE) in the European Union: Belgium. Brussels: Overleg Centrum voor Integratie van Vluchtelingen.
OECD (2003), *Economic Survey of Spain*. Paris: OECD.
— (2005), *Economic Surveys: Belgium*. Paris: OECD.
— (2005), African Economic Outlook: Senegal. Paris: OECD.
— (2005), 'Net Social Expenditure. More comprehensive measures of social support', in *Oecd Social, Employment and Migration Working Papers no. 29*. Paris: OECD.
— (2006), OECD Employment Outlook: Boosting Jobs and Incomes. Paris: OECD.
Ouali, N. (1997), 'Emploi: De La Discrimination à L'Egalité de Traitement?', in Marie-Thérese Coenen & Rosine Lewin (eds.), *La Belgique et Ses Immigrés. Les Politiques Manquées.*, 147-165. Paris and Brussels: De Boeck Université.

Pajares, M. (2004), Inmigración Irregular en Cataluña: Análasis y Propuestas. Barcelona: CCOO, Ceres.
— (2005), Inserción Laboral de la Población Inmigrada en Cataluña. Barcelona: CCOO, Ceres.
Pascual de Sans, Á., J. Cardelús & M. Solana Solana (2000), 'Recent Immigration to Catalonia: Economic Character and Responses', in Russell King, Gabriella Lazaridis & Charalambos Tsardanidis (eds.), *Eldorado or Fortress? Migration in Southern Europe*, 104-124. Basingstoke: Macmillan.
Patton, M. Q. (1990), *Qualitative Evaluation and Research Methods*. Thousand Oaks, London and New Delhi: Sage Publications.
Peraldi, M. (2001), Cabas et Containers. Activités Marchandes Informelles et Réseaux Migrants Transfrontalières. Paris: Maisoneuve et Larose.
Pérez, V. G. e. a. (1995), Inmigrantes Marroquíes y Senegaleses en la Espana Mediterránea. Valencia: Generalitat Valenciana.
PICUM (2001), *Health Care for Undocumented Migrants: Germany, Belgium, The Netherlands, United Kingdom*. Brussels: PICUM (Platform for International Cooperation on Undocumented Migrants).
Piore, M. (1979), Birds of Passage: Migrant Labor and Industrial Societies. Cambridge: Cambridge University Press.
Piore, M. & C. Sabel (1984), The Second Industrial Divide: Possibilities for Prosperity. New York: Basic Books.
Planningscel Antwerpen (2004), *Thuis in het Hart van de Stad: Beleidsvisie Atheneumbuurt.* Antwerp: City of Antwerp.
Portes, A. (1995), 'Economic Sociology and the Sociology of Immigration: A Conceptual Overview', in Alejandro Portes (ed.), *The Economic Sociology of Immigration: Essays on Networks, Ethnicity, and Entrepreneurship*, 87-123. New York: Russell Sage Foundation.
— (1997), 'Immigration Theory for a New Century: Some Problems and Opportunities', *International Migration Review* 31:799-825.
Pugliese, E. (1993), 'Restructuring of the Labour Market and the Role of Third World Migrations in Europe', *Environment and Planning D: Society and Space* 11:513-522.
— (2004), 'L'Immigration Africaine en Italie et en Europe', *Migrations Societé* 16:195-212.

Quassoli, F. (1999), 'Migrants in the Italian Underground Economy', *International Journal of Urban and Regional Research* 23:212-231.
Quiminal, C. (1993), 'Transformations Villageoises et Regroupement Familial', *Hommes & Migrations* 1165:18-22.
— (1995), 'La Famille Soninké en France', *Hommes & Migrations* 1185:26-31.

Rath, J. & R. Kloosterman (1998), 'Economische Incorporatie en Ondernemerschap van Immigranten', in R. Penninx, H. Münstermann & H. Entzinger, *Etnische Minderheden en de multiculturele samenleving*, 689-716. Groningen: Wolters-Noordhoff.

Reitz, J. G. (2002), 'Host Societies and the Reception of Immigrants: Research Themes, Emerging Theories and Methodological Issues', *International Migration Review* XXXVI:1005-1019.

Rigau i Oliver, I. (2003), 'La Inmigración Extranjera en Catalunya: Presente y Futuro', in Gemma Aubarell (ed.), *Perspectivas de la Migración en España*, 9-34. Barcelona: Icaria.

Robin, N. (1996a), 'Transferts, Investissements et Lieux de Fixation des Emigrés Sénégalais', in Emmanuel Ma Mung (ed.), *Mobilités et Investissements des Emigres. Maroc, Tunisie, Turquie, Sénégal*, 249-264. Paris, Montréal: L'Harmattan.

— (1996b), 'La Multipolarisation de la Migration Sénégalaise', in Emmanuel Ma Mung (ed.), *Mobilités et Investissements des Emigres. Maroc, Tunisie, Turquie, Sénégal*, 48-64. Paris, Montréal: L'Harmattan.

Romaniszyn, K. (2000), 'Clandestine Labour Migration from Poland to Greece, Spain and Italy: Anthropological Perspectives', in Russell King, Gabriella Lazaridis & Charalambos Tsardanidis (eds) *Eldorado or Fortress? Migration in Southern Europe*, 125-144. Basingstoke: Macmillan.

Roque, M.-Á. (2003), 'Identidad y Territorio. El Reto de la Integración en Catalunya. La Interculturalidad como Reto y como Oportunidad', in Gemma Aubarell (ed.), *Perspectivas de la Migración en España*, 155-174. Barcelona: Icaria.

Rubin, H. J. & I. S. Rubin (1995), *Qualitative Interviewing. The Art of Hearing Data*. Thousand Oaks, London and New Delhi: Sage Publications.

Salt, J. & J. Stein (1997), 'Migration as a business: The case of trafficking', *International Migration* 35:467-494.

Salzbrunn, M. (2002), 'Hybridization of Religious and Political Practices amongst West African Migrants in Europe', in Deborah Bryceson & Ulla Vuorela (eds.), *The Transnational Family: New European Frontiers and Global Networks*, 217-230. Oxford, New York: Berg.

Santana, A. (2000), 'Los Trabajadores Extranjeros en el Sector Agrícola', *OFRIM Suplementos* June:41-73.

Sassen, S. (1991a), 'The Informal Economy', in John Hull Mollenkopf & Manuel Castells *Dual City: Restructuring New York*, 79-100. New York: Russell Sage Foundation.

— (1991b), 'Introduction to 'The Global City', in Saskia Sassen (ed.), *Introduction to 'The Global City: New York, London, Tokyo'*, 3-15. Princeton: Princeton University Press.

— (1994), 'The Informal Economy – Between New Developments and Old Regulations', *Yale Law Journal* 103:2289-2304.

— (1996), 'New Employment Regimes in Cities: The Impact on Immigrant Workers', *New Community* 22:579-594.

— (1999), *Guests and Aliens*. New York: The New Press.

Sayad, A. (1993), ' "Coûts" et "Profits" de l'Immigration', in Pierre Bourdieu (ed.), *La Misère du Monde*, 270-271. Paris: Editions du Seuil.

Scales-Trent, J. (1990), 'African Women in France: Immigration, Family and Work', *Brooklyn Journal of International Law* XXIV:705-721.

Schierup, C.-U. (2006), 'Transatlantic Convergence or Transatlantic Split? Elements for a Comparative Framework', in Carl-Ulrik Schierup, Peo Hansen, A & Stephen Castles (eds.), *Migration, Citizenship, and the European Welfare State: a European dilemma*, 81-111. Oxford: Oxford University Press.

Schierup, C.-U., P. Hansen, A & S. Castles (2006), *Migration, Citizenship, and the European Welfare State: a European dilemma*. Oxford: Oxford University Press.

Schmidt di Friedberg, O. (1994), 'Le Réseau Sénégalais Mouride en Italie', in Y. Kepel (ed.), *Exils et Royaumes. Les Appartenances au Monde Arabo-Musulman Aujourd'hui*, 301-329. Paris: Presses de la Fondation Nationale des Sciences Politiques.

Schmidt di Friedberg, O. (2000), 'Du Sénégal à New York, Quel Avenir pour la Confrérie Mouride?', *Hommes & Migrations, numéro monographique 'Marseille, Carrefour d'Afrique'* 1224:36-45.

Schneider, F. (2006), *Shadow Economies of 145 Countries all over the World: What do we really know?*. Linz-Auhof: Johannes Kepler University, Department of Economics.

Schuster, L. (2005), 'The Continuing Mobility of Migrants in Italy: Stereotyping, Labelling and 'Nomad Camps'', *Journal of Ethnic and Migration Studies* 31:757-774.

Sheller, M. & J. Urry (2006), 'New Mobilities Paradigm', *Environment and Planning A* 38:207-226.

Sin, C. H. (2005), 'Seeking Informed Consent: Reflections on Research Practice', *Sociology* 39:277-294.

Sinatti, G. (2006), Space, Place and Belonging. Senegalese Migrants Between Translocal Practices and Diasporic Identities. PhD thesis. Milan, Italy: Università di Milano-Bicocca, Urban Studies.

Soenen, H. (2003), 'Survival of the Fittest? Economic Strategies of Undocumented Workers in Brussels', *Kolor* 3:43-54.

Solé, C., N. Ribas, V. Bergalli & S. Parella (1998), 'Irregular Employment Amongst Migrants in Spanish Cities', *Journal of Ethnic and Racial Studies* 24:333-346.

Sow, A. (2001), 'Africains et Asiatiques dans l'Economie Informelle à Marseille', *Hommes & Migrations, numéro monographique 'Marseille, Carrefour d'Afrique'* 1233:58-71.

Sow, P. (2004), 'Prácticas Comerciales Transnacionales y Espacios de Acción de los Senegaleses en España', in A. Escrivá & N. Ribas (eds.), *Migración y Desarrollo. Estudios sobre Remesas y Otras Prácticas Transnacionales en España*, 234-254. Córdoba: CSIC.

Stalker, P. (2002), 'Migration trends and migration policy in Europe', *International Migration* 40:151-179.

— (2003), *De Feiten over Internationale Migratie*. Rotterdam: Lemniscaat.

Staring, R. (1998), ''Scenes from a Fake Marriage': Notes on the Flip-side of Embeddedness', in Khalid Koser & Helma Lutz (eds.), *The New Migration in Europe: Social Constructions and Social Realities*, p. 224-241. Hampshire and London: Macmillan Press Ltd.

Stoller, P. (2002), *Money has no smell: the Africanisation of New York*. Chicago: University of Chicago Press.

Tall, S. M. (1994), 'Les Investissements Immobiliers à Dakar des Emigrants Sénégalais', *Revue Européenne des Migrations Internationales* 10:137-149.

— (2002), 'L'Emigration Internationale Sénégalaise d'Hier à Demain', in Momar Coumba Diop (ed.), *La Société Sénégalaise entre le Local et le Global*, 549-577. Paris: Karthala.

— (2003), Les Emigrés Sénégalais et les Nouvelles Technologies de l'Information et de la Communication. Geneva: UNRISD, paper no. 7.

Tang, N. (2002), 'Interviewer and Interviewee Relationships Between Women', *Sociology* 36:703-721.

Tarrius, A. (1992), *Les 'Fourmis' d'Europe*. Paris: L'Harmattan.

Tarrius, A. (2002), La Mondialisation par le Bas. Les Nouveaux Nomades de l'Economie Souterraine. Paris: Balland.

Taylor, J. E. (2004), 'Remittances, Savings, and Development in Migrant-Sending Areas', in Douglas S. Massey & J. Edward Taylor (eds.), *International Migration: Prospects and Policies in a Global Market*, 157-174. Oxford: Oxford University Press.

Tellegen, N. (2000), 'Afrikanen op de Nederlandse Arbeidsmarkt: Een Eerste Verkenning', in Ineke van Kessel & Nina Tellegen (eds.), *Afrikanen in Nederland*, 165-181. Amsterdam: Koninklijk Instituut voor de Tropen/Leiden: African Studies Centre.
Terrones Ribas, A. (2005). Vivienda e Inmigración. Una Aproximación a los Factores Explicativos de las Condiciones Residenciales de las Personas Inmigradas. Barcelona: Universitat Autónoma de Barcelona, Departamento de Sociología.
Thompson, P. (2000), *The Voice of the Past: Oral History*. Oxford: Oxford University Press.
Tilly, C. (1996), *Big Structures, Large Processes, Huge Comparisons*. New York: Russell Sage Foundation.
Timera, M. (1997), 'Sans-Papiers Africains Face aux "Communautés" d'Origin', in Didier Fassin, Alain Morice & Catherine Quiminal (eds.), *Les Lois de l'Inhospitalité. Les Politiques de l'Immigration a l'Epreuve des Sans-Papiers*, 95-106. Paris: La Découverte.
— (2002), 'Righteous or Rebellious? Social Trajectory of Sahelian Youth in France', in Deborah Bryceson & Ulla Vuorela (eds.), *The Transnational Family: New European Frontiers and Global Networks*, 147-154. Oxford, New York: Berg.
Torres Perez, F. (2004), 'Les Immigrés, le Processus d'Insertion et les Réseaux Sociaux à Valence', *Hommes et Migrations* 1250:24-37.
Traore, S. (1994), 'Les Modèles Migratoires Soninké et Poular de la Vallée du Fleuve Sénégal', *Revue Européenne des Migrations Internationales* 10:61-80.
Trinidad García, M. L. (2003), 'El Trabajo por Cuenta Propia de los Extranjeros en España', *Migraciones* 2003:61-106.

UN (2000), *Replacement Migration: Is It a Solution to Declining and Ageing Populations?*. New York: UN, Department of Economic and Social Affairs, Population Division.
UNDP (2006), The 2006 Human Development Report, New York: UNDP.

Valenzuela, A. J., N. Theodore, E. Meléndez, N. S. University & A. Luz Gonzalez (2006), 'On The Corner: Day Labor in the United States'. Center for the Study of Urban Poverty. www.sscnet.ucla.edu/issr/csup/pubs/papers/item.php?id=31.
Van Bergen, D. (2003), 'De Werk- en Leefsituatie van Migranten in de Mannelijke Prostitutie in Amsterdam', *Migrantenstudies* 2003:240-251.
Van der Leun, J. & R. Kloosterman (1999), 'Loopbanen onder het Legale Plafond', in Jack Burgers and Godfried Engbersen (eds.), *De Ongekende Stad 1. Illegale Vreemdelingen in Rotterdam*, 118-160. Amsterdam: Boom.
— (2006), 'Going Underground: Immigration Policy Changes and Shifts in Modes of Provision of Undocumented Immigrants in the Netherlands', *Tijdschrift voor Economische en Sociale Geografie* 97/1:59-68.
Van Naerssen, T. (2002), 'Waarom Migranten Kleding Maken. Studies over de Kledingindustrie in Amsterdam en Andere Steden', *Migrantenstudies* 18/3:178-182.
Vargas Llovera, M. D. (1997), 'La Inmigración Africana de Venta Ambulante: El Caso de Alicante', in Francisco Checa (ed.), *Africanos en la Otra Orilla. Trabajo, Cultura e Integración en la España Mediterránea*, 61-77. Barcelona: Icaria Antrazyt.
Vengroff, R. & M. Magala (2001), 'Democratic Reform, Transition and Consolidation: Evidence from Senegal's 2000 Presidential Election', *The Journal of Modern African Studies* 39:129-162.
Verbeken, P. (2005), 'Dossier Illegalen: In de Onderbuik van de Belgische Economie', *Humo* 8-13.
Vermorgen, G. (2002), 'De Una Política de Integración a una Política de Diversidad', *Migraciones* 2002:9-23.
Vink, M. (2005), *Limits of European Citizenship*. Hampshire: Palgrave.

Vlaams Minderhedencentrum (2004), Toegang tot Basis-Bankdiensten voor Vreemdelingen met een Precair Verblijfsstatuut. Brussels: Vlaams Minderhedencentrum.
Vlaamse Gemeenschap (2003), Volwassen Anderstalige Nieuwkomers in het Vlaamse Gewest: Aantallen, Profielen, Beleidsaandachtspunten. Brussels: Ministerie van de Vlaamse Gemeenschap.
Vuylsteke, B. (2006), Illegally Resident Third Country Nationals in the EU Member States: State Approaches towards them and their Profile and Social Situation. Brussels: European Union.

Walckiers, L. (2003), 'De Regularisatiecampagne Voor Mensen in Illegale Verblijfssituatie (1999-2002)', *Samenleving en Politiek* 10:4-17.
Wauters, B. & J. Lambrecht (2006), *Zelfstandig ondernemerschap bij asielzoekers en vluchtelingen*, Brussels: ESF-Equalproject 'Rainbow Economy'.
WAV (2000), De Arbeidsmarkt in de Provincie Antwerpen, Jaarboek 1999. Leuven: Acco.
Wets, J. (2001), *Migratie en Asiel: Vluchten Kan Niet Meer*. Brussels: Koning Boudewijn Stichting.
Withol de Wenden, C. (2004), 'Admissions Policies in Europe', in Douglas S. Massey & J. Edward Taylor (eds.), *International Migration: Prospects and Policies in a Global Market*, 286-295. Oxford: Oxford University Press.

Zapata-Barrero, R. (2004), Inmigración, Innovación Política y Cultura de Acomodación en España. Un Análisis Comparativo entre Andalucía, Cataluña, la Comunidad de Madrid y el Gobierno Central. Madrid: CIDOB.

Abstract

This book examines two major social changes experienced by European cities in the last two decades: post-industrial economic restructuring and new immigration flows. The link between both has been extensively discussed throughout a variety of theoretical approaches and in numerous descriptive contributions. Adding to those studies, this research focuses on three elements of migratory experience that have been relatively neglected thus far: a dynamic view of changes over time, the influence of national welfare and legislation frameworks, and the importance of support mechanisms outside the labour market. The material underpinning the arguments is the qualitative life-course analysis of 81 in-depth interviews with Senegambian migrants living in Antwerp and Barcelona.

First, it is shown how a more dynamic approach on the position of newly arrived migrants in receiving economies improves the static perspective common to most theories. I describe how respondents may move from purely survival stages, over phases of looking for a regularisation of their legal status, to a more stable context in which they can work to improve their socio-economic situation. Second, the life course of these migrants is influenced by substantial differences between Antwerp and Barcelona in terms of labour markets, welfare and immigration policies. Despite the undeniable influences of globalisation, the local institutional framework and its implementation are crucial. In addition, immigrants interact with these rules, developing strategies to circumvent the law, limit the consequences of breaking it, or creatively trying to match conditions. Third, it is argued that a purely economic and individual approach cannot grasp the complexity, precariousness, and volatility typical of contemporary migratory experiences. In analysing their life courses, attention is paid to the changing roles of community, social support systems, the legal context, the relationship with home, and the integration schemes. An in-depth insight is given into the lives of migrants, the limits, rights and possibilities for getting by in two different European urban settings.

Extracto

Este libro examina dos grandes cambios sociales experimentados por las ciudades europeas en las últimas dos décadas: la reestructuración económica post-industrial y las nuevas corrientes de inmigración. El vínculo entre ambos procesos ha sido ampliamente debatido desde una gran variedad de enfoques teóricos y disciplinares. Agregando a estos estudios, la presente investigación se centra en tres elementos de la experiencia migratoria que han sido relativamente descuidados hasta la fecha: una visión dinámica de los cambios en el tiempo, la influencia del bienestar nacional y los marcos legislación, así como la importancia de los mecanismos de apoyo externos al mercado de trabajo. El material que sustentan los argumentos aquí planteados es de naturaleza cualitativa basado en el estudio de trayestorias vitales de inmigrantes senegambianos entrevistados residentes en Amberes y Barcelona.

En primer lugar, se muestra cómo un enfoque más dinámico acerca de la posición de los inmigrantes recién llegados en las economías receptoras mejora las perspectivas estáticas comunes a la mayoría de los análisis teorícos. Se describe cómo los informantes pueden moverse desde etapas de pura supervivencia, pasando por fases de buúsqueda de una regularización de su situación legal, hasta un contexto más estable en el que puedan trabajar para mejorar su situación socioeconómica. En segundo lugar, las trayectorias de curso de vida de estos inmigrantes se ven influidas por las diferencias sustanciales entre Amberes y Barcelona en términos de sus mercados de trabajo, las políticas de bienestar y de inmigración. A pesar de los innegables influencias de la globalización, el marco institucional local y su aplicación práctica resulta crucial. Además, los inmigrantes interactuar con estas normas desarrollando estrategias para circunvalar la legislación, limitando las consecuencias de infringir dicha normativa, o tratando de responder a las restricciones de forma creativa . En tercer lugar, se argumenta que un enfoque puramente económico e individualista no puede captar la complejidad, precariedad e inestabilidad típica de la experiencia migratoria contemporánea. Al analizar las trayectorias de curso de vida se presta atención a la evolución de las funciones de la comunidad, los sistemas de apoyo social, el contexto jurídico, la relación con el hogar, y los programas de integración. En este trabajo se presenta un conocimiento en profundidad acerca de las condiciones de vida de los migrantes, los límites, derechos y posibilidades de adaptarte a dos contextos urbanos europeos diferentes.

Samenvatting

Dit boek onderzoekt twee belangrijke sociale veranderingen die Europese over de laatste twee decennia getekend hebben: postindustriële economische herstructurering en nieuwe migrantenstromen. De link tussen beide is uitgebreid bediscussieerd in een reeks theoretische benaderingen en in talrijke beschrijvende bijdragen. In de lijn hiervan focust dit onderzoek op drie elementen van de migratie-ervaring die tot dusver relatief weinig aandacht gekregen hebben: een dynamisch zicht op veranderingen doorheen de tijd, de invloed van nationale welvaartsstaat- en wettelijke kaders, en het belang van hulpmechanismes buiten de arbeidsmarkt. Het empirisch materiaal dat de argumenten onderbouwt is de kwalitatieve levensloopanalyse van 81 diepte-interviews met Senegambiaanse migranten die in Antwerpen en Barcelona wonen.

In de eerste plaats wordt aangetoond hoe een meer dynamische benadering van de positie van nieuw aangekomen migranten in de ontvangende economieën een meerwaarde biedt tegenover het meer statische perspectief van de meeste theorieën. Ik beschrijf hoe respondenten kunnen evolueren van de loutere overlevingsfase, over een periode van zoeken naar regularisatie van hun legale status, tot een stabielere context waarin ze kunnen werken aan het verbeteren van hun sociaaleconomische situatie. Ten twee wordt de levensloop van deze migranten beïnvloed door substantiële verschillen tussen Antwerpen en Barcelona in arbeidsmarkt, sociaal- en migratiebeleid. Ondanks de onmiskenbare invloed van globalisering, blijft het lokale institutionele kader en de implementatie hiervan cruciaal. Bovendien interageren migranten met deze regels, ontwikkelen ze strategieën om de wet te omzeilen, de gevolgen van een inbreuk te beperken, of creatief om te gaan met de omstandigheden. In een derde punt wordt geargumenteerd dat een louter economische en individuele benadering niet de complexiteit, kwetsbaarheid en vluchtigheid kan vatten die typisch zijn voor hedendaagse migratie-ervaringen. Bij de analyse van hun levensloop kan aandacht besteed worden aan de veranderende rol van de gemeenschap, systemen van sociale hulp, de wettelijke context, de relatie met het thuisland, en het integratiebeleid. Er wordt een diepte-inzicht gegeven in de levens van deze migranten, de grenzen, rechten en mogelijkheden om rond te komen in twee verschillende Europese stedelijke contexten.

Other IMISCOE titles

IMISCOE Research

Rinus Penninx, Maria Berger, Karen Kraal, Eds.
The Dynamics of International Migration and Settlement in Europe: A State of the Art
2006 (ISBN 978 90 5356 866 8)
(originally appearing in IMISCOE Joint Studies)

Leo Lucassen, David Feldman, Jochen Oltmer, Eds.
Paths of Integration: Migrants in Western Europe (1880-2004)
2006 (ISBN 978 90 5356 883 5)

Rainer Bauböck, Eva Ersbøll, Kees Groenendijk, Harald Waldrauch, Eds.
Acquisition and Loss of Nationality: Policies and Trends in 15 European Countries, Volume 1: Comparative Analyses
2006 (ISBN 978 90 5356 920 7)

Rainer Bauböck, Eva Ersbøll, Kees Groenendijk, Harald Waldrauch, Eds.
Acquisition and Loss of Nationality: Policies and Trends in 15 European Countries, Volume 2: Country Analyses
2006 (ISBN 978 90 5356 921 4)

Rainer Bauböck, Bernhard Perchinig, Wiebke Sievers, Eds.
Citizenship Policies in the New Europe
2007 (ISBN 978 90 5356 922 1)

Veit Bader
Secularism or Democracy? Associational Governance of Religious Diversity
2007 (ISBN 978 90 5356 999 3)

Holger Kolb & Henrik Egbert, Eds.
Migrants and Markets: Perspectives from Economics and the Other Social Sciences
2008 (ISBN 978 90 5356 684 8)

Ralph Grillo, Ed.
The Family in Question: Immigrant and Ethnic Minorities in Multicultural Europe
2008 (ISBN 978 90 5356 869 9)

Corrado Bonifazi, Marek Okólski, Jeannette Schoorl, Patrick Simon, Eds.
International Migration in Europe: New Trends and New Methods of Analysis
2008 (ISBN 978 90 5356 894 1)

Maurice Crul, Liesbeth Heering, Eds.
The Position of the Turkish and Moroccan Second Generation in Amsterdam and Rotterdam: The TIES Study in the Netherlands
2008 (ISBN 978 90 8964 061 1)

Marlou Schrover, Joanne van der Leun, Leo Lucassen, Chris Quispel, Eds.
Illegal Migration and Gender in a Global and Historical Perspective
2008 (ISBN 978 90 8964 047 5)

IMISCOE Reports

Rainer Bauböck, Ed.
Migration and Citizenship: Legal Status, Rights and Political Participation
2006 (ISBN 978 90 5356 888 0)

Michael Jandl, Ed.
Innovative Concepts for Alternative Migration Policies: Ten Innovative Approaches to the Challenges of Migration in the 21st Century
2007 (ISBN 978 90 5356 990 0)

Jeroen Doomernik, Michael Jandl, Eds.
Modes of Migration Regulation and Control in Europe
2008 (ISBN 978 90 5356 689 3)

IMISCOE Dissertations

Panos Arion Hatziprokopiou
Globalisation, Migration and Socio-Economic Change in Contemporary Greece: Processes of Social Incorporation of Balkan Immigrants in Thessaloniki
2006 (ISBN 978 90 5356 873 6)

Floris Vermeulen
The Immigrant Organising Process: Turkish Organisations in Amsterdam and Berlin and Surinamese Organisations in Amsterdam, 1960-2000
2006 (ISBN 978 90 5356 875 0)

Anastasia Christou
Narratives of Place, Culture and Identity: Second-Generation Greek-Americans Return 'Home'
2006 (ISBN 978 90 5356 878 1)

Katja Rušinović
Dynamic Entrepreneurship: First and Second-Generation Immigrant Entrepreneurs in Dutch Cities
2006 (ISBN 978 90 5356 972 6)

Ilse van Liempt
Navigating Borders: Inside Perspectives on the Process of Human Smuggling into the Netherlands
2007 (ISBN 978 90 5356 930 6)

Myriam Cherti
Paradoxes of Social Capital: A Multi-Generational Study of Moroccans in London
2008 (ISBN 978 90 5356 032 7)

Marc Helbling
Practising Citizenship and Heterogeneous Nationhood: Naturalisations in Swiss Municipalities
2008 (ISBN 978 90 8964 034 5)

Jérôme Jamin
L'Imaginaire du Complot: Discours d'Extrême Droite en France et aux Etats-Unis
2009 (ISBN 978 90 8964 048 2)